THE COMPLETE POEMS
OF W. H. DAVIES

THE
COMPLETE POEMS OF
W. H. DAVIES

With an Introduction by
OSBERT SITWELL

and a Foreword by
DANIEL GEORGE

WESLEYAN UNIVERSITY PRESS
Middletown, Connecticut

© 1963 BY JONATHAN CAPE LIMITED

FIRST AMERICAN EDITION 1965

PRINTED IN GREAT BRITAIN

Contents

[Arranged alphabetically. An Index of first lines is given at the end of the book]

A is for Artist	Page 350
A Beggar's Life	522
A Bird's Anger	285
A Blind Child	59
A Bright Day	446
A Cat's Example	497
A Change of Voice	505
A Chant	304
A Child's Fancy	411
A Child's Mint	435
A Child's Pet	282
A Dog's Grave	442
A Dream	152
A Dream of Winter	411
A Drinking Song	26
A Dull Spirit	399
A Familiar Face	581
A Familiar Voice	528
A Fleeting Passion	210
A Fleeting Wonder	429
A Foolish Tongue	466
A Great Time	215
A Greeting	167
A Happy Life	84
A Life's Love	75
A Lonely Coast	365
A Lovely Day	452
A Lovely Woman	90
A Luckless Pair	517
A Lullaby of Rest	476
A Maiden and Her Hair	80
A May Morning	170
A Merry Hour	524
A Midsummer's Night's Storm	212
A Miracle	334

A Month Ago	Page	538
A Mother to her Sick Child		237
A Mother's Science		554
A New World		483
A Prayer		424
A Richer Freight		83
A Safe Estate		573
A Silver Wonder		412
A Song		279
A Strange City		197
A Strange Meeting		252
A Summer's Noon		512
A Swallow that Flew into the Room		513
A Sweeter Life		432
A Thought		320
A Vagrant's Life		522
A Winter's Night		245
A Woman's Charms		186
A Woman's Glory		558
A Woman's History		324
A Young Thrush		417
Advice		396
Again I Sing		206
Age and Youth		431
Ale		54
All in June		502
All's Well		483
Alone		465
Ambition		408
An Early Love		189
An Epitaph		402
An old House in London		107
Angel and Mystery		256
Angry		113
April		593
April's Charms		228
April's Lambs		278
Armed for War		499
Around that Waist		306
At Night		332
Australian Bill		88

Autumn	Page	23
Aye		441
B is for Beauty		350
Beauty and Brain		476
Beauty and Song		473
Beauty's Bait		558
Beauty's Danger		511
Beauty's Light		23
Beauty's Revenge		549
Beggars' Luck		453
Beggar's Song		305
Bells		452
Bewitched		456
Bird and Brook		285
Bird and Cloud		438
Birds		245
Birthdays		409
Body and Spirit		240
Born of Tears		418
Breast to Breast		447
Breath		339
Broken Hearts		492
Brother Gods		459
Brothers		571
C is for Child		351
Cant		338
Captives		560
Catching the Devil		486
Catharine		57
Charity		410
Charms		234
Child Lovers		239
Childhood's Hours		539
Children at Play		191
Christ, the Man		145
Christmas		171
Circumstance		556
City and Country		512
Clocks		434

Clouds	Page 105
Combing	490
Come Away, Death	367
Come, Honest Boys	115
Come, Let Me Close	566
Come, let us Find	259
Come, Melancholy	432
Come, thou Sweet Wonder	234
Comfort	288
Common Joys	498
Compensation	455
Competitors	467
Confession	242
Cowslips and Larks	250
Crumbs and Guineas	444
D is for Dog	351
Day or Night	416
Day's Black Star	82
Days and Years	500
Days that have Been	142
Days too Short	143
Dead Born	541
Death	27
Death's Game	523
Dogs	443
Down Underground	341
Dreamers	440
Dreaming of Death	550
Dream Tragedies	190
Dreams of the Sea	187
Drink	449
Drinking Song	306
Dust	347
E is for Eyes	351
Eardrops	480
Early Morn	81
Early Spring	204
Earth Love	335
Easter	243

England	Page 258
Epitaph on a Child	433
Epitaph on John Keats	432
Evil	349
Exalted Flower	255
Eyes	449
Eyes and Ears	414
F is for Fiddles	352
Facts	62
Fairies, Take Care	156
Fancy	125
Fancy's Home	141
Farewell to Poesy	97
Father and Son	491
Faults	467
Flirting	478
Flowers	422
Flying Blossoms	446
Following a Bee	500
For Sale	408
Forgiveness	250
Fortunes	468
Francis Thompson	179
Friends	236
Friends Unborn	405
From France	201
Frost	392
G is for Garden	352
Giants	395
Go, Angry One	541
Good and Evil	471
Good Friends	491
Great Lovers	468
H is for Hedge	353
Hand or Mouth	407
Happy Wind	109
Heaven	203
Heaven and Earth	418

Heigh Ho, the Rain	Page 575
Her Absence	216
Her Body's a Fine House	306
Her Merriment	315
Her Mouth and Mine	289
Here am I	421
Hidden Love	183
Hill and Vale	394
His Throne	478
Hope Abandoned	66
How Kind is Sleep	274
How Late	571
How Sordid is this Crowded Life	370
Hunting Joy	417
I is for Implements	354
I am the Poet Davies, William	268
I Could not Love Him More	303
If Love Survives	407
Impudence	313
In a Garden	562
In a Lodging House	30
In Days Gone	540
In June	589
In May	139
In Neath Valley	266
In Silent Groves	567
In Spring-Time	336
In the Country	106
In the End	223
In the Snow	247
In the Wood	545
In Time of War	258
In Winter	419
Infancy	224
Ingratitude	145
J is for Jealousy	354
Jenny	77
Jenny Wren	99
Jewels	433

x

Jove Warns Us	Page 246
Joy	316
Joy and Pleasure	85
Joy Supreme	178
K is for Kings	355
Killed in Action	248
Kiss and Blow	429
Kitty and I	229
Knitting	104
L is for Light	356
Lamorna Cove	317
Last Thoughts	475
Late Singers	263
Laughing Rose	172
Leaves	332
Leisure	140
Let Love Live On	469
Let Me Confess	289
Let Us Lie Close	474
Letters	416
Life	504
Life is Jolly	184
Light and Darkness (i)	401
Light and Darkness (ii)	474
Lines to a Sparrow	33
Little Flower	449
Logic	455
Looks	506
Love Absent	28
Love and Immortality	545
Love and Money	458
Love and the Muse	175
Love Impeached	276
Love in Trouble	485
Love Lights His Fire	463
Love, Like a Drop of Dew	329
Love Me No More	479
Love Speechless	271
Love Ten Years Old	464

Love's Birth   Page 525
Love's Caution   280
Love's Coming   29
Love's Happiness   555
Love's Inspiration   576
Love's Payment   336
Love's Power   543
Love's Rivals   466
Love's Silent Hour   290
Love's Youth   221
Lovely Dames   249
Loyalty   439

M is for Mother   356
Mad   392
Mad Poll   177
Magpies   442
Man   482
Man   554
Mangers   422
March   516
Margery   52
Married Couples   461
Marvellous Ears   472
Men that have Strength   310
Men that Think   502
Molly   248
Money   91
Moss and Feather   413
Music   61
Music's Tragedy   503
My Garden   337
My Lady Comes   569
My Life's Example   419
My Love could Walk   243
My Old Acquaintance   244
My Rockery   445
My Youth   176

N is for Nature   357
Nailsworth Hill   505

Named	Page 487
Nature's Friend	78
Nature's Moods	527
Near a Quiet Stream	222
Nell Barnes	225
New-comers	63
Night is the only Time I Live	311
Night Wanderers	182
No Careless Mind	428
No Idle Gold	270
No Master	102
No Place or Time	440
No-man's Wood	366
Now	514
Now That She Gives	291
Now that the Tears	309
O Happy Blackbird	559
O is for Open	357
Oh for a Glass of Wine!	307
Oh, Sweet Content!	270
Old Acquaintance	267
Old and Crazy	448
Old Autumn	426
Old Friends	425
Old or Young	402
Old Ragan	521
Old Sailors	264
On a Cold Day	450
On Expecting some Books	110
On Finding a Dead Bird Under My Window	443
On Hearing Mrs. Woodhouse play the Harpsichord	262
On the Death of a little Child	542
On the Mountain	223
On What Sweet Banks	305
One by One	393
One Night, when I was Sleeping	367
One Poet Visits Another	445
One Thing Wanting	286
One Token	331

One we Love	Page 591
Our Longer Life	346
Ourselves	438
Our Sussex Downs	320
Owls	448
P is for Pool	358
Parted	64
Passion's Greed	573
Passion's Hounds	276
Past and Present	463
Pastures	315
Peace and Goodwill	405
Peace and Rest	413
Pecking	470
Pity	347
Plants and Men	211
Playmates	437
Poison	424
Poor Kings	175
Pot and Kettle	414
Pride and Humility	494
Property	397
Q is for Question	358
R is for Remembrance	359
Rags and Bones	261
Raptures	241
Regret	460
Return to Nature	192
Rich Companions	493
Rich Days	221
Rich or Poor	147
Robin Redbreast	76
Rogues	331
Rose	100
S is for Swimmer	359
Sadness and Joy	149
Saints and Lodgers	38

xiv

Saturday Night in the Slums	Page 591
Scandal	484
School's Out	84
'Scotty' Bill	55
Scotty's Luck	109
Secrets	345
Seed and Flower	456
See how the Glow-worm's Light	304
See Where Young Love	333
Seeking Beauty	148
Seeking Joy	173
Self Love	544
Selfish Hearts	519
Sheep	142
Ships and Stars	423
Shooting-Stars	398
Shopping	158
Sick Minds	437
Silent Eyes	496
Silver Hours	421
Sleep	24
Slippers	506
Slum Children	556
Smiles	176
Solitude	534
Song of the Miners	490
Songs of Joy	137
Sound and Grace	553
Sound and Light	454
Speed	498
Spirits and Bodies	460
Sport	403
Starers	202
Starlings	423
Stars	565
Stings	475
Storms	397
Strange People	583
Street Criers	484
Strength	322
Strong Moments	166

Success	Page 493
Sun, Tree and Crow	398
Sweet Birds, I Come	577
Sweet Child	219
Sweet Music	532
Sweet Night	204
Sweet Stay-at-Home	168
Sweet Youth	532
T is for Time	360
Taking Stock	495
Telling Fortunes	321
Tell Me, World, and Tell Me, Nature	485
That Day She Seized	251
That Golden Time	507
The Age of Gold	488
The Battle	81
The Beautiful	313
The Bed-sitting-room	160
The Bee Lover	451
The Bell	251
The Best Friend	203
The Bird of Paradise	225
The Bird-Man	180
The Birds of Steel	260
The Birth of Song	481
The Black Cloud	218
The Blest	415
The Blind Boxer	266
The Boy	89
The Bust	369
The Call of the Sea	114
The Calm	582
The Captive Lion	284
The Cat	273
The Cave	340
The Change	518
The Chase	430
The Cheat	530
The Child and the Man	561
The Child and the Mariner	161

xvi

The Child Chatters	Page 563
The Church Organ	181
The City's Ways	579
The Clock	284
The Collar	321
The Collier's Wife	565
The Coming of Peace	278
The Coming of Spring	279
The Conquerors	486
The Cuckoo	447
The Daisy	92
The Dancer	261
The Dark Hour	98
The Dead	450
The Dead Tree	503
The Deed	496
The Den	209
The Distinction	574
The Dog	272
The Doll	344
The Doubtful One	157
The Dragonfly	400
The Dreaming Boy	212
The Dumb World	103
The Dumb World	207
The Dying	580
The East in Gold	149
The Elements	153
The Emigrant	564
The End of Summer	590
The Enemy	436
The Evening Star	401
The Example	138
The Excuse	247
The Faithful One	480
The Fates	342
The Fear	341
The Flirt	283
The Flood	140
The Fog	185
The Force of Love	275

The Forsaken Dead	Page	58
The Ghost		469
The Girl is Mad		572
The Green Tent		101
The Grey-haired Child		552
The Grief of Others		318
The Happiest Life		584
The Happy Child		151
The Harvest Home		147
The Hawk		214
The Heap of Rags		154
The Helpless		578
The Hermit		222
The Hill-side Park		34
The Holly on the Wall		254
The Homeless Man		586
The Hospital Waiting-Room		230
The Hour of Magic		313
The House Builder		516
The Hunt		269
The Idiot		415
The Idiot and the Child		100
The Inexpressible		227
The Inquest		232
The Jealous Lover		479
The Jolly Tramp		65
The Joy of Life		348
The Kingfisher		107
The Lady of Light		436
The Lament of Age		574
The Last Years		501
The Laughers		87
The Laws of Beauty		462
The Legacy		434
The Life Divine		220
The Life of Man		368
The Likeness		53
The Lily of our Valley		489
The Little Devil		457
The Little Man		553
The Little Ones		158

xviii

The Load of Pearls	Page 494
The Lodging House Fire	36
The Loneliest Mountain	494
The Lonely Dreamer	171
The Long Sleep	561
The Lost Sex	265
The Man of Moods	454
The Mask	395
The Meadow	338
The Milkmaid's Call	510
The Milkmaid's Song	510
The Mind Speaks	507
The Mind's Liberty	205
The Mint	287
The Mongrel	488
The Moon	215
The Moon and a Cloud	268
The Moth	82
The Mourner	439
The Muse	508
The Nature Lover	330
The Old Oak Tree	174
The One Real Gem	524
The One Singer	232
The Owl	148
The Ox	56
The Peacemaker	471
The Perfect Life	365
The Philosophical Beggar	117
The Players	481
The Poet	364
The Poet's Horse	328
The Pond	333
The Poor	428
The Poppy	515
The Portrait	318
The Posts	146
The Power of Music	144
The Power of Silence	236
The Prayer of Daft Harry	431
The Primrose	585

	Page	
The Prover		28
The Quarrel		155
The Rabbit		343
The Rain		75
The Rainbow		329
The Rat		273
The Rev. Ebenezer Paul		567
The Richest Stones		406
The Rivals		335
The River Severn		451
The Rock		364
The Sailor to his Parrot		112
The Schemes of Love		337
The Sea		93
The Signs		214
The Shadow		465
The Shameless One		568
The Sleepers		159
The Sluggard		110
The Snowflake		345
The Song of Life		292
The Song of Love		371
The Soul's Companions		254
The Soul's Destroyer		41
The Spoiler		396
The Stars at Work		551
The Start		263
The Starved		169
The Supper		472
The Sweetest Dream		542
The Temper of a Maid		551
The Thieves		531
The Time of Dreams		391
The Toothache		66
The Trance		325
The Treasured Three		370
The Trick		339
The Trickster		536
The Trusting Young		538
The Truth		277
The Tugged Hand		499

xx

The Two Children	Page	233
The Two Flocks		152
The Two Heavens		344
The Two Lives		183
The Two Loves		366
The Two Spirits		560
The Two Stars		342
The Tyrants		477
The Vagabond		453
The Villain		271
The Visitor		228
The Visitor		429
The Voice		242
The Wanderer		217
The Ways of Time		53
The Weeping Child		208
The White Cascade		231
The White Horse		394
The White Monster		238
The Wind		76
The Winged Flower		552
The Witness		487
The Wonder-Maker		188
The Woods and Banks		307
The World Approves		340
The World Dictates		435
The World May Charge		309
The Worms' Contempt		504
They're Taxing Ale Again		257
This Bantam Star		406
This Green Orchard		462
This is a Joy		482
This Night		227
This World		210
Thou Comest, May		230
Three Loves		477
Three Score and Ten		473
Thunderstorms		166
Till I Went Out		253
Time's Justice		533
Time's Rule		580

To a Bore Page 559
To a Butterfly 509
To a Contemporary 404
To a Flirt 526
To a Fool 322
To a Lady Friend 343
To a Rich Lady 557
To a Working Man 546
To Bacchus 323
To my Thoughts 570
To Play Alone 446
To Sparrows Fighting 150
To the New Year 116
To the Wind at Morn 102
To W.S. — On his Wonderful Toys 492
To-day 274
To-morrow 461
To-night 461
Traffic 369
Trails 427
Treasures 546
Trees 281
True or Fickle 464
Truly Great 86
Trust 497
Two Women 314
Tyrants 508

U is for Union 360
Uncertainty 409

V is for Venus 361
Vain Beauty 536
Violet and Oak 348
Violet to the Bee 588
Voices of Scorn 444

W is for Will 361
Waiting 94
War 543
Wasted Hours 314
We Arm to Fight 569

What County?	Page 281
What Light	426
What Thoughts are Mine	256
When and Where	420
When Autumn's Fruit	308
When Diamonds, Nibbling in my Ears	311
When I am Old	201
When I in Praise	219
When I Returned	530
When Leaves Begin	275
When Love is Young	346
When on a Summer's Morn	205
When the Cuckoo Sings	578
When We Forget	457
When Yon Full Moon	253
Where She is Now	310
Where We Agree	458
Where we Differ	92
Whiskey	594
Who Bears in Mind	312
Whom I Know	576
Wild Blossoms	412
Wild Creatures	441
Wild Oats	317
Winter Fire	403
Winter's Beauty	181
Without Contentment, what is Life?	307
With thy Strong Tide of Beauty	312
Woman	501
Wonderful Places	425
Wondering Brown	60
Words and Kisses	470
Worm-Proof	288
Worms	495
X is for Expecting	362
Y is for Youth	363
You Interfering Ladies	291
Young Beauty	182
Z is for Zany	363

FOREWORD

by DANIEL GEORGE

ALTHOUGH I never became personally acquainted with W. H. Davies, I seem to have known him well at the beginning of his literary career through my friends Duncan Williams and Holbrook Jackson who, with Edward Thomas, were among his earliest admirers and practical supporters. None of us who then bought his poems imagined that he would become both prolific and famous and achieve the almost impossible by making a living out of poetry. All we were concerned to do was to enjoy this new poet — new yet old, recalling now Herrick, now Blake — of whom it was said, as of Goldsmith, that he wrote like an angel but (according to those who had met him) talked like poor Poll, except that he was no parrot of other people's opinions. Some of us who were charmed by his artless melodies were equally pleased when he changed his note and uttered a protest against social injustice: he was on our side, we thought. Small volumes from him regularly appeared; his innocent lyricism was miraculously sustained, though its novelty had gone; old admirers yielded to young enthusiasts; anthologists increased his public. He was accepted; our prescience was vindicated.

When in the wartime year of 1943 *Collected Poems of W. H. Davies* was published with an Introduction by Sir Osbert Sitwell the book came to me for review in *Tribune*. From time to time since 1936 Jonathan Cape had enterprisingly issued volumes under the title of *Collected Poems*, which swelled in bulk as they accommodated the poet's increasing output. The 1943 volume (published after the death of Davies in 1940) contained 636 poems, with most of which I could claim to be familiar. I was also familiar with some that had been omitted from the collection.

In my review I deplored the absence of these poems, and drew the inference that they had been deliberately omitted because they were regarded as in too harsh a key for the caged canary that Davies seemed to have become — a pet of Society, a Civil List pensioner, a conformist. What I had in mind were such poems as 'City and Country':

> The City has dull eyes,
>   The City's cheeks are pale;
> The City has black spit,
>   The City's breath is stale ...

and 'The Collier's Wife':

> The Collier's wife has four tall sons
> Brought from the pit's mouth dead,
> And crushed from foot to head ...

— such poems, in short, as appeared to be intense, individual expressions, not echoes; above all, not parodies of himself. My review implied that in what I had mistakenly supposed to be a *complete* collection an important aspect of the poet's work had been suppressed: he was being presented only as an amiable warbler.

Later investigation revealed that the collection had been made by Davies himself with no such intention as I had attributed to him or to his publishers. The omissions were numerous and, as far as I could judge, indiscriminate. There was no evidence of any principle of self-criticism. Carefully checking through the separate volumes, I discovered no fewer than 113 poems not included in the 1943 collection.

All these have been added in the present edition. It will be seen that they exhibit the full range of the poet's interests and talents. Few are below his best, none as weak as his least successful. Here then is a total of 749 poems — a substantial *œuvre* for any poet, and a really wonderful achievement for a man who began with no advantages except his own natural but latent and uncultivated gift for song.

This is not the place for a critical estimate of Davies as poet and prose-writer. He was a 'sport':

> A rainbow and a cuckoo's song
> May never come together again;
>   May never come
> This side the tomb.

Poetry such as his will never be written again in this 'flowery, green, bird-singing land' — or, if written, will remain unpublished.

A full biography of him, by Richard J. Stonesifer, is appearing simultaneously with this volume.

DANIEL GEORGE

INTRODUCTION

by OSBERT SITWELL

NINA HAMNETT, generous with her friends as with her belongings, first took my brother and myself to tea with Davies in 1917; and in the space of the next few weeks we seem to have become old friends. Certainly from that time until he left London in 1925, we saw a great deal of the poet. But though he called me 'Osbert' very shortly after we met, some years went by before I was privileged to call him 'William', for Davies manifested his own individual ways in everything. If he liked a man, he would soon call him by his Christian name, but that man would be expected to continue to call him 'Davies' in return until several years had passed. On the other hand, albeit he called a woman by her first name, she must always call him 'Mr. Davies'. Moreover even these universal laws found an exception where married women were concerned; there his strong sense of propriety, coupled with an innate fear, I think, of husbands enraged at another man's familiarity with their wives, never permitted him to call them by their Christian names. Most certainly he was a man with whom everybody must have wished to be on mutual Christian name terms for his whole nature seemed to have been designed to call out the affection of his friends.

Davies came of Welsh parents and, paternally, of Cornish descent. He was brought up in Newport by his grandfather and grandmother, his father being dead when he first remembered, and his mother — whom he seldom mentioned — having married again. In addition to his grandparents and himself, his home consisted, he says, of 'an imbecile brother, a sister ... a maidservant, a dog, a cat, a parrot, a dove, and a canary bird.'[1] He does not tell us to what profession his father belonged, but his grandfather and uncle, I know, owned their own boats.

Davies' grandmother, a Baptist by denomination, was of a more austere and religious turn of mind than her husband, and he once told me that he remembered her smacking him

[1] This, and other quotations that follow, are from *The Autobiography of a Super-Tramp*, W. H. Davies, with a preface by Bernard Shaw.

severely after some manifestation of childish sin, saying between the blows:

'If-you-go-on-like-this —, you'll-be-no-better-then-that-young-Brodribb-cousin-of-yours, who's-brought-disgrace-upon-the-family!' 'That young Brodribb cousin' was, in fact, known to theatre-going audiences all over the English-speaking world as Sir Henry Irving.

Directly one knew of this relationship it was plain that William Davies bore an unmistakable likeness to Irving. His cast of face was rather long and aquiline, but with broad high cheek bones, and all of it, chin, mouth, long upper lip, nose, and high forehead, was finely sculptured and full of character. Features and hair both exhibited a naturally proud, backward slant or tilt, though there was no arrogance in him. His eyes were dark and gleaming, like those of a blackbird, and his skin possessed an almost nautical tinge. He was broad-shouldered and vigorous-looking, but of less than middle height. Having lost a leg, he wore — for he could not afford the expense of a new metal limb — a heavy wooden stump, which made a wooden sound as he walked, and gave him a slow and very personal gait, making him raise and dip his shoulders as he moved. It never, however, until the very end of his life, prevented him from going for long walks, or enjoying them. When he spoke, his voice, with its soft Welsh rhythm and intonations — he pronounced 'man' as 'mun', and 'Mr. Asquith' as 'Mr. Usquith' — was singularly attractive, but in it was to be traced, too, a disarming and pathetic diffidence, not easy to account for, since, when I knew him, he was sure both of himself and his poems.

Davies, as can be deduced from his work, and in spite of the occasionally austere appearance of his face, was by no means a puritan. He seemed to have inherited in his disposition more qualities from his sailor grandfather than from his nonconformist grandmother. In his autobiography he accounts for his liking for liquor by the fact that he was born in a public-house and 'became acquainted with the taste of drink at a very early age, receiving sups of mulled beer at bed-time, in lieu of cocoa or tea. . . .' Wine made him happy and he loved it. And of course, it always represented to him luxury. Moreover the drinking of it converted a gathering into something more memorable, more festive, 'a party'. And Davies looked forward immensely to parties, though he considered himself ever at a disadvantage in society, for he maintained that having heard so much slang all throughout his early life, his thoughts naturally first decked themselves out in it, and that, this being so, 'the shame and confusion in good company' made him 'take so long to undress and clothe them better ... that other people grow tired of waiting and take upon themselves the honour of entertainers'.

Herein, he shows himself, of course, too humble. He talked always interestingly, he loved seeing his friends, and he looked forward particularly to evening entertainments, because they presented him with the opportunity of wearing evening clothes — more of a symbol, even, than wine — and thus of testifying, to himself as well as to others, to what an altitude above his tramp-status his poems had brought him. But to us, that was neither so mysterious, nor so significant as how it was, that, leading the life he describes in *The Autobiography of a Super-Tramp*, he was able to become a poet.

His education must have been fitful, to say the most of it, but he wrote in a beautiful, small, clear, educated hand. The books which his grandmother read were *Paradise Lost*, *Pilgrim's Progress*, and Young's *Night Thoughts*. Against all others she warned him, but he contrived as a youth to read Shelley, Marlowe, and Shakespeare. At fourteen or fifteen, he was apprenticed to the picture-frame trade, but being consumed with a passion for reading, could not apply himself sufficiently to his craft. (During this period he went so far as to compose and cause to be printed a poem describing a storm at night.) After his apprenticeship was finished, he tried to persuade his grandmother — his grandfather being by now dead — to finance him so that he might go to the New World, but she refused. He then took work for six months in Bristol, whence he was recalled home by the old lady's death. Here he found that her estate was in the hands of a trustee, and that she had left the profits of it to be divided equally, every week, among her three grandchildren. Accordingly, he obtained for himself, 'on account', an advance of fifteen pounds, and embarked for America, where he quickly adapted himself to the life of a tramp.

Through spring and summer and autumn he as a rule

begged his way, though sometimes he was engaged to pick fruit, strawberries being the first crop. Usually he and his fellow tramps, by a convenient arrangement with the conniving Sheriff, spent the winter in prison, so as to be sure of at least a modicum of food and warmth. During this period of five years, he made some eight trips to England with cattle. After the last of these he decided to settle at home for good: but he quickly became dissatisfied once more and resolved this time to seek his fortune in Klondyke. He reached Canada, but in the act of train-jumping there, and through the negligence of a fellow tramp, he met with an accident, and in consequence his leg had to be amputated. As soon as he was well enough, he returned to London.

Here he lived in doss-houses on the money inherited from his grandmother. Shaw, to whose kindness and discernment Davies owed his first fame, says on this point: 'The exact amount of his independent income was ten shillings a week. Finding this too much for his needs, he devoted twenty per cent of it to pensioning necessitous friends in his native place: saved a further percentage to print verses with; and lived modestly on the remainder.' He had now at the age of 34 begun to write poems, and a publisher informed him that he would accept them if Davies would pay twenty-five pounds towards the cost of issuing the book. To raise this sum, he decided to have four short poems printed, and himself to sell them from door to door. Alas, even this printing was estimated to cost thirty-five shillings, and he had only contrived to put aside thirty-one shillings, so he was obliged nearly to starve himself in order to save the missing four shillings, at the rate of a further two shillings a week off his eight-shillings-a-week income. And when the poems were at last ready, he did not sell a single copy, though he made a house-to-house visitation in the suburbs. Most of the people he called upon were poor. They looked at the poet in amazement when he offered them a printed sheet for threepence. One richer woman, with a servant, gave him a penny, but refused altogether to accept the poems in return. When he reached his doss-house again that evening, he burnt every single copy.

Of his days as a tramp, he told me the following story; and though he may have written it somewhere himself, I must relate it ... One cold and wet evening Davies was sitting on a broken wooden box near a large brazier in a Lambeth doss-house. In spite of the suffocating fumes it emitted he was reading by the glow of it, for there was no light. The general noise and rowdiness were insupportable, for it was Saturday night, and everyone who could, or could not, afford it had got drunk. In the whole room he was the only quiet man, except for a mysterious stranger who sat opposite and talked to nobody. He, too, was trying to read, and something in the look of him made Davies wonder who he was. Indeed, he would have liked to enter into conversation, but the man seemed wrapped in his book, or else in melancholy thoughts, and a sort of shyness and restraint came over Davies. Many years later, however, when he consented to take part in a reading by famous modern poets, he saw there, again, on the platform, the stranger of the Lambeth doss-house. It was Francis Thompson.

During the years that I saw most of Davies he lived at 12 Great Russell Street, not far from the British Museum. Notwithstanding the hideousness of the enormous stone Y.M.C.A. palace which occupied the half of the street nearly opposite, his part of it was pretty. There, the houses are set back, so that it becomes a *place* more than a street, being lined with low eighteenth-century houses of three storeys. Davies inhabited a room on the first floor. It had pleasant, low proportions, and two windows, old and well made, but the place was rather dark, because of its wallpaper. In the middle stood a table, covered with his writing apparatus, and one wall supported a large case, full of the signed volumes of poetry presented to him by the authors. In spite of the sociability of his disposition, he liked very much to be his own master, to go and come, or read or work quietly, as he felt inclined, or sometimes just to stay at home and puzzle over various new accomplishments which he still found troublesome. His civil-list pension of seventy-five pounds a year had been doubled by 'Mr. Usquith', and such a sum represented to him a Crœsus-like fortune. Alas! money brought, as well as its pleasure, its own responsibilities.

On a spring afternoon, then, we went to visit him unexpectedly, and found him seated before his table. His face wore a look of mingled gloom and bewilderment. In front of him was a cheque-book. Obviously some connection must exist between his aspect and this object. For a long time he would not confide in us, but, finally, after extracting a promise of secrecy, he explained. He had been asked for a subscription for some object, and the secretary had remarked airily, 'Don't make the cheque out to me, draw it to yourself'. Davies had felt that to ask for an elucidation on this point would impair his status as a man of the world, so he had returned home to pass a miserable hour or two pondering what the mystic phrase could signify? If it got out, the situation would seem so ridiculous, he felt; people would be as surprised and amused at such an unexpected lack of *savoir faire*, as if D'Orsay or Brummel had been found incapable of tying a cravat.

Davies would often come to stay with my brother and myself. He particularly loved the walk by the river from the Houses of Parliament, as far as the Physick Garden, over which our house looked. Usually, therefore, he went the whole distance on foot, carrying a bag. No doubt, if his real leg became tired, he took a short rest and refreshment at one of his favourite public-houses on the way. The attraction to him of the Embankment, however, consisted in the contrast it offered between the warehouses and huge, black factories opposite Pimlico, and the idyllic beauty of the neighbouring Battersea Park which lay at dusk like a sleepy wood across the water. I suppose, though he loved London, he always missed the country.

On a hot evening in July, when he was staying with us, it was growing dark, and the dining-room windows were wide open. I noticed a sudden look of intentness on Davies's face, and he lifted a hand, and said 'Hush! . . . There's an owl!' Our ears could not reach so far, but he had heard it, right across the river, from Battersea Park. In his expression was all the lighted rapture of his country-man's soul — *countryman* is too insufficient a word, and *tramp* too derogatory.

When Davies came to stay with us, we used to take him on Sunday afternoons to hear Violet Gordon Woodhouse play the harpsichord and clavichord in her house in Ovington Square. Being a genius herself, she of course recognized at once in this other extraordinary and fascinating individual the same qualities of fire that he recognized in her. They soon became fast friends, and a result of these visits to her was that Davies wrote and dedicated to her a beautiful poem: he brought it to her with the words, 'A lady like you should live for ever'.

After Davies married, in 1925, he settled at Nailsworth, in Gloucestershire, not far from Mrs. Gordon Woodhouse at Nether Lypiatt, and we saw little of him, except when we went to stay with her. On these occasions, however, she would always arrange for the Davieses to come to dinner. He would talk as if we had met every day, asking after old friends, telling us of Jim, his pet toad whom he fed regularly with saucers of milk — and whom, according to Mrs. Davies, he 'encouraged' — of what he had been writing, and of the trials to which he had been subjected by the cruel overcharging of unworthy members of the medical profession in the neighbourhood.

'Of course, I *can* pay,' I remember him saying, *apropos* of this. 'But it will spoil my Christmas.'

The last time I saw him was at his own house, about a month after the collapse of France. He was too ill to come over to dine, so my hostess motored me over to his home, 'Glendower'. I had not been in the English country-side since I had returned, about six weeks before, from Italy and the South of France, and it seemed to me that it had decked itself out in that particular glory with which it seems to oppose public or private misfortune. A narrow road, with a wonderful view over the long stone town, straggling along the river, wound up the steep side of the hill on which the house was situated. We had been nervous that we might not be able to see Davies, for there had been no way of letting him or Mrs. Davies know that we were coming. However, we were fortunate in finding them at home, and in the fact that he was out of pain at the moment.

I thought William looked very ill, but his head, so typical of him in its rustic or nautical boldness, with the black hair now greying a little, but stiff as ever, surrounding the high, bony forehead, seemed to have acquired an even more sculptural quality. He was full that day of plans for his small, terraced garden that ran along the slopes above the house and caught all the sunshine. Whilst he was on the lawn, talking to Violet Gordon Woodhouse, and explaining what alterations had been made, I was able to ask Mrs. Davies the nature of his illness. She told me that his heart showed alarming symptoms of weakness, and that the doctors attributed its condition to the continual dragging weight of his wooden leg. Mrs. Davies, with her solicitude for him, never allowed him to realize the seriousness of his illness, for, in his gentle way, he was already nervous about himself. And I can still hear the puzzled tones of his voice, full of pathos, as he said to me:

'I've never been ill before, really, except when I had that accident and lost my leg . . . And, d'you know, I grow so irritable when I've got that pain, I can't bear the sound of people's voices.' And then, after an instant's pause, he added:

'Sometimes I feel I should like to turn over on my side and die.'

I am sure, all the same, that he did not know he was going to die. The rest of his talk was most cheerful and reassuring.

I asked to see Jim, the toad, but it was dead . . . Then one of the party said what a pity it was that a house in front and a little below, blocked part of the view, and Davies told us how, some fifty years before, it had been built, especially for that obstructive purpose by a spiteful neighbour who, when he had finished his wicked work, dropped dead. As he related the story of this old feud, of which the four stout walls in front of us were the solid materialization, he contrived, because of his own simplicity and concern at the evil of the action, to invest the narrative with a palpitating Homeric interest.

Alas, he died three months later, and this was the final talk we were ever to enjoy with this extraordinary and memorable being, who, for all his humility, bore about him something of the primitive splendour and directness of the Elizabethan age: in which, as his appearance testified, he would have been equally at home. No one who knew him will, or ever could, forget him, even had he never written so many lovely poems, fresh and exquisite as flowers, to keep his memory alive; and no one who knew him will ever be able to recall him without a smile of pleasure and regret, without tenderness, and without gratitude for a character that was no less remarkable in itself than in the genius it supported and nourished, and of which even the little blemishes and flaws were singularly endearing.

THE COMPLETE POEMS
OF W. H. DAVIES

1. Autumn

Autumn grows old: he, like some simple one,
In Summer's castaway is strangely clad;
Such withered things the winds in frolic mad
Shake from his feeble hand and forehead wan.

Autumn is sighing for his early gold,
And in his tremble dropping his remains;
The brook talks more, as one bereft of brains,
Who singeth loud, delirious with the cold.

O now with drowsy June one hour to be!
Scarce waking strength to hear the hum of bees,
Or cattle lowing under shady trees,
Knee deep in waters loitering to the sea.

I would that drowsy June awhile were here,
The amorous South wind carrying all the vale –
Save that white lily true to star as pale,
Whose secret day-dream Phoebus burns to hear.

2. Beauty's Light

Think not her face is patched with pink,
Or is a jumbled mess to seem,
As berries red, that neither sink
Nor swim in shallows of pale cream –
Oh, no! her face it is not white,
Nor red, nor brown, nor dark, nor fair,

Nor yellow sure, though all the light
Of gold and yellow flower meets there;
So radiant is my loved one's face
There's not one colour there to trace.

I know not where the light turns on:
Whether that wondrous ball of hair
And golden fire reflects upon
Her cheeks, creating sunbeams there,
I cannot tell; but it is sweet
Back of that column white as snow
To let my fingers link and meet
Under her hair falls, and to know
Her mine; where it feels warm; a nest
Just emptied by the birds at rest.

A thousand sunbeams on each cheek
Are crowding eager to o'erleap
Her blue eyes' fence rails, where they seek
To drown themselves in pools so deep;
And leapt them seems that many have,
Yet, strange to say, not one could drown,
But may be seen afloat the wave,
Bobbing their bodies up and down;
And not a beam that leapt the fence
Lost its soul's light in consequence.

3. Sleep

Life's angel half, sweet Sleep,
When, like the mermaid, thou
In all thy loveliness
Dost rise from out the deep

Where Life is foul to see –
Men wake to scheme and sin,
But thou dost keep them pure
In that sweet hour with thee.

The flower upon the hill,
Where caves and crags and peaks
Carry the thunder on
After the heavens are still,
Knows thee: as that cared flower
Within some sheltering wood,
And houses built by men,
And in my lady's bower.

If Age hath followed Truth,
A conscience clean and pure
Is unto him as is
Sweet Innocence to Youth;
But Age and Innocence
Dost thou, sweet Sleep, reward:
Thou givest rest to both,
To both art recompense.

Yet thou hast awful power
When thou art lying still
And breathing quietly!
Was it not such an hour
Dark Murder slunk away,
Fearing thy innocence
More than the watchfulness
Of men in armed array?

Thou makest War to cease
Awhile, and armies pause;
And in the midst of strife
Thou bringest them to peace;
The tyrant must delay
The cruel deed at thy command;
Oppressed ones know thy balm
Can take their fears away.

4.   A Drinking Song

A Bee goes mumbling homeward pleased,
He has not slaved away his hours;
He's drunken with a thousand healths
Of love and kind regard for flowers.
Pour out the wine,
His joy be mine.

Forgetful of affairs at home,
He has sipped oft and merrily;
Forgetful of his duty – Oh!
What can he say to his queen bee?
He says in wine,
'Boo to her shrine!'

The coward dog that wags his tail,
And rubs the nose with mangy curs,
And fearful says, 'Come play, not fight,'
Knows not the draught to drown his fears;
Knows not the wine,
The ruby shine.

Poor beggar, breathless in yon barn,
Who fears a mouse to move thy straw,
Must Conscience pester thee all night,
And fear oppress with thoughts of law?
O dearth of wine,
No sleep is thine.

Is Bacchus not the god of gods,
Who gives to Beauty's cheeks their shine?
O Love, thou art a wingless worm;
Wouldst thou be winged, fill thee with wine;
Fill thee with wine,
And wings be thine.

Then, Bacchus, rule thy merry race,
And laws like thine who would not keep?
And when fools weep to hear us laugh,
We'll laugh, ha! ha! to see them weep.
O god of wine,
My soul be thine.

5. Death

Beauty'll be no fairer than
Agèd dame so shrunk and wan,
Whom she looks on proudly. Now,
Did Death strike them sudden low,
Strike them down, a little while
Vanished Beauty's velvet smile,
Ugly grinner she, and few
Mark the difference 'tween these two.
Nothing here shall arbitrate,
Chivalry intimidate,

27

Hour of doom, or change Death's laws;
Kings hire no ambassadors.
Death makes monarchs grinning clowns,
Fits their skulls for bells, not crowns.

6. Love Absent

Where wert thou, love, when from Twm Barlum turned
The moon's face full the way of Alteryn,
And from his wood's dark cage the nightingale
Drave out clear notes across the open sheen?

I stood alone to see the ripples run
From light to shade, and shade to light in play;
Like fearsome children stealing guilty moves
When Age is dozing – when thou wert away.

The banks of Alteryn are no less sweet,
Nor Malpas brook more chary of his flower,
And I unchanged as they; but thou, dear love,
Allowest Time to part us with his hours.

7. The Prover

If Life gives friends,
'Tis Death that keeps them true;
When living long
Time proves them false and few;
So Life's a boon
When Death is coming soon.

Life has no joy
Except we cherish some
Illusive dream:
If Wisdom come,
Life were no boon –
Did Death not come more soon.

I loved a maid
Time has proved false to be;
Would Death had come
When true that maid to me!
Life were a boon
Had Death been coming soon.

8.   Love's Coming

An hour or more she's gone,
And we are left alone,
I and her bird.
At last he twittered sweet,
To hear my loved one's feet,
And I, too, heard.

When she had entered,
He tilted then his head,
If right or wrong;
But when her voice was heard
A frenzy seized the bird
To rave in song.

'Peace, pet, my love is near,
Her voice I cannot hear
In such a din;

29

Thou couldst not call more loud
Unto a smiling cloud
That May hides in.'

Now, what his thoughts could be –
If she still spake and he
In harmony;
Or had forgetful grown,
Enamoured of his own
Sweet melody –

Is not my say; I know
I out with her must go
To hear her story.
We left that raving thing –
Made worse by laughter – sing
Out his mad glory.

9.   In a Lodging House

'Get to thy room,' a voice told me,
'From sottish lips in blasphemy';
And I said this: 'If I go there,
Silence will send me to Despair;
Then my weak What I Am will be
Mocked by that one I wish to be;
And leeches of regret will lie
On me to palely stupefy,
Close sucking at my heart's content' –
Yet I arose, to my room went.
I knew't : scarce off my garments were
When came the funeral gathering there

To bury my dead hopes, as night
By night to mock my Fancy's sight.
There was a meeting-house adjoined,
Where rich ones, rare and few of kind,
Fed little children, came to cheer
Parents with music sweet to hear.
While now I grieved a real voice stole
Into my room, and sang this soul
To heaven from hell, though I knew well
Silence would drift it back to hell
When that sweet sound was heard no more.
She sang to me a chanted shore
Where seamaids' dripping tresses spread
And made the rocks gold carpeted;
She sang me back to childhood's way,
To fields with lambs to see at play,
And sheep that coughed like men. Again
I saw quaint treasures of the main,
Dried fishes, model ships, and shells,
And coral stalks, and seaweed bells,
In my grandfather's house. Ah! sweet
To bear his boast through school and street –
'Master of my own ship was I.'
Again I heard his footsteps nigh,
As to and fro the passage dark
He walked, as though on his own bark;
When granny, I, a sister, brother,
Huddled under cosy cover.
Now have I lived my score and ten,
Yet less my hope than older men.
No collier bowelled in the earth
But Hope shall flush with rosy breath;
No seaman drowning in the main,
Nor traveller perished on a plain,

Where all is silent, and the wind
Prowls day and night in vain to find
A living thing to make a moan,
Or mountaineer was lost – nay, none
Of these but Hope makes less afraid,
And flatters to some call for aid.
Yet here lives one a score and ten,
And less his hope than older men.
I cared not for that singer's grace,
If plain she were or fair of face,
Or what her station, age might be –
She was a Voice, no more to me,
But such an one, so sweet and fresh,
I made no judgment on her flesh.
It seemed a spirit there to float,
Alighting with such raptured note
That it must ease its heart of. Oh,
Woman; thy sweet voice none others know
As those to whom thou'rt seldom heard;
Who have no flower to tend, no bird
For pet, no child to play – to give
A cultured joy to ones that live
In common lodging house. To hear
A sweet voice is to me more dear
Than sound of organs, bands, or bells.
Discordant bursts lead out soft swells
Of instrumental harmony –
Love's voice is from all discord free,
Here darkly die, die darkly here,
And lack e'en Friendship's common tear;
A wreck of men, one score and ten,
And less thy hope than older men.

10. Lines to a Sparrow

What shall we call thee – mouse o' the air,
To raid our buds, make our trees bare,
To rob the sunlight of its grain,
More mischievous than April's rain;
To rob our orchards, and to knock
Young blossoms down, to spoil and pock
Nature's fair face, in spite and wrath –
As he, thy brother of the earth,
Who creeps at night-time slyly forth
To tear our satins, silks, and what
He cannot munch makes wanton rot?
Nay, not like him art thou, for he
Doth from his own poor shadow flee,
And is a fearsome wretch, to show
A guilt his conscience should not know;
And so ridiculous his fear
That Innocence, without a tear
Delights to prison him; but thou
Art guiltier than we will allow.
It is in wintry weather when
The robin turns a beggar, then
Jays, pigeons, steal the squirrel's store;
But, when the winter's stress is o'er,
They are dishonourable no more –
Yet thou art thief, despoiler ever,
Through sunny and through stormy weather.
Time was thou didst perform great work,
And slay slugs, bugs, and things that lurk
In pioneer's path; of late
Thou hast incurred our mortal hate,
And we would hunt thee out of life –
Were't not for such unequal strife;

Our gins and traps, we must confess,
Are vain, and powder powerless;
And all our cunning arts are vain,
The triumph thine, and ours the pain.
Man cannot shake thee off: as though
A billow reared and plunged to throw
The wind that on its archèd crest
Jockeyed from shore to shore, and rest
Not for a moment gave – e'en so
Thy triumph none can overthrow.
With all this fuss of thee, I doubt
Thou art all bad, as men make out;
Not Cocky Sparrow, nor Jim Mouse,
O foolish man, that robs thy house:
If thou wouldst know what takes thy feed,
Set trap for hand of human greed;
'Tis not that sparrows, mice are sly –
On men who govern men keep eye.
Brown sparrow, with us everywhere,
Go, multiply without a care:
When larks sing over fields unroamed,
And sealèd woods by night are stormed,
Surrendering unto nightingales –
When cuckoos call to hills from vales,
Thou, Sparrow mine, art here and near,
To find all times, come year, go year.

11. The Hill-side Park

Some banks cropped close, and lawns smooth mown
    and green,
Where, when a daisy's guiltless face was seen,

Its pretty head came sacrifice to pride
Of human taste – I saw upon the side
Of a steep hill. Without a branch of wood
Plants, giant-leaved, like boneless bodies stood.
The flowers had colonies, not one was seen
To go astray from its allotted green,
But to the light like mermaids' faces came
From waves of green, and scarce two greens the same.
And everywhere man's ingenuity
On fence and bordering: for I could see
The tiny scaffolding to hold the heads
And faces overgrown of flowers in beds
On which their weak-developed frames must fall,
Had they not such support upright and tall.
There was a fountain, and its waters' leap
Was under a full-quivered Cupid's keep.
And from his mother's lip the spray was blown
Upon adjusted rock, selected stone;
And so was placed that all the waters fell
Into a small ravine in a small dell,
And made a stream, where that wee river raved,
As gold his rocks and margent amber paved.
This park, it was a miracle of care,
But sweeter far to me the prospects there:
The far beyond, where lived Romance near seas
And pools in haze, and in far realms of trees.
I saw where Severn had run wide and free,
Out where the Holms lie flat upon a sea
Whose wrinkles wizard Distance smoothed away,
And still sails flecked its face of silver-grey.

12. The Lodging House Fire

My birthday – yesterday,
Its hours were twenty-four;
Four hours I lived lukewarm,
And killed a score.

I woke eight times and rose,
Came to our fire below,
Then sat four hours and watched
Its sullen glow.

Then out four hours I walked,
The lukewarm four I live,
And felt no other joy
Than air can give.

My mind durst know no thought
It knew my life too well:
'Twas hell before, behind,
And round me hell.

Back to that fire again,
Ten hours I watch it now,
And take to bed dim eyes,
And fever's brow.

Ten hours I give to sleep,
More than my need, I know;
But I escape my mind
And that fire's glow.

For listen: it is death
To watch that fire's glow;
For, as it burns more red
Men paler grow.

O better in foul room
That's warm, make life away,
Than homeless out of doors,
Cold night and day.

Pile on the coke, make fire,
Rouse its death-dealing glow;
Men are borne dead away
Ere they can know.

I lie; I cannot watch
Its glare from hour to hour;
It makes one sleep, to wake
Out of my power.

I close my eyes and swear
It shall not wield its power;
No use, I wake to find
A murdered hour

Lying between us there!
That fire drowsed me deep,
And I wrought murder's deed –
Did it in sleep.

I count us, thirty men,
Huddled from Winter's blow,
Helpless to move away
From that fire's glow.

So goes my life each day –
Its hours are twenty-four –
Four hours I live lukewarm,
And kill a score.

No man lives life so wise
But unto Time he throws
Morsels to hunger for
At his life's close.

Were all such morsels heaped –
Time greedily devours,
When man sits still – he'd mourn
So few wise hours.

But all my day is waste,
I live a lukewarm four
And make a red coke fire
Poison the score

13. Saints and Lodgers

Ye saints, that sing in rooms above,
Do ye want souls to consecrate?
Here's 'Boosy' Bob, 'Pease Pudding' Joe,
And 'Fishy Fat,' of Billingsgate.

Such language only they can speak,
It juggles heaven and hell together;
One threatens, with a fearful oath,
To slit a nose like a pig's trotter.

Here's sporting Fred, swears he is robbed,
And out of fifteen shillings done
By his own pal, who would not lend
Sixpence to back a horse that won.

Here's Davie, he's so used to drink,
When sober he is most bemuddled;
He steers his craft with better skill,
And grows quite sly when he is fuddled.

Here's 'Brummy' Tom, a little man,
Who proudly throws his weight in drink;
He knows men think him poor when sober,
And then, ashamed, to bed doth slink.

The 'Masher' who, by his kind deeds,
The friendship of our house hath lost;
He lent out cash that's not repaid –
They hate him worst who owe him most.

Here's 'Irish' Tim, outspoken wretch,
Insult him, he is thy staunch friend;
But say 'Good morning,' civil like,
He'll damn thee then to thy life's end.

What use are friends if not to bear
Our venom and malicious spleen!
Which, on our life! we dare not give
To foes who'll question what we mean.

Come down, ye saints, to old 'Barge' Bill,
And make his wicked heart to quake,
His stomach nothing can upset,
He boils his tea an hour to make.

Ye saints above, come to these sinners:
To 'Sunny' James, and 'Skilly' Bob,
'The Major,' 'Dodger,' 'Tinker' George,
And 'Deafy,' he's the lodgers' snob.

Here's 'Yank,' we call 'All Legs and Wings,'
He's so erratic in his motion;
And poor wee 'Punch,' a sickly man –
He's worse when he hath ta'en his lotion.

'Haymaker' George, a pig for pickles,
And 'Brass' for old clay pipes swops new;
Here's 'Balmy' Joe, he's cursèd clean,
Sweeps beetles in one's mutton stew.

'Australian' Bill, ta'en sick away,
Came home to find his wife hath slid
To other arms; he's done with Liz,
But in his heart he wants the kid.

Here's Jack, so mean he begs from beggars,
Who make scant living door to door;
Here's 'Slim,' a quiet man awake,
Whose sleep's a twenty-horse-power snore.

Here's 'Sailor,' pacing to and fro,
Twice on his four hours' watch to see;
Ten paces forward, ten go aft –
A silent man and mystery.

'The Watchman' takes twelve naps a day
And at each wake his mouth is foul;
When he shall wake from his last sleep
He'll have good cause to curse his soul.

Here's gentle Will, who knows most things,
Throws light on Egypt and the Nile –
And many more to consecrate,
If, Christian folk, ye think worth while.

Toy-sellers, fish-men, paper-men,
A few work barges, few are cadgers;
Some make up flowers from wire and wool,
Some pensions take – such are our lodgers.

14. The Soul's Destroyer

London! What utterance the mind finds here!
In its academy of art, more rich
Than that proud temple which made Ophir poor,
And the resources famed of Sheba's Queen.
And its museums, hoarding up the past,
With their rare bones of animals extinct;
And woven stuffs embroidered by the East
Ere other hemispheres could know that Peace
Had trophies pleasanter to win than War;
The great man, wrought to very life in stone –
Of genius, that raises spirits that
It cannot lay until their will is wrought –
Till in their eyes we seek to wander awed,
Lost in the mind's immensity, to find
The passage barred, the spirit gone away.
And not without sweet sounds to hear: as I
Have heard the music, like a hiding child,
Low chuckling its delight behind a wall,
Which, with a sudden burst and joyous cry,

Out leapt and on my heart threw its sweet weight –
When strolling in the palace-bounded parks
Of our great city on a summer's morn.
Now, one who lives for long in London town
Doth feel his love divided 'tween the two –
A city's noise and Nature's quiet call:
His heart is as a mother's, that can hear
Voices of absent children o'er the sea
Calling to her, and children's words at home.
E'en when old Thames rolls in his fog, and men
Are lost, and only blind men know their way;
When Morning borrows of the Evening's lamps,
Or when bewildered millions battle home
With stifled throats, and eyes that burn with pain
Still are there lovers faithful to such moods.
But in thy slums, where I have seen men gaunt,
In their vile prisons where they wander starved
Without a jailer for their common needs –
Heard children whimper to their mother's moan;
Where rich ones, had they love, with willing hands,
Have privilege to win their godhead soon
By charity that's needless in new realms –
Oh, who can love thy slums with starving ones!
Where children live, like flowers in Ocean's dells,
Unvisited by light or balmy wind:
As daffodils, that plead with their sweet smiles
Our charity for their rude father March.
Thy place is in the slums, O Charity,
These are thy churches for thy visitings;
The charity that seeks is nobler far
Than charity that must at home be sought.
This London served my life for full five years.
In sheer disgust to know intemperance
And poverty, and leaning to the sot

42

Who lays this precious intellect to sleep,
As though no beauty was in all the world,
With heaven and earth scarce worthy of a thought,
And helpless grown of every future joy –
Methought return to Nature might restore
Youth's early peace and faith's simplicity.
Though Hope be an illusion, yet our life
Were never so bewildered as without it;
An April day of sunny promises
When we are suffering actual cold and want,
And child of Discontent – without such hints
Of coming joy Life's name were Vanity.
Hopeless had I become, a wreck of men;
A derelict that neither sinks nor floats,
Is drifting out of sight of heaven and earth,
Not of the ways of men, but *in* their ways.
And there lived one, now to another wed,
Whom I had secret wish to look upon,
With sweet remembrance of our earlier years.
Her presence then a pool of deep repose
To break Life's dual run from Innocence
To Manhood, and from Manhood unto Age,
And a sweet pause for all my murmuring;
Until a way, for which is no account,
Set me to run again, and she received
Into her favour one who was my friend.
Oft had I mourned those days for ever gone
We went together side by side to school,
Together had our holidays in fields
Made golden by June's buttercups; in woods,
Where under ferns fresh pulled I buried her,
And called her forth like Lazarus from the grave
She'd laughing come, to shake her curls until
Methought to hear full half a hundred bells.

A grown-up world took playful notice soon,
Made me feel shame that grew a greater love;
She was more chary of her laughter then,
And more subdued her voice, as soft and sweet
As Autumn's, blowing through his golden reeds.
In her sweet sympathies she was a woman
When scarcely she was more than child in years,
And yet one angry moment parted us,
And days of longing never joined us more.

One morning I awoke with lips gone dry,
The tongue an obstacle to choke the throat,
And aching body weighted with more heads
Than Pluto's dog; the features hard and set,
As though encasèd in a plaster cast;
With limbs all sore through falling here and there
To drink the various ales the Borough kept
From London Bridge to Newington, and streets
Adjoining, alleys, lanes obscure from them,
Then thought of home and of the purer life,
Of Nature's air, and having room to breathe,
A sunny sky, green field, and water's sound;
Of peaceful rivers not yet fretful grown
As when their mouths have tasted Ocean's salt;
And where the rabbits sit amid their ferns,
Or leap, to flash the white of their brown tails.
Less time a grey crow picks the partridge clean,
I was apparelled, and, with impulse that
Was wonderful in one of many sprees,
Went onward rapidly from street to street.
I still had vision clear of Nature's face,
Though muddled in my senses to the ways
And doings of the days and nights before.

44

I heard the city roaring like a beast
That's wronged by one that feared an open strife
And triumphed by his cunning – as I walked.
It followed on for hours with rushing sound,
As some great cataract had burst all bounds
And was oncoming with its mingled pines –
The fallen sentinels – to choke the sea.
Once in awhile the sound, though not less near,
Seemed distant, barred by dwellings closely joined,
But at a corner's turn heard full again;
Yet lessened soon and sure to softer ways
Of a low murmuring – as though it found
Anger was vain, and coaxed for my return.
All day walked I, and that same night, I scorned
The shelter of a house, lay peaceful down
Beneath the glorious stars; beneath that nest
Of singing stars men call the Milky Way;
Thought it, maybe, the way that spirits take,
And heavenly choir to sing triumphal march
For dead men for the New Jerusalem.
I was alone: had left the Borough in
Safe care of my old cronies, who would keep
Its reputation from becoming changed
Into a quiet neighbourhood.

As with a shipwrecked seaman cast ashore,
And carried to a land's interior
By the rude natives, there to work and slave
Quarries and mines of their barbaric king;
Who after years escapes his servitude
To wander lost, at last to see before
Him mountains which he climbs to see beyond,
When on their top he stands – beholds the sea'

And, wonders more, a fleet of friendly flags
Lying at anchor for his signalling –
Such joy a hundred times a day was mine
To see at every bend of the road the face
Of Nature different. And oft I sat
To hear the lark from his first twitter pass
To greater things as he soared nearer heaven;
Or to the throstle, singing nearer home,
With less of that abandon and wild fire,
But steady, like a sheltered light from wind.
What joy was mine, sweet Nature, to return!
The flower so wild, reared on thine own pure milk
Of dew and rain, and by thy sunbeams warmed,
Speckled the green with light of various hues;
The hawthorn it caught slippery Mercury,
And smothered him to smell of where he'd been;
And everything that had a voice made sound,
The speechless things were gladsome in dumb smiles.
It was a day of rest in heaven, which seemed
A blue grass field thick dotted with white tents
Which Life slept late in, as 'twere holiday.
Yon lord or squire in his great house,
Who himself busies guessing all his days
The age of horses and the weight of hogs,
The breed of hounds – not such as he has held
The ear to Nature's quiet heart-beat. No;
He overlooks the flower to spy the fox,
Ignores the lark's song for the halloing horn,
Nor hears the echo of that horn he loves –
Not such as he is rich in Nature's stores.
I've seen proud Autumn in more gold arrayed,
Ere cold October strips and blows him bare,
Than ever delved from earth or ta'en from water's
    wash;

More pearls seen scattered to a summer's morn
Than Ocean e'er possessed in depths or out,
Though in his water's workshop – like a slave.
Who sees a cobweb strung with dew pearls, sees
A finer work than jewelled crowns of gold.
Few are thy friends, sweet Nature, in these days,
But thou art still the Solitary's love.
The glory of the river's long since gone,
The land is sped and beauty unrevealed.
The motor-car goes humming down the road,
Like some huge bee that warns us from its way.
On, on, we speed by fire on slippery rails,
And earth goes spinning back from whence we came,
And through the trees, or on the hills' smooth tops
That cut the heaven clean – the day's one orb
Goes with us till he sinks before the dark,
Clouds towering with him, to his back and front;
We speed our way through tunnels under ground,
Where one sees naught but faces of his kind.
Let others praise thy parts, sweet Nature; I
Who cannot know the barley from the oats,
Nor call the bird by note, nor name a star,
Claim thy heart's fulness through the face of things.
The lonely shepherd in his hut at night
Will dream of Beauty in the feverous towns,
Of Love and Gaiety, of Song and Dance;
With fore-paws on his master's crook, the dog
Sleeps dreaming his life's duty – though his flocks
Are countless, and the hills on which they roam:
So faithful I to thee, like shepherd's dog,
To follow thee with joy in all thy moods,
As docile as the lamb that Una led.
When man shall stand apart from this dear world,
And have his vision's manifold increase,

47

To see it rolled at morning when the sun
Makes lamps of domes and lighthouses of fanes,
With its green fields, blue waters, and its hills,
And smiling valleys filled with brooks and flowers;
To hear the music of the world once his,
Singing in unison with other spheres –
He shall exclaim, 'I have God's second heaven
Ere I have known the wonder of His first.'

Six days had gone, and I at length near home,
Where toil the Cymry deep in sunless pits,
And emptying all their hills to warm the world.
Soon saw familiar scenes, and saw no change:
The rookery, where never silence seemed –
For every hour seemed it to be disturbed
By strange new-comers, aliens to invade;
Or, maybe, known ones bringing envied stores
Which stay-at-homes would clamour to divide.
And near that rookery a river ran,
And over it a bridge too small for piers;
Another crossing, of irregular stones,
Was seen, which in the springtime flooded o'er;
And I had heard the river tell their number
And spell – like letters of an alphabet,
That it would never tire repeating day
And night. When young I oft had bared my feet
To go from bank to bank, leapt stone to stone,
My ankles wetted on a sunken one.
Beyond the bridge was seen the village spire –
My courage failed. I feared to see in life
Her who was now the heroine of dreams,
And sweet familiar of my solitude
And silence, and whose shadowy hand kept full

48

The cup of memory; and in such mood
Entered an inn, to seek that courage which
Makes man abuse his friends, and wish them foes;
Or puts unnatural pity in his mind
To help strange ones, forgetful of his own.
Not one known face had met my own, or voice
To recognize, until that moment came;
And then such sight to see that had the man
Been other than he was had not surprised:
He who had wed my love stood shaking there
While to his lips another held the glass
Which his own hand lacked power to raise unspilled;
And there stood he, in manner of a beast
That's drinking from a trough, but more the greed.
We greeted as old friends; few moments passed
When I inquired of her, in casual way,
On which a fearful change came over him:
'Why, she hath filled the house with merry men
To mock her husband,' he replied, and turned
His head in fear. And well I knew his thoughts,
And of such demons in a drunkard's dream,
The sleepless dream that wearies flesh and brain.
This curse of drink, in village and in town,
The curse of nations, their decline and fall,
Ere they can question purpose of this life;
And so 'twill be until the mind is reared
To see the beauty that is in the world,
Of science, art, and Nature at all times;
To know that temperance and sobriety
Is truer joy – e'en though the grave ends all –
Than an unnatural merriment that brings
A thousand tortures for its hundred joys.
He now seemed worse and moved about the room,
And many a sound of triumph, anguish made,

49

Though from his unseen foes receiving knocks
And giving in return. We stood in awe!
One looked at me and said: 'He should be home,
And we are much to blame for him; wouldst thou
See him safe there? for none can censure thee.'
'Nay, I would rather tread his threshold floor,
And dare all devils of his fancy there,
Than front his wife and children innocent.'
As some lone hunter might at sunrise see,
Upon the margent of a woodland pool,
Huge prints of something alien to his lore,
And know not if 'twere fowl or beast, or freak
Of man – so awed, amazed I stood; until
He grew more calm, and then we coaxed him home.

We reached his home, a cottage lone and small
And such a place was my ideal to live,
Where I might walk it round, touch its four sides,
Free to the sun in every latitude,
Unto the first and final look on earth.
And at its door three little Aprils played,
Three little children, little Aprils all,
So full were they of April's strife and love;
Who, when they saw us coming, ran to meet us,
To make a bridal entry with their laughter;
But saw a stranger, and their father cold,
Fell back, and followed hushed, a funeral train.
Sure, thought I, our whole duty is to leave
Our children's state exalted 'bove our own:
Equipping them with kinder thoughts than ours,
And they do likewise in their day; so through
The generations to at last attain
The climax of our mortal purity.

Had I so failed to these poor little ones
If she and I were sharing of their lives?
We entered, and we stood before her face,
And it was stern, as woe affects the man,
Not that sweet resignation of her sex.
She looked on me as one unjustly served,
A look regretful, part resigned, as if
Some retribution was my right to claim.
Her once blue sapphire eyes had not a gleam,
As they would never smile or weep again,
And had no light to draw the waters up
Which staled upon her heart. To me all seemed
So plain: that she had loved without avail,
And reasoned, then had widowed her own self,
A widowhood in which Death claimed no part.
All night he raved, and in his madness died,
And I have seen his death-look on a beast
Baring the teeth 'twas powerless to use
Against a foe of greater strength, and there
Lay dead, intentions hatefully revealed.
Such his dread look: the vicious show of teeth
Made bare in hatred to his unseen foes.
Such is this drink that fathers half our sins;
It makes a simple one responsible
For deeds which memory makes no count to save,
And proves man guilty in his innocence.
When he shall stand before his judging God
He needs must answer charges strange to him
And his own mind – to One who sees all things;
And what He sees, He never can forget.
May God have mercy on our frailties!
Sure we, though set a thousand years of pain,
Nor once should murmur at vicissitude,
Yet ill deserve those promises fulfilled

Of an eternity of bliss with Him;
And who can know the thoughts of him in hell,
Who sacrificed eternity of joy
To gratify this little life on earth!
Were't not for God Almighty's mercy, trees
Would 'scape the thunderbolt, th' unfeeling rocks
The lightning's blast; all ills would fall on man,
Who hides his conscience in a covered cage,
As dumb and silent as a moulting bird.

15. Margery

The Butterfly loves Mignonette,
    And every moment deeper sips;
When Winds do shake him by his wings,
    He fastens tighter with his lips;
So let the whole world make me shake,
I will not from my true love break.

The bird is perched alone and sings,
    Not all the rain can make him stop;
In sooth he singeth more, as though
    He'd sing one note for each rain-drop;
So, like that bird, to his heart true,
I'll sing through showers that wet me through.

A thousand trees to every house,
    A singing bird in every tree;
And in the midst of these she dwells,
    And lives for me – doth Margery;
Where we can take our sweet love's fill
Shut in a garden green and still.

16. The Ways of Time

As butterflies are but winged flowers,
    Half sorry for their change, who fain,
So still and long they lie on leaves,
    Would be thought flowers again –

E'en so my thoughts, that should expand,
    And grow to higher themes above,
Return like butterflies to lie
    On the old things I love.

17. The Likeness

When I came forth this morn I saw
    Quite twenty cloudlets in the air;
And then I saw a flock of sheep,
    Which told me how those clouds came there.

That flock of sheep, on that green grass,
    Well it might lie so still and proud!
Its likeness had been drawn in heaven,
    On a blue sky, in silvery cloud.

I gazed me up, I gazed me down,
    And swore, though good the likeness was,
'Twas a long way from justice done
    To such white wool, such sparkling grass.

18. Ale

Now do I hear thee weep and groan,
　　Who hast a comrade sunk at sea?
Then quaff thee of my good old ale,
　　And it will raise him up for thee;
Thou'lt think as little of him then
As when he moved with living men.

If thou hast hopes to move the world,
　　And every effort it doth fail,
Then to thy side call Jack and Jim,
　　And bid them drink with thee good ale;
So may the world, that would not hear,
Perish in hell with all your care.

One quart of good old ale, and I
　　Feel then what life immortal is:
The brain is empty of all thought,
　　The heart is brimming o'er with bliss;
Time's first child, Life, doth live; but Death,
The second, hath not yet his breath.

Give me a quart of good old ale,
　　Am I a homeless man on earth?
Nay, I want not your roof and quilt,
　　I'll lie warm at the moon's cold hearth,
No grumbling ghost to grudge my bed,
His grave, ha! ha! holds up my head.

54

19. 'Scotty' Bill

There's 'Scotty' Bill, four score of years,
   Who, every morning when we rise,
Will swear that summer's not yet come,
   And questions us – 'Where are the flies?'

His age, methought, unsettled him,
   Yet still I felt some strange surprise
When, every day, he damned and raved
   That Summer had not brought more flies.

I asked a lodger – 'Tell me why
   Bill swears, and where his trouble lies.'
'Old Bill makes sticky papers, and
   He makes his living catching flies.'

Now what though Summer brings sweet flowers,
   They'll not make glad his aged eyes.
Tell him not then that Summer's come,
   If she hath come without her flies.

And Bill, he knows a thing or two,
   For here he strikes the cursèd cause
That robbed sweet Summer of her flies –
   ''Tis those damn sanitation laws.'

With better food, and half a home,
   I'd back Bill for a hundred years:
Death failed to blow his light out thrice,
   Expecting help from hopeless tears.

20. The Ox

Why should I pause, poor beast, to praise
  Thy back so red, thy sides so white;
And on thy brow those curls in which
  Thy mournful eyes take no delight?

I dare not make fast friends with kine,
  Nor sheep, nor fowl that cannot fly;
For they live not for Nature's voice,
  Since 'tis man's will when they must die.

So, if I call thee some pet name,
  And give thee of my care to-day,
Where wilt thou be to-morrow morn,
  When I turn curious eyes thy way?

Nay, I'll not miss what I'll not find,
  And I'll find no fond cares for thee;
So take away those great sad eyes
  That stare across yon fence at me.

See you that Robin, by himseh,
  Perched on that leafless apple branch,
His breast like one red apple left –
  The last and best of all – by chance?

If I do but give heed to him,
  He will come daily to my door;
And 'tis the will of God, not Man,
  When Robin Redbreast comes no more.

21. Catharine

We children every morn would wait
For Catharine, at the garden gate;
Behind school-time, her sunny hair
Would melt the master's frown of care,
What time his hand but threatened pain,
Shaking aloft his awful cane;
So here one summer's morn we wait
For Catharine at the garden gate.
To Dave I say – 'There's sure to be
Some coral isle unknown at sea,
And – if I see it first – 'tis mine!
But I'll give it to Catharine.'
'When she grows up,' says Dave to me,
'Some ruler in a far countree,
Where every voice but his is dumb,
Owner of pearls, and gold, and gum,
Will build for her a shining throne,
Higher than his, and near his own;
And he, who would not list before,
Will listen to Catharine, and adore
Her face and form; and,' Dave went on –
When came a man there pale and wan,
Whose face was dark and wet though kind,
He, coming there, seemed like a wind
Whose breath is rain, yet will not stop
To give the parchèd flowers a drop:
'Go, children, to your school,' he said –
'And tell the master Catharine's dead.'

57

22.　The Forsaken Dead

What tyrant starved the living out, and kept
Their dead in this deserted settlement?
There is no voice at home, no eyes to look
Down from their windows on these gardens wild;
A tyrant hath refused his people work,
Since they had claimed a right to share his spoils,
And they have left their dead forsaken here.
Here will I sit upon this fallen tree,
Beside these ancient ruins, ivy-crowned,
Where Nature makes green mosses ooze and spread
Out of the pores of their decaying walls –
Here will I sit to mourn that people gone.
Where are they gone that there's no maiden left
To weep the fall of this sweet village lost,
Down where its waters pass the empty mills?
No living thing except one tethered lamb,
That hath been crying full an hour in vain,
And, on that green where children played their games,
Hath browsed his circle bare, and bleats to see
More dewy pastures all beyond his reach.
Where is maid Margaret, whom I saw crowned
Queen of the May before so many eyes?
And scornful Maud, of her rare beauty proud –
That cruel rosebud, with her close hard heart,
Between whose folds no mercy drop could lodge:
And where the men who threw the hammer's weight,
And leapt this common but three moons ago
When unto heaven they sent a deafening shout
Like wild Pacific, when he leaps and falls
At Raratonga, off a coral reef:
Then, in Life's glorious deep they swam and laughed,

And felt no nameless substance touch their limbs
To make them sick with dread of things unseen.
Some other tyrant, in some other shire,
Will drive his people forth, and they will come
Hither, to be this other tyrant's slaves.
Then back, ye famished strangers, or haste on:
There is no joy here, save in one short change;
Be warned to see these dead forsaken here.
Had they no dreamer here who might remain
To sing for them these desolated scenes?
One who might on a starvèd body take
Strong flights beyond the fiery larks in song,
With awful music, passionate with hate?
Were I that bard, and that poor people mine,
I would make strangers curse that tyrant's day:
Would call on Sleep, compeller of strange dreams,
Who leads the unbeliever to the Heaven he doubts,
And makes a false one fear the Hell he scorns –
Would call on Sleep to bring him ghastly dreams,
And haunt that tyrant's night without repose.

23. A Blind Child

Her baby brother laughed last night,
    The blind child asked her mother why;
    It was the light that caught his eye.
Would she might laugh to see that light!

The presence of a stiffened corse
    Is sad enough; but, to my mind,
    The presence of a child that's blind,
In a green garden, is far worse.

She felt my cloth – for worldly place;
  She felt my face – if I was good;
  My face lost more than half its blood,
For fear her hand would wrongly trace.

We're in the garden, where are bees
  And flowers, and birds, and butterflies;
  One greedy fledgling runs and cries
For all the food his parent sees!

I see them all: flowers of all kind,
  The sheep and cattle on the leas;
  The houses up the hills, the trees –
But I am dumb, for she is blind.

24. Wondering Brown

There came a man to sell his shirt,
  A drunken man, in life low down!
When Riley, who was sitting near,
  Made use of these strange words to Brown.

'Yon fallen man, that's just gone past,
  I knew in better days than these;
Three shillings he could make a day,
  As an adept at picking peas.'

'God help us all! I never heard –
  'Tis scarce believable,' said Brown;
'To think that man was what you say,
  And now to be so low and down!

'Now, Riley, had another told me,
    What you have just remarked,' said Brown,
'I would have doubted – help us, Heaven!
    That 'tis as you have said' – cried Brown.

'You'd scarcely credit it, I knew
    A man in this same house, low down,
Who owns a fish-shop now – believe
    Me, or believe me not,' said Brown.

'He was a civil sort of cove,
    But did queer things, for one low down:
Oft have I watched him clean his teeth –
    As true as Heaven's above!' cried Brown.

25. Music

Let Fortune gift on gift bestow
When Music plays it bringeth woe
For something dearer Time hath ta'en,
Which never can be ours again.
The aged beggar-man hath heard,
And tear-drops trickle down his beard
For loss of kinder looks and home,
And days that never more can come.
Here in this smoky capital,
With scarce aught seen but grimy wall
And human faces – bring to me,
Music, the things of old: the bee
Humming as Summer's months were three,
Winter had nine; bring birds and flowers,
And the green earth of childhood's hours,

With sparkling dews at early morn;
The murmuring streams; and show the corn;
And break its golden roof to show
Poppies and blueflowers where they grow.
O happy days of childhood, when
We taught shy Echo in the glen
Words she had never used before –
Ere Age lost heart to summon her.
Life's river, with its early rush,
Falls into a mysterious hush
When nearing the eternal sea:
Yet we would not forgetful be,
In these deep, silent days so wise,
Of shallows making mighty noise
When we were young, when we were gay,
And never thought Death lived – that day.

26. Facts

One night poor Jim had not a sou,
    Mike had enough for his own bed;
'Take it: I'll walk the streets to-night,'
    Said Mike, 'and you lie down instead.'

So Mike walked out, but ne'er came back;
    We know not whether he is drowned,
Or used his hands unlawfully;
    Is sick, or in some prison bound.

Now Jim was dying fast, and he
    Took to the workhouse his old bones;
To earn some water, bread, and sleep,
    They made that dying man break stones,

He swooned upon his heavy task:
  They carried him to a black coach,
And tearless strangers took him out –
  A corpse! at the infirmary's porch.

Since Jesus came with mercy and love,
  'Tis nineteen hundred years and five:
They made that dying man break stones,
  In faith that Christ is still alive.

27. New-comers

So many birds have come along,
The nightingale brings her sweet song,
With lease to charm, by her own self,
The nights of this best month in twelve.
To sit up all a night in June
With that sweet bird and a full moon –
The moon with all Heav'n for her worth,
The nightingale to have this earth,
And there we are for joy – we three.
And here's the swallow, wild and free,
Prince flyer of the air by day;
For doth he not, in human way,
Dive, float and use side strokes, like men
Swimming in some clear lake? And then,
See how he skates the iceless pond!
And lo! the lark springs from the land;
He sees a ladder to Heaven's gate,
And, step by step, without abate,

He mounts it singing, back and forth;
Till twenty steps or more from earth,
On his return, then without sound
He jumps, and stone-like drops to ground
And here are butterflies; poor things
Amazed with new-created wings;
They in the air-waves roll distrest
Like ships at sea; and when they rest
They cannot help but ope and close
Their wings, like babies with their toes.

28. Parted

Alack for life!
Worn to a stalk since yesterday
Is the flower with whom the bee did stay,
And he was but one night away.
Alack for life, I say.

Alack for life!
A flower put on her fine array,
In hopes a bee would come her way,
Who's dying in his hive this day.
Alack for life, I say.

Alack for life!
If Death like Love would throw his dart
And pierce at once a double heart,
And not to strike away one part –
Alack for life, who'd say?

29. The Jolly Tramp

I am a jolly tramp: I whine to you,
Then whistle till I meet another fool.
I call the labourer sir, the boy young man,
The maid young lady, and the mother I
Will flatter through the youngest child that walks.
In sooth, there's no joy in a poor man's house,
Save when the little baby walks or swears;
Still do they pity my pretended grief.
When, like that fallen oak stripped of its bark,
Showing the naked muscles of its limbs
Flat on the ground – I lie with my coat off,
Hidden in deep green grass that's high enough
To miss a baby in, I pity half the world.
If it be summer time, then what care I
For naked feet, and flesh through tattered garb?
O foolish Pride, discomfort is thy due;
That made a savage take an axe to chop
His feet that were too large to fit small shoes.
What though I read few books, I can read men,
And weigh a face for what the heart is worth,
Far better than the fools who think they know.
So that the sun shines bright, I like to rest
All day, to let the body lie in sloth,
And make imagination do the work;
Such work is sweet, and brings no sweat or ache.
Their questions and their pity make me laugh,
But idle men can always find excuse.
Alas! I do not always laugh: for see
How fine was yester morn; the heavens clear;
Then came a golden cloud with three dark ones –
Three pirates following a peaceful barque;

The heavy rain tugged with its might for hours,
And almost pulled the heavens down to earth;
And then came torrents, and no jolly tramp
Was I, but whined in truth most pitiful.

30. The Toothache

Last night, though I had fifty souls,
I had been bankrupt ere the day;
    And all because this body slight
    That ill maintained its spirit's light
Had made me swear my souls away;

Had sent them humming into hell:
And all because an ivory mite
    Was by a nerve-surge pounded, bent,
    And by fierce lightnings blasted, rent,
That made the force of Nature slight.

I never heard Love's voice sound harsh,
Until it sought to soothe this evil;
    And when it said – 'Pray, do not fret:
    Be patient and – sure cure – forget,'
I could not help cry out – 'The Devil!'

31. Hope Abandoned

The drinking man maybe hath gold, and then
Ofttimes he vomits food before starved men:
But one I met had seedy clothes which shone,
So many suns had poured their fires upon.

Man! king of that strange world where none bend knee,
Whose subjects pay mock reverence to thee –
The Shadows, Coloured Imps, Fantastic Crews
Swarming a hulk condemned that rolls in boose:

Enchanter Drink! the world's half, small and great,
Mock Death by lying fearless in Death's state;
They pawn their finest tools: they know not what
In life there is to make, why they should not.

Thou leering Imp, create of flame and fume,
Who quenched such hopes as did yon mind illume,
Now, like a babe, he is near blind again,
And sees but from one corner of his brain.

The light of Love, though it from Heaven came.
It cannot now outburn Lust's fiercer flame;
This man would do a shameful deed at once,
Were he not saved from it by blessèd Chance.

Now, as the cuckoo, where he holds no right,
Attempts to put the lawful young to flight,
So I with my own reason would essay
That mind, to scatter its own thoughts away.

And so began: 'Canst thou, O man, find naught
Above in Heaven or under worth thy thought?
Why waste Life's flower, and leave behind no seed,
When such sweet joy is in pure thought and deed?

'Thou canst not know life as a pleasant thing,
Though much to practise sham manœuvring;
Or know of Nature with her glint and peep
Of flowers and dewy fields, and brooks that leap.

'Thou canst escape these slums in half a mile
For works of Art, and Music to beguile:
See hoary buildings with Time's frosted towers,
Midst spaces green and young in summer hours.

'There's beauty in our streets, and beauty seen
From river's banks that are no longer green;
Barges half sunk with bales of golden hay,
Or coals that sparkle more in sunny ray.

'I passed a carvèd porch in yonder street,
To hear a woman's voice half-timid, sweet;
Then heard a wondrous chorus burst to end,
When, confident in numbers, many blend.

'There's music in the leaves, the shaken tree;
Aye, in the ocean, cruel though it be –
That will not leave the poor drowned boy unmoved,
But cuts with rocks that face his mother loved.

'The waves that splash the sides of iron ships,
When the lone watch at night with whistling lips
Paces the deck in tune; and in the tones
Of rills, for ever polishing their stones.

'To hear the larks when higher than yon cloud,
A gale of music's blowing in heaven loud;
Or hear the mavis when the bees' time come
At eve to take their bags of honey home.

"'Tis music takes from toiler's sweat the burn,
Carries the labourer's load; there's music stern
When clouds do thunder in the mountain's caves
Sounds heard by trembling vales below, and waves.

'Hear how the axes make melodious ring
In winter, and the woodmen stir in spring,
When cracks the ice so loud, and flood-time floats
Vast forests down to fill the deep-sea boats.

'As light is first to take the infant's eyes,
So Music brings his ears their first surprise,
Who then in sport will toss his toes and bounce,
And would outleap the mother's arms at once.

'Nay, why say more? with all these charms around,
Scenes for thine eyes, and for thine ears such sound;
Yet dost thou blind those precious orbs from choice,
And into gibberish turn that human voice.

'I know thy fall: those sins we grow to love
Were only done at first that Youth might prove
Courage to follow Age; which now at last
Are sinful habits that have bound him fast,

'So came thy sins at first, and made thee bound,
Till Death shall surely find thee – as he found
The clammy thing that hid its life away,
Hutched in a hollowed rock from day to day.

'A bite of food, a pot of ale or stout,
A murder every day to talk about –
And though the sun with crimson fills the sky
Thou wilt not raise thine eyes to him on high.'

Said he: 'Are they more wise who sigh and weep,
To hear the drunkard laugh, and see him sleep?
Drink frees a mortal from the Future's dread,
And lays the Past of all its ghostly dead.

'There live some spirits made so fine and frail,
Who strive for joy and all their efforts fail.
Must steep their minds in some dark deadening stain
Be mad awhile, or else till Death insane.

'Give to the child a faded flower to be
From home to school its only company,
'Tis well content – though once or twice is heard
That simple voice cry wonder to a bird.

'The urchin in his fancy slays galore
To keep his mouth in sweetmeats every hour:
And such is Childhood, that clear well to drink,
Ere Wisdom's toad hath chanced upon its brink.

'When Age complains the year is weeping leaves,
They're tossed to give him sport – a child believes;
Who sees a sparkle warm on ice and snow,
And thinks Jack Frost the merriest wight to know.

'Youth comes with all his hopes; the loss of few
Makes others left more spirited to do:
As one at war sees comrades stricken down,
And feels their spirits work to help his own.

'The hopeful youth believes to rap until
He'll make the world give answer to his will:
As Woodpecker makes the oak's heart to fear,
And cry aloud for all the woods to hear.

'Now count those small mechanics where they toil
To show above the sea their coral isle:
As well count them as count youth's many schemes
To thwart Old Age, who frowns on his young dreams.

When our young days are o'er, Life's sad in sooth:
To change his place with that poor homeless youth
Whose chattering teeth can sing away the cold
The grey-haired millionaire would give his gold.

'Those days are gone: think of those winters told,
When Youth's warm blood did ne'er complain of cold;
And dost thou make new friends the present day,
'Tis but to talk of old friends passed away.

'Had I not hopes to feed one fond Desire,
Till Dark Despair gave me a torch of fire –
Intoxication – bade me burn my brain
And body up, for joy to kill my pain?

'I heard the voice of Fame, and I did come
To these loud parts, where ever is her home;
And day and night sought those sweet favours she
Conferred on one less worthy scorning me.

'For one drop's sake to scent Time's robe, I sought:
Distilled a hundred flowers and one of Thought;
And still to fail, though they who set the word
In hopes a thought would venture in were heard.

'Life, like that berg from Polar seas, doth show
A smiling top, with horrors hid below;
A virgin soil to mine, and it appears
Fools find the gold and wise men stones for tears.

'A thing of beauty shall created be,
Methought, and I will then sit quietly,
And in old age enjoy its sound: of course,
Necessity prevents that deed by force.

71

'And still I struggled, struggled still to fail,
Deep thinking night and day without avail
Until I came to herd with hopeless men,
To drink with them through lost ambition then.

'And oft when Inspiration came from Heaven free,
I let the sacred fire die out of me,
Since dribbling drunkards came and hemmed me in,
And sober men as bad who laughed at sin.

'And then my soul with wonder ceased to burn,
Nor sweet surprises startled me each turn:
Age early found me; Fancy hid her stores;
Self dared my Thoughts to venture out of doors.

'I have gone past my hunger now for joy,
The pleasantries of other men annoy;
I envy them the shining of their lives,
And mope in darkness as a bird that grieves.

'As that vexed Owl, on top of his dark tree,
Seeing the moon above, looks down to see
The Hunter dares to burn night fires – will shout
Till morn, and hoot till both their fires are out.

'Here in these slums to sleep and wake again,
Fretted at night by brutal cries of pain,
Year after year: I who alone had hours
With Nature to share woods and fields of flowers.

'In this strange world of little spaces, where
The millions starve, and die for want of air;
Yet mighty wastes that have for ages lain
Silent to hear the step of man in vain.

'Here in these crowded marts where reeks the stain
On bloody stalls of creatures newly slain;
On those red lumps the starvers stare with might,
And well-fed people wish no fairer sight.

'Hear how the brook will cease to shout and rave,
Passing the willow's deep and teary grave;
Who soon forgets to make his little moans,
To find more shallows wait with heaps of stones.

'But all Life's play and game is left behind,
I out of this sad pool no way can find;
Though hunger doth not make a man his prey,
Foul air will never leave him night or day.

'Sweet Nature hath her slums, where crowds of flowers
Can thrive, and not make short each other's hours;
Where swarmèd birds can for their young provide,
And no life pales, save pallor be its pride.

'Whilst wooing Fame in this her native town,
Death stripped my home, and struck my dear ones
        down;
Death hath his duty, and it would not fail
Though all the infants in the world did wail.

'When young thou dost delay returning home,
Thinking the greater joy at last to come;
But never more will come those moments dear
Of kinder eyes and voices sweet to hear.

'The farther Life goes on, more clear his eye,
To probe the past and glean Time's mystery:
But Time will never tell what Death hath done –
We can but guess – with thy belovèd one.

'When she who gave thee birth lies cold and dead,
And thou hast found no hand or voice instead –
No hand to lay that gentle spirit down,
No voice to answer for thy cheerless own:

'Old age brings then no twilight hour for thee,
Remembrances as stars to Memory;
And now thou knowest where Death's sting can be,
And how the grave hath made its victory.

"'Tis true great spirits are by Sorrow taught,
With intervals to make their feelings thought,
The world, indifferent to the man, would know –
So true that happy spirits feign such woe.

'What time the vine's roots reached the sewer's drains,
There grew more grapes than grew in former reigns;
The flower that lives most in the shade, and leaf
Grow large, as doth a human mind in grief.

'But rain without a break succeeding rain,
Will wash the buried seed out, rot the grain,
Make genius blind whose mind is with the lark
To see the dawn while others are in dark.

'The man doth choose his star, and if he fail
Inhabit that, what shall to him avail
A thousand others that would give him home?
Give him his star, or let the darkness come!'

He ceased: he who had fallen in the strife,
And might have sucked some honey out of life
And lodged it in the world's hive to its joy –
But failed, since none would give his brain employ.

32. The Rain

I hear leaves drinking rain;
   I hear rich leaves on top
Giving the poor beneath
   Drop after drop;
'Tis a sweet noise to hear
These green leaves drinking near.

And when the Sun comes out,
   After this rain shall stop,
A wondrous light will fill
   Each dark, round drop;
I hope the Sun shines bright;
'Twill be a lovely sight.

33. A Life's Love

How I do love to sit and dream
   Of that sweet passion, when I meet
The lady I must love for life!
   The very thought makes my Soul beat
Its wings, as though it saw that light
Silver the rims of my black night.

I see her bring a crimson mouth
   To open at a kiss, and close;
I see her bring her two fair cheeks,
   That I may paint on each a rose;
I see her two hands, like doves white,
Fly into mine and hide from sight.

In fancy hear her soft, sweet voice;
　　My eager Soul, to catch her words,
Waits at the ear, with Noah's haste
　　To take God's message-bearing Birds;
What passion she will in me move –
That Lady I for life must love!

34.　Robin Redbreast

Robin on a leafless bough,
　　Lord in Heaven, how he sings!
Now cold Winter's cruel Wind
　　Makes playmates of poor, dead things.

How he sings for joy this morn!
　　How his breast doth pant and glow!
Look you how he stands and sings,
　　Half-way up his legs in snow!

If these crumbs of bread were pearls,
　　And I had no bread at home,
He should have them for that song;
　　Pretty Robin Redbreast, Come.

35.　The Wind

Sometimes he roars among the leafy trees
Such sounds as in a narrow cove, when Seas
Rush in between high rocks; or grandly roll'd,
Like music heard in churches that are old.

Sometimes he makes the children's happy sound,
When they play hide and seek, and one is found.
Sometimes he whineth like a dog in sleep,
Bit by the merciless, small fleas; then deep
And hollow sounds come from him, as starved men
Oft hear rise from their empty parts; and then
He'll hum a hollow groan, like one sick lain,
Who fears a move will but increase his pain.
And now he makes an awful wail, as when
From dark coal-pits are brought up crushed, dead men
To frantic wives. When he's on mischief bent,
He breeds more ill than that strange Parliament
Held by the witches, in the Hebrides;
He's here, he's there, to do whate'er he please.
For well he knows the spirits' tricks at night,
Of slamming doors, and blowing out our light,
And tapping at our windows, rattling pails,
And making sighs and moans, and shouts and wails.
'Twas he no doubt made that young man's hair white,
Who slept alone in a strange house one night,
And was an old man in the morn and crazed,
And all who saw and heard him were amazed.

36. Jenny

Now I grow old, and flowers are weeds,
    I think of days when weeds were flowers;
When Jenny lived across the way,
    And shared with me her childhood hours.

Her little teeth did seem so sharp,
    So bright and bold, when they were shown,
You'd think if passion stirred her she
    Could bite and hurt a man of stone.

Her curls, like golden snakes, would lie
   Upon each shoulder's front, as though
To guard her face on either side –
   They raised themselves when Winds did blow.

How sly they were! I could not see,
   Nor she feel them begin to climb
Across her lips, till there they were,
   To be forced back time after time.

If I could see an Elm in May
   Turn all his dark leaves into pearls,
And shake them in the light of noon –
   That sight had not shamed Jenny's curls.

And, like the hay, I swear her hair
   Was getting golder every day;
Yes, golder when 'twas harvested,
   Under a bonnet stacked away.

Ah, Jenny's gone, I know not where;
   Her face I cannot hope to see;
And every time I think of her
   The world seems one big grave to me.

37. Nature's Friend

Say what you like,
   All things love me!
I pick no flowers –
   That wins the Bee.

The Summer's Moths
   Think my hand one –
To touch their wings –
   With Wind and Sun.

The garden Mouse
   Comes near to play;
Indeed, he turns
   His eyes away.

The Wren knows well
   I rob no nest;
When I look in,
   She still will rest.

The hedge stops Cows,
   Or they would come
After my voice
   Right to my home.

The Horse can tell,
   Straight from my lip,
My hand could not
   Hold any whip.

Say what you like,
   All things love me!
Horse, Cow, and Mouse,
   Bird, Moth and Bee.

38. A Maiden and Her Hair

Her cruel hands go in and out,
  Like two pale woodmen working there,
To make a nut-brown thicket clear –
  The full, wild foliage of her hair.

Her hands now work far up the North
  Then, fearing for the South's extreme,
They into her dark waves of hair
  Dive down so quick – it seems a dream.

They're in the light again with speed,
  Tossing the loose hair to and fro,
Until, like tamèd snakes, the coils
  Lie on her bosom in a row.

For wise inspection, up and down
  One coil her busy hands now run;
To screw and twist, to turn and shape,
  And here and there to work like one.

And now those white hands, still like one,
  Are working at the perilous end;
Where they must knot those nut-brown coils,
  Which will hold fast, though still they'll bend.

Sometimes one hand must fetch strange tools,
  The other then must work alone;
But when more instruments are brought,
  See both make up the time that's gone.

Now that her hair is bound secure,
  Coil top of coil, in smaller space,
Ah, now I see how smooth her brow,
  And her simplicity of face.

39. Early Morn

When I did wake this morn from sleep,
  It seemed I heard birds in a dream;
Then I arose to take the air –
  The lovely air that made birds scream;
Just as green hill launched the ship
Of gold, to take its first clear dip.

And it began its journey then,
  As I came forth to take the air;
The timid Stars had vanished quite,
  The Moon was dying with a stare;
Horses, and kine, and sheep were seen
As still as pictures, in fields green.

It seemed as though I had surprised
  And trespassed in a golden world
That should have passed while men still slept!
  The joyful birds, the ship of gold,
The horses, kine and sheep did seem
As they would vanish for a dream.

40. The Battle

There was a battle in her face,
  Between a Lily and a Rose:
My Love would have the Lily win
  And I the Lily lose.

I saw with joy that strife, first one,
  And then the other uppermost;
Until the Rose roused all its blood,
  And then the Lily lost.

81

When she's alone, the Lily rules,
  By her consent, without mistake:
But when I come that red Rose leaps
  To battle for my sake.

41. The Moth

Say, silent Moth,
  Why thou hast let
The midnight come,
  And no dance yet?

Man's life is years,
  Thy life a day;
Is thine too long
  To be all play?

Man's life is long,
  He lives for years;
So long a time
  Breeds many fears.

Thy life is short:
  Whate'er its span,
Life's worth seems small
  Be't Moth or Man

42. Day's Black Star

Is it that small black star,
  Twinkling in broad daylight,
Upon the bosom of
  Yon cloud so white –
Is it that small black thing
Makes earth and all Heaven ring!

Sing, you black star; and soar
　　Until, alas! too soon
You fall to earth in one
　　Long singing swoon;
But you will rise again
To heaven, from this green plain.

Sing, sing, sweet star; though black,
　　Your company's more bright
Than any star that shines
　　With a white light;
Sing, Skylark, sing; and give
To me thy joy to live.

43.　A Richer Freight

You Nightingales, that came so far,
　　From Afric's shore;
With these rich notes, unloaded now
　　Against my door;

Most true they are far richer freight
　　Than ships can hold;
That come from there with ivory tusks,
　　And pearls, and gold.

But you'll return more rich, sweet birds,
　　By many notes,
When you take my Love's sweeter oncs
　　Back in your throats,

And Afric's coast will be enriched
　　By how you sing!
What! you'll bring others back with you,
　　To learn – next Spring.

44. School's Out

Girls scream,
    Boys shout;
Dogs bark,
    School's out.

Cats run,
    Horses shy;
Into trees
    Birds fly.

Babes wake
    Open-eyed;
If they can,
    Tramps hide.

Old man,
    Hobble home;
Merry mites,
    Welcome.

45. A Happy Life

O what a life is this I lead,
Far from the hum of human greed;
Where Crows, like merchants dressed in black,
Go leisurely to work and back;
Where Swallows leap and dive and float,
And Cuckoo sounds his cheerful note;
Where Skylarks now in clouds do rave,
Half mad with fret that their souls have
By hundreds far more joyous notes

Than they can manage with their throats.
The ploughman's heavy horses run
The field as if in fright – for fun,
Or stand and laugh in voices shrill;
Or roll upon their backs until
The sky's kicked small enough – they think;
Then to a pool they go and drink.
The kine are chewing their old cud,
Dreaming, and never think to add
Fresh matter that will taste – as they
Lie motionless, and dream away.

I hear the sheep a-coughing near;
Like little children, when they hear
Their elders' sympathy – so these
Sheep force their coughs on me, and please;
And many a pretty lamb I see,
Who stops his play on seeing me,
And runs and tells his mother then.
Lord, who would live in towns with men,
And hear the hum of human greed –
With such a life as this to lead?

46. Joy and Pleasure

Now, Joy is born of parents poor,
    And Pleasure of our richer kind;
Though Pleasure's free, she cannot sing
    As sweet a song as Joy confined.

Pleasure's a Moth, that sleeps by day
    And dances by false glare at night;
But Joy's a Butterfly, that loves
    To spread its wings in Nature's light.

Joy's like a Bee that gently sucks
    Away on blossoms his sweet hour;
But Pleasure's like a greedy Wasp,
    That plums and cherries would devour.

Joy's like a Lark that lives alone,
    Whose ties are very strong, though few;
But Pleasure like a Cuckoo roams,
    Makes much acquaintance, no friends true.

Joy from her heart doth sing at home,
    With little care if others hear;
But Pleasure then is cold and dumb,
    And sings and laughs with strangers near.

47. Truly Great

My walls outside must have some flowers,
    My walls within must have some books;
A house that's small; a garden large,
    And in it leafy nooks.

A little gold that's sure each week;
    That comes not from my living kind,
But from a dead man in his grave,
    Who cannot change his mind.

A lovely wife, and gentle too;
    Contented that no eyes but mine
Can see her many charms, nor voice
    To call her beauty fine.

Where she would in that stone cage live,
  A self-made prisoner, with me;
While many a wild bird sang around,
  On gate, on bush, on tree.

And she sometimes to answer them,
  In her far sweeter voice than all;
Till birds, that loved to look on leaves,
  Will doat on a stone wall.

With this small house, this garden large,
  This little gold, this lovely mate,
With health in body, peace at heart –
  Show me a man more great.

48. The Laughers

Mary and Maud have met at the door,
  Oh, now for a din; I told you so:
They're laughing at once with sweet, round mouths,
  Laughing for what? does anyone know?

Is it known to the bird in the cage,
  That shrieketh for joy his high top notes,
After a silence so long and grave –
  What started at once those two sweet throats?

Is it known to the Wind that he takes
  Advantage at once and comes right in?
Is it known to the cock in the yard,
  That crows – the cause of that merry din?

Is it known to the babe that he shouts?
  Is it known to the old, purring cat?
Is it known to the dog, that he barks
  For joy – what Mary and Maud laugh at?

Is it known to themselves? It is not,
  But beware of their great shining eyes;
For Mary and Maud will soon, I swear,
  Find a cause to make far merrier cries.

49. Australian Bill

Australian Bill is dying fast,
  For he's a drunken fool:
He either sits in an alehouse,
  Or stands outside a school.

He left this house of ours at seven,
  And he was drunk by nine;
And when I passed him near a school
  He nods his head to mine.

When Bill took to the hospital,
  Sick, money he had none –
He came forth well, but lo! his home,
  His wife and child had gone.

'I'll watch a strange school every day,
  Until the child I see;
For Liz will send the child to school –
  No doubt of that,' says he.

And 'Balmy' Tom is near as bad,
   A-drinking ale till blind:
No absent child grieves he, but there's
   A dead love on his mind.

But Bill, poor Bill, is dying fast,
   For he's the greater fool;
He either sits in an alehouse
   Or stands outside a school.

50. The Boy

Go, little boy,
Fill thee with joy;
   For Time gives thee
Unlicensed hours,
   To run in fields,
And roll in flowers.

A little boy
Can life enjoy;
   If but to see
The horses pass,
   When shut indoors
Behind the glass

Go, little boy,
Fill thee with joy;
   Fear not, like man,
The kick of wrath,
   That you do lie
In some one's path.

Time is to thee
Eternity,
  As to a bird
Or butterfly;
  And in that faith
True joy doth lie.

51. A Lovely Woman

Now I can see what Helen was:
Men cannot see this woman pass
And be not stirred; as Summer's Breeze
Sets leaves in battle on the trees.
A woman moving gracefully,
With golden hair enough for three,
Which, mercifully! is not loose,
But lies in coils to her head close;
With lovely eyes, so dark and blue,
So deep, so warm, they burn me through.
I see men follow her, as though
Their homes were where her steps should go.
She seemed as sent to our cold race
For fear the beauty of her face
Made Paradise in flames like Troy –
I could have gazed all day with joy.
In fancy I could see her stand
Before a savage, fighting band,
And make them, with her words and looks,
Exchange their spears for shepherds' crooks,
And sing to sheep in quiet nooks;
In fancy saw her beauty make
A thousand gentle priests uptake

Arms for her sake, and shed men's blood.
The fairest piece of womanhood,
Lovely in feature, form and grace,
I ever saw, in any place.

52. Money

When I had money, money, O!
  I knew no joy till I went poor;
For many a false man as a friend
  Came knocking all day at my door.

Then felt I like a child that holds
  A trumpet that he must not blow
Because a man is dead; I dared
  Not speak to let this false world know.

Much have I thought of life, and seen
  How poor men's hearts are ever light;
And how their wives do hum like bees
  About their work from morn till night.

So, when I hear these poor ones laugh,
  And see the rich ones coldly frown –
Poor men, think I, need not go up
  So much as rich men should come down.

When I had money, money, O!
  My many friends proved all untrue;
But now I have no money, O!
  My friends are real, though very few.

53. Where we Differ

To think my thoughts all hers,
    Not one of hers is mine;
She laughs – while I must sigh;
    She sings – while I must whine.

She eats – while I must fast;
    She reads – while I am blind;
She sleeps – while I must wake;
    Free – I no freedom find.

To think the world for me
    Contains but her alone,
And that her eyes prefer
    Some ribbon, scarf, or stone.

54. The Daisy

I know not why thy beauty should
    Remind me of the cold, dark grave –
Thou Flower, as fair as Moonlight, when
    She kissed the mouth of a black Cave.

All other Flowers can coax the Bees,
    All other Flowers are sought but thee:
Dost thou remind them all of Death,
    Sweet Flower, as thou remindest me?

Thou seemest like a blessèd ghost,
    So white, so cold, though crowned with gold·
Among these glazèd Buttercups,
    And purple Thistles, rough and bold.

When I am dead, nor thought of more,
    Out of all human memory –
Grow you on my forsaken grave,
    And win for me a stranger's sigh.

A day or two the lilies fade;
    A month, aye less, no friends are seen:
Then, claimant to forgotten graves,
    Share my lost place with the wild green.

55. The Sea

Her cheeks were white, her eyes were wild,
Her heart was with her sea-gone child.
'Men say you know and love the sea?
It is ten days, my child left me;
Ten days, and still he doth not come,
And I am weary of my home.'

I thought of waves that ran the deep
And flashed like rabbits, when they leap,
The white part of their tails; the glee
Of captains that take brides to sea,
And own the ships they steer; how seas
Played leapfrog over ships with ease.

The great Sea-Wind, so rough and kind;
Ho, ho! his strength; the great Sea-Wind
Blows iron tons across the sea!
Ho, ho! his strength; how wild and free!
He breaks the waves, to our amaze,
Into ten thousand little sprays!

'Nay, have no fear'; I laughed with joy,
'That you have lost a sea-gone boy;

The Sea's wild horses, they are far
More safe than Land's tamed horses are;
They kick with padded hoofs, and bite
With teeth that leave no marks in sight.

'True, Waves will howl when, all day long,
The Wind keeps piping loud and strong;
For in ships' sails the wild Sea-Breeze
Pipes sweeter than your birds in trees;
But have no fear' – I laughed with joy,
'That you have lost a sea-gone boy.'

That night I saw ten thousand bones
Coffined in ships, in weeds and stones;
Saw how the Sea's strong jaws could take
Big iron ships like rats to shake;
Heard him still moan his discontent
For one man or a continent.

I saw that woman go from place
To place, hungry for her child's face;
I heard her crying, crying, crying;
Then, in a flash! saw the Sea trying,
With savage joy, and efforts wild,
To smash his rocks with a dead child.

56. Waiting

Who can abide indoors this morn,
Now sunny May is ten days born,
In his house caged, a moping thing,
When all the merry free birds sing?

It is a pleasant time, and all
The sky's so full of cloudlets small,
That white doth seem Heaven's natural hue,
And clouds themselves are painted blue.
Now lusty May doth grow and burst
Her bodice green; her hawthorn breast,
Breaking those laces once so tight,
Doth more than peep its lovely white.
Come forth, my Love, for Nature wears
This hour her bridal smile; she hears
Ten thousand bantering birds, as they
Do hop upon her blossomed way.
The Sun doth shine, all things rejoice;
The cows forget the milkmaid's voice;
Of gardeners flowers have little care,
The sheep care not where shepherds are,
Dewdrops are in the grass, and they
Are twenty times more bright than day;
And if we look them close their rays
Will even make our own eyes daze;
But from that red and fiery Sun
Some timid drops of dew have run
Down the green blades of grass, and found
At once a cool place underground;
The birds sing at their high, sweet pitch,
And bees sing basso deep and rich.
May is Love's month: her flowers and voice
Call youth and maiden to rejoice,
And fill their hearts with Love's sweet pains;
They meet with laughter in green lanes,
And then they turn to whispering,
Under the leaves where the birds sing.
Fie, fie, my love; you wait too long
To hear that old black kettle's song;

He'll keep thee suffering long for him,
And a true lover for his whim
I've seen where you did stand last night,
Near the old stile: that spot is white
With daisies, and I swear, they were
Never in that green place before;
But that those sweet flowers came to sight
Since we two parted there last night,
At sunset, when that western world
Had four green rainbows rimmed with gold.
You indoors when the skylark long
Has sung on high his matin song!
The humble bees, dressed in black cloth,
Like mourners for the dead, come forth
With their false groans – for soon they'll stop
With red-faced flowers to drink a drop;
Until they are so tight with drink,
They must lie down awhile and think.
So quiet lie the Butterflies,
Some Bees can scarce believe their eyes,
But what they're Blossoms, lovelier far,
And sweeter than all others are.
But one black Bee did come along,
A big, black bully, fat and strong,
And saw my Lady Butterfly,
Who, dreaming sweet romance, did lie
Lazy on a red flower; and he,
Vexed she'd not toil like Ant or Bee,
Buzzed in her ears, and grumbled so –
She must at last arise and go.
Come, Love, and breathe on these small flowers,
So they may live a few more hours.
Had I been near, you had not ta'en
Sleep's second draught and drowsed again,

But waked for good at my first kiss –
As Phoebus made these flowers with his.
Young Buds are here, that wait to see
How you do part your lips for me,
Ere they ope theirs the least – who wait
Your coming, Love, which is so late.
We'll miss, when summer is no more,
The very weed that chokes a flower.
Alas! too soon the time must come
When leaves will fall, and birds be dumb;
And but red Robin's breast will show
How the late fruits and flowers did glow.
The leafy Elm, that now has made
For twenty kine a pleasant shade,
Will in its scraggy bones stand bare,
With not one leaf seen anywhere.
The Stream will take and bury one
By one, till Willow's leaves are gone;
The Hedge – see how it dances now!
Will stand to its broad waist in snow.
Yet what care I? If I have thee,
'Twill still be summer time to me;
Though no Sun shines, when you come forth
A light must fall across the earth.

57. Farewell to Poesy

Sweet Poesy, why art thou dumb?
  I loved thee as my captive bird,
That sang me songs when spring was gone,
  And birds of freedom were not heard;
Nor dreamt thou wouldst turn false and cold
  When needed most, by men grown old.

Sweet Poesy, why art thou dumb?
  I fear thy singing days are done;
The poet in my soul is dying,
  And every charm in life is gone;
In vain birds scold and flowers do plead –
  The poet dies, his heart doth bleed.

58. The Dark Hour

And now, when merry winds do blow,
  And rain makes trees look fresh,
An overpowering staleness holds
  This mortal flesh.

Though I do love to feel the rain,
  And be by winds well blown –
The mystery of mortal life
  Doth press me down.

And, in this mood, come now what will,
  Shine Rainbow, Cuckoo call;
There is no thing in Heaven or Earth
  Can lift my soul.

I know not where this state comes from –
  No cause for grief I know;
The Earth around is fresh and green,
  Flowers near me grow.

I sit between two fair Rose trees;
  Red roses on my right,
And on my left side roses are
  A lovely white.

The little birds are full of joy,
   Lambs bleating all the day;
The colt runs after the old mare,
   And children play.

And still there comes this dark, dark hour –
   Which is not born of Care;
Into my heart it creeps before
   I am aware.

59. Jenny Wren

Her sight is short, she comes quite near;
A foot to me's a mile to her;
And she is known as Jenny Wren,
The smallest bird in England. When
I heard that little bird at first,
Methought her frame would surely burst
With earnest song. Oft had I seen
Her running under leaves so green,
Or in the grass when fresh and wet,
As though her wings she would forget.
And, seeing this, I said to her –
'My pretty runner, you prefer
To be a thing to run unheard
Through leaves and grass, and not a bird!'
'Twas then she burst, to prove me wrong,
Into a sudden storm of song;
So very loud and earnest, I
Feared she would break her heart and die.
'Nay, nay,' I laughed, 'be you no thing
To run unheard, sweet scold, but sing!

O I could hear your voice near me,
Above the din in that oak tree,
When almost all the twigs on top
Had starlings singing without stop.'

60. The Idiot and the Child

There was a house where an old dame
  Lived with a son, his child and wife;
And with a son of fifty years,
  An idiot all his life.

When others wept this idiot laughed,
  When others laughed he then would weep:
The married pair took oath his eyes
  Did never close in sleep.

Death came that way, and which, think you,
  Fell under that old tyrant's spell?
He breathed upon that little child,
  Who loved her life so well.

This made the idiot chuckle hard:
  The old dame looked at that child dead
And him she loved – 'Ah, well; thank God
  It is no worse!' she said.

61. Rose

Sweet Margaret's laugh can make
Her whole plump body shake.

Jane's cherry lips can show
Their white stones in a row.

A soft June smile steals out
Of Mary's April pout.

Sweet creatures swim and play
In Maud's blue pools all day.

But when Rose walks abroad,
Jane, Margaret, Mary, Maud,

Do stand as little chance
To throw a lovely glance,

As the Moon that's in the sky
While still the Sun is high.

62. The Green Tent

Summer has spread a cool, green tent
   Upon the bare poles of this tree;
Where 'tis a joy to sit all day,
   And hear the small birds' melody;
To see the sheep stand bolt upright,
   Nibbling at grass almost their height.

And much I marvel now how men
   Can waste their fleeting days in greed;
That one man should desire more gold
   Than twenty men should truly need;
For is not this green tent more sweet
   Than any chamber of the great?

This tent, at which I spend my day,
   Was made at Nature's cost, not mine,
And when night comes, and I must sleep,
   No matter if my room be fine
Or common, for Content and Health
   Can sleep without the power of Wealth.

63. To the Wind at Morn

Is it for you
   The Larks sing loud,
The Leaves clap hands,
   The Lilies nod?
Do they forget
   The screams so wild,
Heard all the night –
   Where is that child?

64. No Master

Indeed this is sweet life! my hand
Is under no proud man's command;
There is no voice to break my rest
Before a bird has left its nest;
There is no man to change my mood,
Would I go nutting in the wood;
No man to pluck my sleeve and say –
I want thy labour for this day;
No man to keep me out of sight,
When that dear Sun is shining bright.
None but my friends shall have command
Upon my time, my heart and hand;

I'll rise from sleep to help a friend,
But let no stranger orders send,
Or hear my curses fast and thick,
Which in his purse-proud throat will stick
Like burrs. If I cannot be free
To do such work as pleases me,
Near woodland pools and under trees,
You'll get no work at all; for I
Would rather live this life and die
A beggar or a thief, than be
A working slave with no days free.

65. The Dumb World

I cannot see the short, white curls
    Upon the forehead of an Ox,
But what I see them dripping with
    That poor thing's blood, and hear the axe;
When I see calves and lambs, I see
    Them led to death; I see no bird
Or rabbit cross the open field
    But what a sudden shot is heard;
A shout that tells me men aim true,
    For death or wound, doth chill me through.

The shot that kills a hare or bird
    Doth pass through me; I feel the wound
When those poor things find peace in death,
    And when I hear no more that sound.
These cat-like men do hate to see
    Small lives in happy motion; I

Would almost rather hide my face
From Nature than pass these men by;
And rather see a battle than
A dumb thing near a drunken man.

66. Knitting

E'en though her tongue may by its force
Leave me as helpless as a horse,
When saucy pup doth bark at him –
I'll love her better for that whim.
No steady summer's love for me,
But let her still uncertain be;
Like spring, whose gusts, and frowns, and showers,
Do grow us fresher, lovelier flowers.
No substances on earth can make
The joy I from her shadow take;
When first I saw her face, I could
Not help draw near her where she stood;
I felt more joy than when a Bee
Sees in a garden a Plum tree
All blossoms and no leaves, and he
Leaps o'er the fence imme liately.
I like to see her when she sits –
Not dreaming I look on – and knits;
To see her hands, with grace so light,
Stabbing the wool that's red or white;
With shining needles, sharp and long,
That never seem to go far wrong.
And that sight better pleases me
Than green hills in the sun; to see
The beach, what time the tide goes out,
And leaves his gold spread all about.

67. Clouds

My Fancy loves to play with Clouds
   That hour by hour can change Heaven's face;
For I am sure of my delight,
   In green or stony place.

Sometimes they on tall mountains pile
   Mountains of silver, twice as high;
And then they break and lie like rocks
   All over the wide sky.

And then I see flocks very fair;
   And sometimes, near their fleeces white,
Are small, black lambs that soon will grow
   And hide their mothers quite.

Sometimes, like little fishes, they
   Are all one size, and one great shoal;
Sometimes they, like big sailing ships,
   Across the blue sky roll.

Sometimes I see small Cloudlets tow
   Big, heavy Clouds across those skies –
Like little Ants that carry off
   Dead Moths ten times their size.

Sometimes I see at morn bright Clouds
   That stand so still, they make me stare;
It seems as they had trained all night
   To make no motion there.

68. In the Country

This life is sweetest; in this wood
I hear no children cry for food;
I see no woman, white with care;
No man, with muscles wasting here.

No doubt it is a selfish thing
To fly from human suffering;
No doubt he is a selfish man,
Who shuns poor creatures sad and wan.

But 'tis a wretched life to face
Hunger in almost every place;
Cursed with a hand that's empty, when
The heart is full to help all men.

Can I admire the statue great,
When living men starve at its feet?
Can I admire the park's green tree,
A roof for homeless misery?

When I can see few men in need,
I then have power to help by deed,
Nor lose my cheerfulness in pity –
Which I must do in every city.

For when I am in those great places,
I see ten thousand suffering faces;
Before me stares a wolfish eye,
Behind me creeps a groan or sigh.

69. The Kingfisher

It was the Rainbow gave thee birth,
   And left thee all her lovely hues;
And, as her mother's name was Tears,
   So runs it in my blood to choose
For haunts the lonely pools, and keep
In company with trees that weep.

Go you and, with such glorious hues,
   Live with proud Peacocks in green parks;
On lawns as smooth as shining glass,
   Let every feather show its marks;
Get thee on boughs and clap thy wings
Before the windows of proud kings.

Nay, lovely Bird, thou art not vain;
   Thou hast no proud, ambitious mind;
I also love a quiet place
   That's green, away from all mankind;
A lonely pool, and let a tree
Sigh with her bosom over me.

70. An old House in London

In fancy I can see thee stand
Again in the green meadow-land;
As in thine infancy, long past,
When Southwark was a lovely waste;
And Larks and Blackbirds sang around,
As common as their children found
So far away in these late days.

And thou didst like a lighthouse raise
Thy windows, that their light could show
Across the broad, green calm below;
And there were trees, beneath whose boughs
Stood happy horses, sheep and cows,
And wilful brooks, that would not yield
To hedges, to mark out each field,
But every field that they passed through
Was by them cut and counted two.
From thy back windows thou couldst see,
Half-way between St. Paul's and thee,
Swans with their shadows, and the barge
Of state old Thames took in his charge.
Ah, wert thou now what thou wert then,
There were no need to fly from men.
Instead of those green meadows, now
Three hundred hungry children show
Rags and white faces at thy door
For charity. We see no more
Green lanes, but alleys dark instead;
Where none can walk but fear to tread
On babes that crawl in dirt and slime.
And from thy windows, at this time,
Thou canst not see ten yards beyond,
For the high blocks that stand around;
Buildings that ofttimes only give
One room in which five souls must live,
With but one window for their air.
Foul art thou now with lives of care,
For hungry children and men poor
Seek food and lodging at thy door;
Thou that didst hear, in thy first hours,
Birds sing, and saw the sweet wild flowers.

71. Scotty's Luck

'Fatty,' one day, called 'Red-nosed Scot'
    A viper! and then punched his nose;
Poor 'Scotty' swore to have revenge
    Before the week could close.

Now 'Scotty' was a gambling man,
    And, when his eyes were glassed and framed,
He saw in print, to his amaze,
    A horse called 'Viper' named.

At once that superstitious man
    Backed 'Viper' for the highest place;
And heard ere long, to his great joy,
    That horse had won the race.

'Fatty,' said 'Scot,' with grateful tears,
    'You called me "Viper," to my shame –
But it was heavenly Providence
    To call me by that name.'

72. Happy Wind

Oh, happy wind, how sweet
    Thy life must be!
The great, proud fields of gold
    Run after thee:
And here are flowers, with heads
    To nod and shake;
And dreaming butterflies
    To tease and wake,
Oh, happy wind, I say,
    To be alive this day.

73. The Sluggard

A jar of cider and my pipe,
    In summer, under shady tree;
A book of one that made his mind
    Live by its sweet simplicity:
Then must I laugh at kings who sit
    In richest chambers, signing scrolls;
And princes cheered in public ways,
    And stared at by a thousand fools.

Let me be free to wear my dreams,
    Like weeds in some mad maiden's hair,
When she doth think the earth has not
    Another maid so rich and fair;
And proudly smiles on rich and poor,
    The queen of all fair women then:
So I, dressed in my idle dreams,
    Will think myself the king of men.

74. On Expecting some Books

To-morrow they will come. I know
How rich their sweet contents are, so
Upon their dress let Fancy play –
Will it be blue, red, green or grey?
Sweet Books that I have oft heard named,
And seen stand up like blossoms framed,
Through many a common window shown –
When I was moneyless in town;
But never touched their leaves, nor bent
Close to them and inhaled their scent.

They'll come like snowdrops to a Bee
That, tired of empty dreams, can see
Real flowers at last. Until this time,
Now on the threshold of my prime,
I did not guess my poverty;
That none of these rich Books, that lie
Untouched on many a shelf – save when
A housemaid, dreaming of young men
And music, sport, and dance, and dress,
Will bang them for their dustiness –
That none of these were in my care;
To-morrow I will have them here.
Well do I know their value; they
Will not be purses found, which may
Be full of coppers, nails or keys –
They will not disappoint, like these.
Books I can always trust; for they
Will not tell neighbours what I say,
What time I go to bed and rise,
What eat and drink. They'll make no
    cries
For cloth to suit the season; no
Oft going out, to make me grow
Jealous of their long absence. When
I'm visited by living men,
They will not sulk and cast black looks
When left unflattered. These sweet
    Books
Will not be heard to grumble that
I keep the room too cold or hot;
The one in leather will not chide
To feel a cloth one touch his side.
O may their coming never cease!
May my book-family increase;

Clothes, pictures, ornaments of show,
Trinkets and mirrors – these can go
Outside, that all my Books may be
Together in one room with me.

75. The Sailor to his Parrot

Thou foul-mouthed wretch! Why dost thou choose
  To learn bad language, and no good;
Canst thou not say 'The Lord be praised'
  As easy as 'Hell's fire and blood'?

Why didst thou call the gentle priest
  A thief and a damned rogue; and tell
The deacon's wife, who came to pray,
  To hold her jaw and go to hell?

Thou art a foe, no friend of mine,
  For all my thoughts thou givest away;
Whate'er I say in confidence,
  Thou dost in evil hours betray.

Thy mind's for ever set on bad;
  I cannot mutter one small curse,
But thou dost make it endless song,
  And shout it to a neighbour's house.

Aye, swear to thy delight and ours,
  When here I welcome shipmates home,
And thou canst see abundant grog –
  But hold thy tongue when landsmen come.

Be dumb when widow Johnson's near,
  Be dumb until our wedding day;
And after that – but not before –
  She will enjoy the worst you say.

There is a time to speak and not;
  When we're together, all is well;
But damn thy soul – What! you damn *mine!*
  And you tell *me* to go to hell!

76. Angry

My Love sits angry; see!
  Her foot shakes in the light;
Her timid, little foot,
  That else would hide from sight

Her left hand props her cheek;
  Its little finger plays
Upon her under-lip,
  And makes a harp-like noise.

Her lip's red manuscript
  She has unrolled and spread;
So I may read ill news,
  And hang my guilty head.

My Love sits angry; see!
  She's red up to her eyes;
And was her face flogged by
  The wings of Butterflies?

113

Her right hand's in her lap,
    So small, so soft, so white;
She in her anger makes
    Five fingers hide from sight.

Two golden curls have now
    Dropped out of their silk net;
There they must stop, for she
    Will not restore them yet.

My Love, she is so fair
    When in this angry way,
That did she guess my thoughts,
    She'd quarrel every day.

77. The Call of the Sea

Gone are the days of canvas sails!
No more great sailors tell their tales
In country taverns, barter pearls
For kisses from strange little girls;
And when the landlord's merry daughter
Heard their rough jokes and shrieked with laughter,
They threw a muffler of rare fur,
That hid her neck from ear to ear.
Ho, ho! my merry men; they know
Where gold is plentiful – Sail ho!
How they did love the rude wild Sea!
The rude, unflattering Sea; for he
Will not lie down for monarch's yacht,
No more than merchant's barge; he'll not
Keep graves with marks of wood or stone
For fish or fowl, or human bone.

The Sea is loth to lose a friend;
Men of one voyage, who did spend
Six months with him, hear his vexed cry
Haunting their houses till they die.
And for the sake of him they let
The winds blow them, and raindrops wet
Their foreheads with fresh water sprays –
Thinking of his wild, salty days.
And well they love to saunter near
A river, and its motion hear;
And see ships lying in calm beds,
That danced upon seas' living heads;
And in their dreams they hear again
Men's voices in a hurricane –
Like ghosts complaining that their graves
Are moved by sacrilegious waves.
And they do love to stand and hear
The old seafaring men that fear
Land more than water; carts and trains
More than wild waves and hurricanes.
And they do walk with love and pride
The tattooed mariner beside –
Chains, anchors on his arm, and Ships –
And listen to his bearded lips.
Aye, they will hear the Sea's vexed cry
Haunting their houses till they die.

78. Come, Honest Boys

Ye who have nothing to conceal,
    Come, honest boys, and drink with me;
Come, drink with me the sparkling ale,
    And we'll not whisper calumny,

But laugh with all the power we can;
   But all pale schemers who incline
To rise above your fellow man,
   Touch not the sparkling ale or wine.

Give me strong ale to fire my blood,
   Content me with a lot that's bad;
That is to me both drink and food,
   And warms me though I am ill-clad;
A pot of ale, man owns the world:
   The poet hears his songs all sung,
Inventor sees his patents sold,
   The painter sees his pictures hung.

The creeds remind us oft of Death;
   But man's best creed is to forget
Death all the hours that he takes breath,
   And quaff the sparkling ale, and let
Creeds shout until they burst their lungs;
   For what is better than to be
A-drinking ale and singing songs,
   In summer, under some green tree?

79. To the New Year

Welcome, New Year, but be more kind
Than thy dead father left behind;
If I may kiss no mouth that's red,
Give me the open mouth instead
Of a black bottle of old wine
To gurgle in its neck and mine.

Let not my belly once complain
For want of meat, or fruit, or grain;
But keep it always tight and quiet –
No matter if with drink or diet.
And, New Year, may I never need
In vain a pipeful of strong weed,
That sends my baby clouds on high
To join big brothers in the sky.
No gold I ask, but that I may
Have some small silver every day.
Not for one night let sleep forsake
My side, and show the Morning break;
Let me not hear Time's strokes in bed,
And feel the pain of one thought dead,
Who hears the earth cast in his grave.
I care not what poor clothes I have;
I'll only think it shame and sin
To show my naked thigh or shin
When the wind blows. Give me, New Year,
Tobacco, bread and meat, and beer.
Also a few old books, so I
Can read about an age gone by;
But as for how the present goes –
I'll thank the Lord the Devil knows.

80. The Philosophical Beggar

When I went in the woods this morn to sleep,
I saw an old man looking on the ground.
Said he: 'Here, where a beggar ate his crust,
We see ten thousand little ants at work,
And they are earning now their winter's ease.

117

As for myself, I cannot rest from work,
I have no patience with those idle fools
That waste their days in mourning wasted time –
My brain must ever be at work. They say
Much work, and just a little pleasure mixed,
Is best for life; as flowers that live in shade
For twenty hours and sunlight four keep fresh
The longest and enjoy the longest life;
They do say this – but all my pleasure's work.
I work on small, when great themes fail my mind –
As cats, when they can catch no mice, content
Themselves with flies. If once I take a rest,
Then sudden famine takes my mind for days,
Which seeks but cannot find the barest feast.
How it doth fret my active Heart to see
The sloven Mind recovering from a day
Of idleness – letting Thoughts peep and none come
    out.
Ah, wretched hours that follow rest! when men
Have no desire for pleasure, and would work,
But still their Minds do sulk from past neglect.
This world, this mystery of Time, of Life
And Death, where every riddle men explain
Does make another one, or many more –
Can always keep the human mind employed;
Old men that do persuade themselves life's work
Is but half done, must all die happy men.
E'en though we think the world and all things vain,
There lives a noble impulse in our minds
To strive and help to reach the perfect state.
Work, work, and thou hast joy; it matters not
If thou dost start upon a quest as vain
As children, when they seek a cuckoo's nest –
The joy is on the way, not at the end.

When I am in this world's society,
Then do I feel like some poor bird that would
Attend its young when people loiter near;
I see my thoughts like blossoms fade, and know
That they will die and never turn to fruit.
What juicy joints I threw away when young!
To think of those rich joints makes this meat sweet,
Near to the bone, which Time doth offer now.
Work, work, I say; sleep is sufficient rest;
It is the wage that Nature pays to all,
And when we spend our days in idleness,
She gives short time; and they that earn the least
Do grumble most, when she keeps back full pay.
'Now, woodman, do thy work, and I'll do mine –
An active man can almost break Death's heart.'
Then with a pencil and a book he went
Mumbling and writing, into the deep woods.

Now, what an old, mad fool is that, methought;
He tries to make one hour do work for two,
To keep away the ghosts of murdered ones
He foully did to death when a small boy.
He'll work his brains, and then the world will rob
His hive of its pure honey; in its place
Put for his food cheap syrup of weak praise.
His mind's a garden, all the flowers are his;
But when he markets his sweet honey goods,
Then scoundrel bees, that have their hives else-
     where,
Will make themselves rich on his flowers' sweets.
I count the tramp as noble as that man
Who lives in idleness on wealth bequeathed,
And far more wise than yon old thinking fool.
Show me one happier than the tramp who has
His belly full, and good boots not too tight.

His careless heart has buried kin that live,
Those that have died he resurrects no more.
He does not know the farmer's spiteful joy,
Who, envying his near neighbour, laughs to see
The wild birds knock that man's fruit blossoms down;
He does not laugh to spite a bachelor,
As mothers do, that hear their babies scream.
We scorn the men that toil, as deep-sea men
Scorn those that sail on shallow lakes and streams –
Yet by our civil tongues we live and thrive.
Our tongues may be as venomous as those
Small flies that make the lazy oxen leap;
Like a ship's parrot I maybe could swear;
Like a ship's monkey for my cunning tricks –
But I have found a gently uttered lie
And civil tongue sufficient for my ends;
For we can find excuse for our escape –
As rats and mice pursued can find dark holes.
Is there a sound more cheerful than the tramp's
'Good morning, sir'? For in that sound he puts
His whole heart's gratitude that you do work
And sweat, and then make sacrifice for him.
His lips do whine, but how his heart does laugh!
To think that he is free to roam at will,
While others toil to keep that thing 'Respect,'
Which makes them starve – if they become like
    him.
If I hear not my belly's voice, nor feel
The cold; if I toil not for other men –
I ask no more; contented with my bread
Ten times outweighing meat, and water fresh.
When I this morn did beg a rich man's house,
'Go to the bees, thou sluggard' – he replied.
'And to the devil, you' – I answered him.

Then stood and cursed him, worse than farmer
    when
He sees the Crows turn his green meadow black.
Go to the bees, thou sluggard! Me! From *him!*
And must I be a slave, like thousands more,
To rise before the Sun, and go – in spite
Of fog, rain, wind or hail – to serve his like?
And if perchance I'm hungry at my work,
I still must fast until a certain hour;
If I am sleepy still, when I should rise,
I must not sleep, but up and work for him!
Nature gave me no extra bone for this;
The rich man cannot know a poor man's life –
No more than hands, that are unwiped and wet,
Can feel if clothes are dry. Go, sluggard, work!
It makes me laugh; Care has them soon her slaves
Who dream of duty to their fellow-men
And set a value on each passing hour.
If rich men are the winter's kings, the kings
Of summer are true beggars – that be sure.
Then, happy beggars can recline on stones
With more content than lords sit cushioned chairs;
Their pleasant houses are the leafy trees,
Whose floors are carpeted with grass or moss;
They sleep upon the new-mown hay at night,
And in the daytime to their liking mix
The sun and shade. Oft in forsaken house –
Where spirits drove the living out – they sleep;
Ghosts cannot deal with beggars bold, who have
Less reverence than the spiders that weave webs
Inside the sacred nostrils of a joss.
And see our health; we live on sun and air,
Plain food and water, and outlive rich men,
With all their physic, wines and cleanliness.

Ah, cleanliness! That strikes a woeful note
To those poor tramps that seek the workhouse oft,
That fear to beg, and should be working men;
For, after they have ta'en a workhouse bath,
And their clothes cleaned, how lonely they must
    feel
When all the fleas that tickled them are dead.
Of Death – who still surprises foolish men,
As though he came but yesterday – the tramp
Thinks not; or takes a little laugh at Death
Ere Death grins everlastingly at him.
The happy tramp cares not if he doth lie
At last between white sheets or on cows' dung.
He has no squeamish taste: he could almost
Eat things alive, in little bits, like birds –
Or lick the streets like Turkey's sacred dogs.
Ah, dogs! that strikes another woeful note.
Many a village have I left through them,
When one had cause – or thought he had – to bark,
And in a while a score of others joined,
Barking because he barked, and nothing more,
And hungry I have had to leave that place.
Some dogs will bite; those small dogs with big heads –
It is the size of these dogs' *heads* we fear,
And not so much how big their bodies are.
If one thing spoils our life it is the dog.
    Now, wherefore should I work my flesh or mind?
I knew Will Davies well; a beggar once,
Till he went mad and started writing books.
Nature, I swear, did ne'er commit worse crime
Than when she gives out genius to the poor;
He is a leper every man would shun;
A lighthouse fast upon the rocks of Want,
To warn men, with his light, to keep away;

And so they do – as far as body goes –
So that they may not witness his distress,
But still they pester him from distant parts.
A beggar's body has far better friends
In nibbling fleas that will not let him sleep,
Than any people's poet whose soul has
More friends than wanted, but scarce one
Real friend to question how his body fares.
Fame's like a nightingale, so sweet at first,
Whose voice soon like a common frog doth croak,
Until we wonder if we hear the same sweet bird.
I cannot see at all why I should work
My mind or body for this cruel world –
I'm no mad poet, like the one I name.
'Tis work, work, work – in every place; it haunts
Me like a painted lady whose sad eyes
Can watch us still, whichever way we look.
Now, let me eat; here's cake, and bread and jam –
I wonder if there's butter in between.
And here's a Christian journal a kind dame
Wrapped round the food to help my happy soul.
What! here's a poem by the poet-tramp.

        Out, life of care!
          Man lives to fret
        For some vain thing
          He cannot get.

        The Cities crave
          Green solitude;
        The Country craves
          A multitude.

Man lives to want;
   The rich man's lot
Is to want things
   The poor know not.

And no man dies
   But must look back
With sorrow on
   His own past track.

If beggar has
   No child or wife,
He, of all men,
   Enjoys most life.

When rich men loathe
   Their meat and wine,
He thinks dry bread
   And water fine.

When Fame's as sick
   As Failure is,
He snores on straw,
   In quiet bliss.

A truthful song, but 'twill not pay his rent.
An English poet! Where's the milk? Me-aw!
If he would thrive, let him be false as hell,
And bow-wow fierce at France or Germany.
   What makes us tramps the happiest of all men?
Our hearts are free of envy, care and greed.
The miser thinks the Sun has not one flower
As fair as his gold heap the dark has grown;

He trembles if the Moon at night comes through
His lattice, with her silver of no worth;
True beggars laugh at him, and do not shake
With greed, like rats that hear a glutton eat,
When they behold a man more richly clad.
Nay, let plain food but keep their bellies tight,
And they will envy none their cloth or land.

81. Fancy

How sad my life had been were't not for her,
I know not; everywhere I looked were heaps
Of moving flesh, silk dresses mixed with rags,
And solid blocks of stone, with squares of glass –
Hard to my sight. That dreadful din! My nerve
Fell all apart, e'en as a wave, impaled
Upon a rock, breaks into quivering drops.
There, men were sat with neither home nor hope,
Ungreeted – save by some lost dog or cat.
There saw I cold and ragged, hungry men
Sit at the feet of statues which the rich
Admired, nor heeded those poor men of flesh.
And as that thief, the Wind, will drink the dew
While Phoebus fights the Clouds, so did the rich
Cheat honest workers of their just reward.
Where'er I looked I saw no beauty there;
Plenty of shops and markets with dead meat,
And other stuff to satisfy man's flesh,
But little for man's soul. A dreadful life,
To live in that stone town without a change;
As though men's souls did not need Nature's charms,
And putting out to grass, like common beasts,

To keep life healthy, fresh and of good cheer.
I blessed sweet Fancy for her favour then;
That oft she robbed my outward eyes of power
To fill the mind with common objects, and
My ears of power to take in common sounds.
And when I saw that here – where thousands lived
In houses without gardens, and the air
Was no true friend to any thing that lived,
And little beauty was – when I saw she,
In spite of that dull town, could bring delight –
Fancy, I cried, thou shalt be my life's Love.
If I do so exalt thee in my life,
There'll be no fear that Death will take thee first,
For we must die together, as we lived.
Much am I pleased with thee; for thou hast more
Sweet antics than a Squirrel on the boughs,
Who, after he has made the green leaves fight,
Slides to the ground for safety. I am sick
Of this loud noise and sights of poverty;
Here, where the poor do either pass away,
Quiet as winds at sundown, starved and lost –
Or drink, and fight like cats that arch their backs
And stretch their legs to twice their common length.

To which she said: He who can sit alone
In solitude, content with his own thoughts,
Can have life's best and cheapest joy; which needs
No purse of gold, no pride of outward show,
Like joy that's purchased from society;
And only by my power canst thou do this.
Thou dost not know true joy of living yet:
Thy mind is as a port that takes ships in,
But when alone with me in solitude,
A greater joy will be to send ships out.

Sweet Thoughts shall tease and romp with thee all
          day,
Till Sleep will pity thy joy-weary Mind,
And sink thee in her depths – but thou shalt still
Be followed by those Torments sweet and wild.
Aye, I will make thy life of purest joy;
A fire that has no smoke, a thornless rose;
A love without one breath of jealousy –
A heaven that has no knowledge of mankind.
For I will then with my sweet visions clear
Thy memory of these scenes depraved and sad,
Of hungry children and their parents drunk.
Thou night and day shalt sing; I'll give two souls
In one – the Lark's and Nightingale's; to sing
By Sun and Moon; and songs as sweet as birds
Make at the birth of April, when Spring crowns
His first day with a rainbow – thou shalt sing.
And I will give thy Mind such dreams that when
Thy Body, her blackmailer, threatens her,
To satisfy his greed for worldly things –
Thou wilt have courage to say nay. And thou
Shalt see again the Ocean bear the Sun
Into the arms of Heaven, his smiling nurse;
And see again the Sun that sank long since
At Severn's Mouth, with that great sail of gold,
That covered all the west; and many more
Scenes, dear to Memory, I will show thy Mind.
For thou shalt see that Meadow burned in two
By fiery Malpas Brook; and hear again
The voice of Ebbw in his lovely park,
Counting its ferns, its rabbits, sheep and deer;
And sweeter music he shall make for thee
Than seamaid ever wasted, when she tried,
With every trick known to her throat, to stop

The Phantom Ship. Come, let us settle then
In some small village which the Cuckoo loves
To haunt and startle. I will give each day
Far sweeter dreams than Love gives her first night.
Much fairer Clouds are there, and brighter Suns,
And Skies more clear and blue; and Night's small Star
Can shine as bright as Mars and Venus here.
There, many a happy wood can hear a Brook
Enjoy his everlasting holiday,
When Birds are silent and no Children come.
Come then, and I will be as true to thee
As snow to the high Mountain, or the Wind
That never leaves the Ocean for a day.

Yes, Sweet, I answered, we will live alone
In some green Village that awake is far
More happy than a City in its sleep.

So we departed, hand in hand for joy;
And, when arrived in that green world, I found
Such peace and ease as only sailors know,
When they return to the wild elements
After a Port has robbed and beaten them.
O I was like a Wasp for joy, when he's
Inside a juicy plum, and near the stone
Where it is sweetest. I could never know
That cunning Time was plucking me alive
Of youth and strength and beauty – when I looked
Into the eyes of horses, sheep and cows,
Sure that their hearts were innocent of sin.
And she had power to change all common forms
Into things lovely or of interest;
Could give a man's face to the rock or tree,
And bodies of fair women to the Clouds.

She was a sweet wild flower, that much preferred
Wild brooks to fountains and hedge banks to lawns.
It was a joy to hear the horses crop
The sweet, short grass; and see the dappled cows
Knee-deep in grass or water; and to watch
The green leaves smoking, when their puffs made me
Expect to hear them smack their lips like men,
Or show some fire; and hear the summer's Wind
Whispering in the ears of corn – and Birds
That whistled while the leaves were drinking rain.
And by her sweet translation I could read
The language of all flowers, and birds and clouds,
And was a master of their tongues. I saw
Among the leaves the cobweb starred with dew,
Saw Rainbows that had tunnelled half the sky;
And as the Lark, that hails the rising Sun,
Will not forget to praise him when he sets –
So did I bless at night each happy day.
And in their turn all things gave up their charms;
One day it was a Cloud, the next a Flower;
Then 'twas a Bird, the Rain or Wind; and then
A full survey of Nature. Sweet to hear
Red Robin sing, and seek among the leaves
The body of that piercing sweetness; or
The Nightingales, paced by a thunderstorm,
Sing at their highest pitch; or to walk forth
At early morn in Spring, when all was still,
And hear the small Birds screaming in the trees,
Before the human world doth wake from sleep.
For it was Springtime then – when I was led
By Fancy into that green solitude,
And all the Birds were happy day and night;
When Day's sweet Birds had done, I could not sleep
For Nightingales, whose notes were links to make

One chain of song to run through all the Spring.
The cunning Cuckoo changed his place each time,
Now North, now South, now East, now West was
    heard —
Knowing that trick would make his voice keep fresh.
Then, saw the Primrose on a distant bank,
And, guided by his golden light, drew close
And found a Violet at his side — sweet thing!
A joy to walk abroad with Fancy then;
When I beheld a Rainbow or fair Cloud,
She gave my Mind free copies, which would last
When their originals were perished quite;
And for my copies I pay no man rent,
Nor need insure them — which are proof
'Gainst loss by water, thieves and fire. When I
Awoke, would hasten forth to see the Sun
Dance with another happy Day; for soon
He in his summer's strength could laugh at Clouds.
And we would walk green lanes, so still and lone
That Reynard walked them without hurry, and
Felt safer than in woods; down some green lane
That's only ten feet wide, and only one
Foot in the centre white; which is the time
When June, with her abundant leaves and grass,
Makes narrow paths of lanes, and lanes of roads;
When she in all her leafy glory comes,
And clothes the naked trees in every limb.
Not much I missed, with Fancy at my side,
Of living things or dead: the Moon, alone,
That set her sheet to sail the heavenly Sea,
To test if safe for piloting the Stars;
Or we would watch the Squirrel hide his nuts,
And stand the blades of grass upright again,
And still eye it suspiciously; or Crows,

Tossing their bright black bodies in the Sun,
And looking like white Pigeons. Wonderful
That Paradise which Fancy gave my Mind,
In which the body had no luxury
Of either food or drink or furniture.
Where'er I was, let her be near and then
My Body trembled like a sucking Bee's;
Life was a joy, no matter if the hour
Was wet and windy, cold or dry and calm,
Sometimes there was not wind enough to shake
The lifeless leaf caught by a spider's thread,
And held suspended; and no sound of life –
Save distant bark of dog, the moo of cow
Or calf, the baa of sheep; or the church bell,
That made forgetful birds renew their songs.
And when, in that still hour, from Traffic's stir,
I looked upon the Sun in Heaven, his eye
Seemed burning with a great intelligence.
She sometimes sang at morn a song so sweet
That I must banish her until my soul
Repeated it a hundred times and more.
She kept me safe from that strong company
Of Gambling, Gluttony, and Drink, and Lust,
That ruin many. She could wake me in
The night to sing, as May wakes sleeping birds;
With visions of the hills and valleys, woods
And streams, and clouds; and all the flowers that
          came
Between the Snowdrop and Chrysanthemum.

And well she entertained my Winter nights;
For by her power I heard a kettle sing
As sweet a song as any bird made, when
In May the Sun was drying his wet wings.

That voice was small, but O what passion! like
A Skylark's voice, were he a Wasp in size.
All troubles did escape my Mind, when I,
With Fancy near, looked into my red fire;
To hear the battle of its blaze, or see
It in a red spell deep. To see two flames
Crouch low to box, and then stand tall; and then
To hear the blows distinct, and hard and fast –
Like carpet hung and beaten by a stick.
Aye, with that Maid it was a joy to live,
No matter had I Nature's Sun outdoors,
Or my own sun made out of wood and coal.
Then travelled we to many a pleasant land,
Where lovely fruit did grow so plentiful
That men that stole it were not counted thieves.
And we did cross high mountains white and bleak,
Which nothing with two feet or four had crossed,
Save birds on wings; and other mountains that
Could take the name of forests with their own.
We heard the water wash the island beach
Where giant turtles lay; and heard the roar
Of captains in a hurricane. Saw ships
Rolled by the waves, and the Pacific make
His waterspouts, that rolled ships far away –
And whirlpools strongest ships could not pass through.
And by her power I saw Thames' face as clear
As Heaven's above, when he had grass to kiss
Twice in twelve hours. I saw the town of Troy
With Helen there, that time when she made Jove
And his Queen almost empty Heaven, to fight
For her cause or against. Black walls saw I
Of castles old, part leafy and part bare;
And lonely abbeys tumbling down, that once
Were rich enough to ruin a king's soul.

With her I saw the rocks that Orpheus moved,
And trees that to his music danced like men;
And we did visit Mab's bright court, when it
Was all alight for foreign fairies; I
Saw by her power the golden barge that made
The black Nile clear in every place it went.
She to my Mind made it a common sight
To see the secret pails and bowls of pearls
Owned by a shah or sultan; she did make
My room more rich than theirs, with stuff that fire
Burned not, nor water spoiled, nor the winds tore.
My mind could watch the shepherd move his sheep
That, like drilled soldiers, one pace kept; and when
One ran, all ran; and when he stopped, all stopped.
We walked the woods and fields; sometimes in shade,
And sometimes out; and crouched behind green
      banks,
To spy on Ariel in the wind.
                        Alas!
Soon she began to make her absence known.
Then to my heart came dark Despondency,
And perched on it, e'en as a Hell's black rook
Will stand upon the head of a white Ewe.
Fool that I was to give her my whole heart!
I should have kept sweet Wine, or Dance, or Dress,
To take her place with pleasure – as a bird
Sings for the rain when Phoebus hides his light.
Ah, misery! that I should think this Maid
Would answer to my call whene'er I wished;
That when my Heart desired her she would come
And set my Mind in motion – foolish thought!
As though the Mind had not its milking hours,
And never failed. So, every night, alone,
When Fancy had been absent all the day,

Late would I sit, in hope she'd charm me yet
With one sweet little verse ere sleep could come,
And oft I sat and yearned for her in vain.
Come to me now, Love, while this blackbird sings;
Now, while the Butterfly's on that warm stone;
Come, while the bosom of yon cloud is white
And full to bursting – nay, she would not come.
It was a dreadful life, when she was gone,
To own a restless sea no vessel sailed.
My bread went stale and sour; I felt no joy,
Though Skylarks sang in Heaven and Rainbows
        shone.
O it was Hell! That I had sacrificed
All entertainment of Society,
Music, and Wine, and Woman for her sake,
And she to leave me, taking every charm
Away with her, of water, earth and sky.
Since I came here to live for her alone,
Then what is life, if she forsakes me now?
A little child that has no speech at all
Is happy with a sound none understand;
But when I heard the tell-tale Lark at morn,
Counting Earth's dewdrops to the eager Sun;
And when I saw the Evening gay with clouds
Of various hues, like flags upon a ship
That entertains its captain's new-made bride,
And, left by Fancy, had no power to speak –
Then O that I had no more speech than babes,
So happy with a simple cry! When she
Was gone, the birds seemed idle chatterers;
The flowers were common smirks that forced their
        charms,
No better than the leaves seen everywhere,
Made common by their number and one hue.

When she was near, my house was like that one
That has a living heir just born; when absent –
'Twas like a house that has an heir born dead.
When she was near, I could not hear the clock
Cry out the hour; but, in her absence, heard
Its smallest whisper, every tick it made.
And so I grieved, but she no sooner came
Than I with joy forgave her with a kiss;
And in that sudden blaze of pleasure, all
My smoky wrath went soon; my anger dropped –
Though for a week my curses had not ceased;
Dropped like a timid Star that cannot stand
Its bright society.
              When for a month
She had not visited my waiting Mind,
'Twas then I spake out loud and bitterly.

  Thou, false as that bright Sun, when he doth coax
Bees out ere Spring is ready with her flowers –
Why didst thou lead me here and then forsake me?
Thy voice as sweet and false as hers of old,
The last thing Merlin heard. Didst thou not say
That with thy company I should not wish
For ale or wine, or voice of man or woman;
That one thought like a lovely star should come,
And others follow, till my Heaven was full;
That one bright ray of Inspiration's light
Would warm my Soul, till it arose and cheered
As lusty as Dawn's streak makes Chanticleer;
And that no ink should dry upon my pen
Till every little black drop did produce
Fancies with thoughts that sparkled a pure white?
Didst thou not promise I should see bright gems
To startle me, though I put down secure

The hatches on my mortal eyes; promise
To give me these, that maybe would outshine
Some of these solid pearls that took long years
Ere they grew rich? Where art thou? Thou hast left
My spirit like a sea without a ship
In sight; no half-built ships are on my stocks,
And in my harbour float no finished ones
Ready to sail. Since thou hast gone, my life
Has courted sleep so oft that she grows sick
Of one that claims her service for so long;
And thou didst promise I would even mock
Sweet sleep, with thoughts of some sweet task undone –
So wouldst thou occupy my Mind.

And now, when I desire thee most – since Time
Has sent forth one white hair to draw the black
Into that treason which dethrones my youth –
Thou hast forsaken me. Since that is so,
There is no help I know of; I must plunge
Into a sea of flesh again – a sea
That's full of things to drag strong swimmers down.
Go then, false Fancy, show thy face no more;
For I will live with Pleasure in the crowd,
With her attendants, Fashion, Dance and Wine.
If thou dost come again, I'll strike thee dead –
As honest seamen, on a raft at sea,
Must strike a madman down for their life's sake.

E'en as I spake these words I felt my Mind
Possessed by Fancy, and forgot my wrath,
And all my heart inclined to hear her speak.

Thou art my life-long Love, I said; I'll not
Return to Pleasure in a city's crowd.
Pleasure can give no true and lasting joy;

Her voice is like a torrent's, in whose sound
The little birds of joy must sing unheard.
Aye, Pleasure is a planet dark, that shines
By the reflection of admiring eyes,
But Joy has her own light — and thou art Joy.
All Pleasure's thoughts are centred in her flesh,
To eat and drink, to dress, to dance, and ride,
And be where there are many eyes and ears;
And vain she is, and proud — she cannot see
One inch beyond her own two feet of hair.
I courted that false goddess once, alas!
Blind and deceived with Jacob's joy, when he
Knew not his best loved son — e'en so was I;
Until my sight returned, and I could see
Through Pleasure's silk, and saw her many faults.
Come then, sweet Fancy — surnamed Joy by me.

82. Songs of Joy

Sing out, my Soul, thy songs of joy;
    Such as a happy bird will sing
Beneath a Rainbow's lovely arch
    In early spring.

Think not of Death in thy young days;
    Why shouldst thou that grim tyrant fear,
And fear him not when thou art old,
    And he is near?

Strive not for gold, for greedy fools
    Measure themselves by poor men never;
Their standard still being richer men,
    Makes them poor ever.

Train up thy mind to feel content,
 What matters then how low thy store?
What we enjoy, and not possess,
 Makes rich or poor.

Filled with sweet thought, then happy I
 Take not my state from others' eyes;
What's in my mind – not on my flesh
 Or theirs – I prize.

Sing, happy Soul, thy songs of joy;
 Such as a Brook sings in the wood,
That all night has been strengthened by
 Heaven's purer flood.

83. The Example

Here's an example from
 A Butterfly;
That on a rough, hard rock
 Happy can lie;
Friendless and all alone
On this unsweetened stone.

Now let my bed be hard,
 No care take I;
I'll make my joy like this
 Small Butterfly;
Whose happy heart has power
To make a stone a flower.

84. In May

Yes, I will spend the livelong day
With Nature in this month of May;
And sit beneath the trees, and share
My bread with birds whose homes are there;
While cows lie down to eat, and sheep
Stand to their necks in grass so deep;
While birds do sing with all their might,
As though they felt the earth in flight.
This is the hour I dreamed of, when
I sat surrounded by poor men;
And thought of how the Arab sat
Alone at evening, gazing at
The stars that bubbled in clear skies;

And of young dreamers, when their eyes
Enjoyed methought a precious boon
In the adventures of the Moon
Whose light, behind the Clouds' dark bars,
Searched for her stolen flocks of stars.
When I, hemmed in by wrecks of men,
Thought of some lonely cottage then,
Full of sweet books; and miles of sea,
With passing ships, in front of me;
And having, on the other hand,
A flowery, green, bird-singing land.

85. The Flood

I thought my true love slept;
Behind her chair I crept
   And pulled out a long pin;
The golden flood came out,
She shook it all about,
   With both our faces in.

Ah! little wren, I know
Your mossy, small nest now
   A windy, cold place is;
No eye can see my face,
Howe'er it watch the place
   Where I half drown in bliss.

When I am drowned half dead,
She laughs and shakes her head;
   Flogged by her hair-waves, I
Withdraw my face from there;
But never once, I swear,
   She heard a mercy-cry.

86. Leisure

What is this life if, full of care,
We have no time to stand and stare.

No time to stand beneath the boughs
And stare as long as sheep or cows.

No time to see, when woods we pass,
Where squirrels hide their nuts in grass.

No time to see, in broad daylight,
Streams full of stars like skies at night.

No time to turn at Beauty's glance,
And watch her feet, how they can dance.

No time to wait till her mouth can
Enrich that smile her eyes began.

A poor life this if, full of care,
We have no time to stand and stare.

87.   Fancy's Home

Tell me, Fancy, sweetest child,
    Of thy parents and thy birth;
Had they silk, and had they gold
    And a park to wander forth,
With a castle green and old?

In a cottage I was born,
    My kind father was Content,
My dear mother Innocence;
    On wild fruits of wonderment
I have nourished ever since.

88.   Sheep

When I was once in Baltimore,
   A man came up to me and cried,
'Come, I have eighteen hundred sheep,
   And we will sail on Tuesday's tide.

'If you will sail with me, young man,
   I'll pay you fifty shillings down;
These eighteen hundred sheep I take
   From Baltimore to Glasgow town.'

He paid me fifty shillings down,
   I sailed with eighteen hundred sheep;
We soon had cleared the harbour's mouth,
   We soon were in the salt sea deep.

The first night we were out at sea
   Those sheep were quiet in their mind;
The second night they cried with fear –
   They smelt no pastures in the wind.

They sniffed, poor things, for their green fields,
   They cried so loud I could not sleep:
For fifty thousand shillings down
   I would not sail again with sheep.

89.   Days that have Been

Can I forget the sweet days that have been,
   When poetry first began to warm my blood;
When from the hills of Gwent I saw the earth
   Burned into two by Severn's silver flood:

When I would go alone at night to see
    The moonlight, like a big white butterfly,
Dreaming on that old castle near Caerleon,
    While at its side the Usk went softly by:

When I would stare at lovely clouds in Heaven,
    Or watch them when reported by deep streams;
When feeling pressed like thunder, but would not
    Break into that grand music of my dreams?

Can I forget the sweet days that have been,
    The villages so green I have been in;
Llantarnam, Magor, Malpas, and Llanwern,
    Liswery, old Caerleon, and Alteryn?

Can I forget the banks of Malpas Brook,
    Or Ebbw's voice in such a wild delight,
As on he dashed with pebbles in his throat,
    Gurgling towards the sea with all his might?

Ah, when I see a leafy village now,
    I sigh and ask it for Llantarnam's green;
I ask each river where is Ebbw's voice –
    In memory of the sweet days that have been.

90. Days too Short

When primroses are out in Spring,
    And small, blue violets come between;
    When merry birds sing on boughs green,
And rills, as soon as born, must sing;

When butterflies will make side-leaps,
    As though escaped from Nature's hand
    Ere perfect quite; and bees will stand
Upon their heads in fragrant deeps;

When small clouds are so silvery white
    Each seems a broken rimmèd moon—
    When such things are, this world too soon,
For me, doth wear the veil of Night.

91. The Power of Music

O those sweet notes, so soft and faint; that seemed
    Locked up inside a thick walled house of stone;
And then that sudden rush of sound, as though
    The doors and windows were wide-open thrown.

Do with me, O sweet music, as thou wilt,
    I am thy slave to either laugh or weep;
Thy power can make thy slave a lover proud,
    Or friendless man that has no place to sleep.

I hear thy gentle whisper and again
    Hear ripples lap the quays of sheltered docks;
I hear thy thunder and it brings to mind
    Dark Colorado scaling his huge rocks.

I hear thy joyous cries and think of birds
    Delirious when the sun doth rise in May;
I hear thy moans and think me of poor cows
    That miss at night the calves they licked by day.

I hear thee wail and think of that sad queen
    Who saw her lover's disappearing mast;
How she, who drank and wasted a rich pearl –
    To prove her love – was left to wail at last.

Do with me, O sweet Music, as thou wilt;
    Till even thou art robbed by jealous Sleep
Of those sweet senses thou hast forced from me –
    And I can neither laugh with thee nor weep.

92.   Christ, the Man

Lord, I say nothing; I profess
    No faith in thee nor Christ thy Son:
Yet no man ever heard me mock
    A true believing one.

If knowledge is not great enough
    To give a man believing power,
Lord, he must wait in thy great hand
    Till revelation's hour.

Meanwhile he'll follow Christ, the man
    In that humanity he taught,
Which to the poor and the oppressed
    Gives its best time and thought.

93.   Ingratitude

Am I a fool?
    So let it be,
For half the world
    Will pity me.

145

Ingratitude
    Is not my name;
Thieves, called by that,
    Are dumb for shame.

A fool – the world
    Will pity me;
Ungrateful – let
    No mercy be.

94.   The Posts

A year's a post, on which
        It saith
The distance – growing less –
        To Death.

Some posts I missed, beguiled
        By Song
And Beauty, as I passed
        Along.

But sad am I to think
        This day
Of forty posts passed on
        My way.

For not one post I now
        Must pass
Will 'scape these eyes of mine,
        Alas!

95. Rich or Poor

With thy true love I have more wealth
    Than Charon's piled-up bank doth hold;
Where he makes kings lay down their crowns
    And lifelong misers leave their gold.

Without thy love I've no more wealth
    Than seen upon that other shore;
That cold, bare bank he rows them to –
    Those kings and misers made so poor.

96. The Harvest Home

The Harvest Home's a home indeed;
    If my lord bishop drank ale there,
He'd want to kiss the beggar wench,
    And change his gown with her, I swear.

The Harvest Home's a place to love,
    There is no better booze on sale;
Angels in Heaven – I take my oath –
    Can find no better glass of ale.

There's courage in such booze as that:
    Old Dicky drank but one small mug,
And then, to please the harvest girls,
    Said, 'Look!' and swallowed a live frog.

The landlord draws to suit my taste,
    I never knew his wife to fail;
But, somehow, what the daughter draws
    Is – by my soul and body – Ale!

97. Seeking Beauty

Cold winds can never freeze, nor thunder sour
  The cup of cheer that Beauty draws for me
Out of those azure Heavens and this green Earth –
  I drink and drink, and thirst the more I see.

To see the dewdrops thrill the blades of grass,
  Makes my whole body shake; for here's my choice
Of either sun or shade, and both are green –
  A Chaffinch laughs in his melodious voice.

The banks are stormed by Speedwell, that blue flower
  So like a little Heaven with one star out;
I see an amber lake of Buttercups,
  And Hawthorn foams the hedges round about.

The old Oak tree looks now so green and young,
  That even Swallows perch awhile and sing:
This is that time of year, so sweet and warm,
  When Bats wait not for Stars ere they take wing.

As long as I love Beauty I am young,
  Am young or old as I love more or less;
When Beauty is not heeded or seems stale,
  My life's a cheat, let Death end my distress.

98. The Owl

The boding Owl, that in despair
  Doth moan and shiver on warm nights –
Shall that bird prophesy for me
  The fall of Heaven's eternal lights?

When in the thistled field of Age
   I take my final walk on earth,
Still will I make that Owl's despair
   A thing to fill my heart with mirth.

99. The East in Gold

Somehow this world is wonderful at times,
   As it has been from early morn in May;
Since first I heard the cock-a-doodle-do –
   Timekeeper on green farms – at break of day.

Soon after that I heard ten thousand birds,
   Which made me think an angel brought a bin
Of golden grain, and none was scattered yet –
   To rouse those birds to make that merry din.

I could not sleep again, for such wild cries,
   And went out early into their green world;
And then I saw what set their little tongues
   To scream for joy – they saw the East in gold.

100. Sadness and Joy

I pray you, Sadness, leave me soon,
   In sweet invention thou art poor!
Thy sister Joy can make ten songs
   While thou art making four.

One hour with thee is sweet enough;
   But when we find the whole day gone
And no created thing is left –
   We mourn the evil done.

Thou art too slow to shape thy thoughts
  In stone, on canvas, or in song;
But Joy, being full of active heat,
  Must do some deed ere long.

Thy sighs are gentle, sweet thy tears;
  But if thou canst not help a man
To prove in substance what he feels –
  Then give me Joy, who can.

Therefore, sweet Sadness, leave me soon,
  Let thy bright sister Joy come more;
For she can make ten lovely songs
  While thou art making four.

101. To Sparrows Fighting

Stop, feathered bullies!
  Peace, angry birds;
You common Sparrows that,
  For a few words,
Roll fighting in wet mud,
To shed each other's blood.

Look at those Linnets, they
  Like ladies sing;
See how those Swallows, too,
  Play on the wing;
All other birds close by
Are gentle, clean and shy.

And yet maybe your life's
   As sweet as theirs;
The common poor that fight
   Live not for years
In one long frozen state
Of anger, like the great.

102. The Happy Child

I saw this day sweet flowers grow thick –
But not one like the child did pick.

I heard the pack-hounds in green park –
But no dog like the child heard bark.

I heard this day bird after bird –
But not one like the child has heard.

A hundred butterflies saw I –
But not one like the child saw fly.

I saw the horses roll in grass –
But no horse like the child saw pass.

My world this day has lovely been –
But not like what the child has seen.

103. The Two Flocks

Where are you going to now, white sheep,
  Walking the green hill-side;
To join that whiter flock on top,
  And share their pride?

Stay where you are, you silly sheep:
  When you arrive up there,
You'll find that whiter flock on top
  Clouds in the air!

104. A Dream

I met her in the leafy woods,
Early a Summer's night;
I saw her white teeth in the dark,
  There was no better light.

Had she not come up close and made
  Those lilies their light spread,
I had not proved her mouth a rose,
  So round, so fresh, so red.

Her voice was gentle, soft and sweet,
  In words she was not strong;
Yet her low twitter had more charm
  Than any full-mouthed song.

We walked in silence to her cave,
  With but few words to say;
But ever and anon she stopped
  For kisses on the way.

And after every burning kiss
    She laughed and danced around;
Back-bending, with her breasts straight up,
    Her hair it touched the ground.

When we lay down, she held me fast,
    She held me like a leech;
Ho, ho! I know what her red tongue
    Is made for, if not speech.

And what is this, how strange, how sweet!
    Her teeth are made to bite
The man she gives her passion to,
    And not to boast their white.

O night of Joy! O morning's grief!
    For when, with passion done,
Rocked on her breast I fell asleep,
    I woke, and lay alone.

105. The Elements

No house of stone
    Was built for me;
When the Sun shines –
    I am a bee.

No sooner comes
    The Rain so warm,
I come to light –
    I am a worm.

When the Winds blow,
  I do not strip,
But set my sails –
  I am a ship.

When Lightning comes,
  It plays with me
And I with it –
  I am a tree.

When drowned men rise
  At Thunder's word,
Sings Nightingale –
  I am a bird.

106. The Heap of Rags

One night when I went down
Thames' side, in London Town,
A heap of rags saw I,
And sat me down close by.
That thing could shout and bawl,
But showed no face at all;
When any steamer passed
And blew a loud shrill blast,
That heap of rags would sit
And make a sound like it;
When struck the clock's deep bell,
It made those peals as well.
When winds did moan around,
It mocked them with that sound.

When all was quiet, it
Fell into a strange fit;
Would sigh, and moan and roar,
It laughed, and blessed, and swore.
Yet that poor thing, I know,
Had neither friend nor foe;
Its blessing or its curse
Made no one better or worse.
I left it in that place –
The thing that showed no face.
Was it a man that had
Suffered till he went mad?
So many showers and not
One rainbow in the lot;
Too many bitter fears
To make a pearl from tears?

107. The Quarrel

Hear me, thou proud, deceitful maid,
Tell how thy charms must droop and fade;
Long ere thy days are done, thou'lt be
Alive for Memory's mockery.
Soft flesh will soon hang hard and dry
Like seaweed on the rocks; that eye
Soon lose its clearness, like a flood
Where late the drinking cows have stood.
Thy berry-lips, now full and red,
Will dry and crack, like snakeskins shed;
And those white stones they keep inside,
Will blacken, break, and then you'll hide.

155

That hair which like a golden net
Hangs loose and free, a trap well set
To catch my silly fingers now –
Will soon cause thee much grief to show.
Thy voice, now like a flawless bell,
Which thou dost ring so sweet and well –
Will shame thee into silence soon.
Thy form, tied like a silk balloon,
Full of sweet gas, straining to rise
From common earth, and sail those skies –
Will sit all huddled in a chair,
Cold at a fire, and springtime there.
These things I told a maid one day,
And laughed with scorn, and went my way;
I laughed with scorn, as home I stept –
Ah, but all night I sighed and wept.

108. Fairies, Take Care

A thousand blessings, Puck, on you
For knotting that long grass which threw
Into my arms a maid; for we
Have told our love and kissed, and she
Will lie a-bed in a sweet fright.
So, all ye Fairies who to-night
May take that stormy passage where
Her bosom's quicksands are, take care
Of whirlpools too: beware all you
Of that great tempest Love must brew.
The waves will rock your breath near out
First sunk, then tossed and rolled about,

Now on your heads, now on your feet –
You'll be near swamped and, for life sweet,
Be glad to cross that stormy main,
And stand on something firm again.
Would I could see her while she sleeps,
And smiles to feel you climb those steeps,
Where you at last will stand up clear
Upon their cherry tops, and cheer.
And that ye are not lost, take care,
In that deep forest of her hair:
Yet ye may enter naked stark,
It gets more warm as it gets dark.
So, Fairies, fear not any harm,
While in those woods so dark and warm.

109. The Doubtful One

When tigers flee from fire, the deer
Have nothing but that fire to fear;
So, driven by Love's flames I see
No danger save thy cruelty.

Let not thy breast, to which I fly
For pity's milk, be hard and dry:
Let not thy heart, to which I come,
Refuse my homeless life a home.

Now, wrecked and cuffed by many a sea,
I swim for safety unto thee;
Let not sharp rocks that poor wretch cut,
Who for his life clings hand and foot.

110. The Little Ones

The little ones are put in bed,
   And both are laughing, lying down;
Their father, and their mother too,
   Are gone on Christmas eve to town.

'Old Santa Claus will bring a horse,
   Gee up:' cried little Will, with glee;
'If I am good, I'll have a doll
   From Santa Claus' – laughed Emily.

The little ones are gone to sleep,
   Their father and their mother now
Are coming home, with many more –
   They're drunk, and make a merry row.

The little ones on Christmas morn
   Jump up, like skylarks from the grass;
And then they stand as still as stones,
   And just as cold as stones, Alas!

No horse, no doll beside their bed,
   No sadder little ones could be;
'We did some wrong,' said little Will –
   'We must have sinned,' sobbed Emily.

111. Shopping

When thou hast emptied thy soft purse,
   Take not from men more merchandise:
Full well I know they'd trust thy looks,
And enter no accounts in books
   Of goods bought by thy lovely eyes.

Take not advantage of that hand,
  That men, admiring it too much,
Forget the value of their stuff,
And think that empty hand enough –
  To make poor bankrupt men of such.

Let not that voice of thine, like silk
  Translated into sound, commend
Plain cloth to Jews, lest they should raise
The price of it to match thy praise,
  And the poor suffer in the end.

112. The Sleepers

As I walked down the waterside
  This silent morning, wet and dark;
Before the cocks in farmyards crowed,
  Before the dogs began to bark;
Before the hour of five was struck
By old Westminster's mighty clock:

As I walked down the waterside
  This morning, in the cold damp air,
I saw a hundred women and men
  Huddled in rags and sleeping there:
These people have no work, thought I,
And long before their time they die.

That moment, on the waterside,
  A lighted car came at a bound;
I looked inside, and saw a score
  Of pale and weary men that frowned;
Each man sat in a huddled heap,
Carried to work while fast asleep.

Ten cars rushed down the waterside
   Like lighted coffins in the dark;
With twenty dead men in each car,
   That must be brought alive by work:
These people work too hard, thought I,
And long before their time they die.

113. The Bed-sitting-room

Must I live here, with Scripture on my walls,
Death-cards with rocks and anchors; on my shelf
Plain men and women with plain histories
A proud landlady knows, and no one else?
Let me have pictures of a richer kind:
Scenes in low taverns, with their beggar rogues
Singing and drinking ale; who buy more joy
With a few pence than others can with pounds.
Show gipsies on wild commons, camped at fires
Close to their caravans; where they cook flesh
They have not bought, and plants not sold to them.
Show me the picture of a drinking monk
With his round belly like a mare in foal,
Belted, to keep his guts from falling out
When he laughs hearty; or a maid's bare back,
Who teases me with a bewitching smile
Thrown over her white shoulder. Let me see
The picture of a sleeping damosel,
Who has a stream of shining hair to fill
Up that deep channel banked by her white breasts.
Has Beauty never smiled from off these walls,
Has Genius never entered in a book?
Nay, Madam, keep your room; for in my box
I have a lovely picture of young Eve,

Before she knew what sewing was. Alas!
If I hung on your wall her naked form,
Among your graves and crosses, Scripture texts,
Your death-cards with their anchors and their rocks –
What then? I think this life a joyful thing,
And, like a bird that sees a sleeping cat,
I leave with haste your death-preparing room.

114. The Child and the Mariner

A dear old couple my grandparents were,
And kind to all dumb things; they saw in Heaven
The lamb that Jesus petted when a child:
Their faith was never draped by Doubt: to them
Death was a rainbow in Eternity,
That promised everlasting brightness soon.
An old seafaring man was he; a rough
Old man, but kind; and hairy, like the nut
Full of sweet milk. All day on shore he watched
The winds for sailors' wives, and told what ships
Enjoyed fair weather, and what ships had storms;
He watched the sky, and he could tell for sure
What afternoons would follow stormy morns,
If quiet nights would end wild afternoons.
He leapt away from scandal with a roar,
And if a whisper still possessed his mind,
He walked about and cursed it for a plague.
He took offence at Heaven when beggars passed,
And sternly called them back to give them help.
In this old captain's house I lived, and things
That house contained were in ships' cabins once;

Sea-shells and charts and pebbles, model ships;
Green weeds, dried fishes stuffed, and coral stalks;
Old wooden trunks with handles of spliced rope,
With copper saucers full of monies strange,
That seemed the savings of dead men, not touched
To keep them warm since their real owners died;
Strings of red beads, methought were dipped in blood,
And swinging lamps, as though the house might move;
An ivory lighthouse built on ivory rocks,
The bones of fishes and three bottled ships.
And many a thing was there which sailors make
In idle hours, when on long voyages,
Of marvellous patience, to no lovely end.
And on those charts I saw the small black dots
That were called islands, and I knew they had
Turtles and palms, and pirates' buried gold.
There came a stranger to my grandad's house,
The old man's nephew, a seafarer too;
A big, strong able man who could have walked
Twm Barlum's hill all clad in iron mail;
So strong he could have made one man his club
To knock down others – Henry was his name,
No other name was uttered by his kin.
And here he was, in sooth ill-clad, but oh,
Thought I, what secrets of the sea are his!
This man knows coral islands in the sea,
And dusky girls heart-broken for white men;
This sailor knows of wondrous lands afar,
More rich than Spain, when the Phoenicians shipped
Silver for common ballast, and they saw
Horses at silver mangers eating grain;
This man has seen the wind blow up a mermaid's hair
Which, like a golden serpent, reared and stretched
To feel the air away beyond her head.

He begged my pennies, which I gave with joy –
He will most certainly return some time
A self-made king of some new land, and rich.
Alas that he, the hero of my dreams,
Should be his people's scorn; for they had rose
To proud command of ships, whilst he had toiled
Before the mast for years, and well content;
Him they despised, and only Death could bring
A likeness in his face to show like them.
For he drank all his pay, nor went to sea
As long as ale was easy got on shore.
Now, in his last long voyage he had sailed
From Plymouth Sound to where sweet odours fan
The Cingalese at work, and then back home –
But came not near his kin till pay was spent.
He was not old, yet seemed so; for his face
Looked like the drowned man's in the morgue, when
     it
Has struck the wooden wharves and keels of ships.
And all his flesh was pricked with Indian ink,
His body marked as rare and delicate
As dead men struck by lightning under trees,
And pictured with fine twigs and curlèd ferns;
Chains on his neck and anchors on his arms;
Rings on his fingers, bracelets on his wrist;
And on his breast the *Jane* of Appledore
Was schooner rigged, and in full sail at sea.
He could not whisper with his strong hoarse voice,
No more than could a horse creep quietly;
He laughed to scorn the men that muffled close
For fear of wind, till all their neck was hid,
Like Indian corn wrapped up in long green leaves;
He knew no flowers but seaweeds brown and green,
He knew no birds but those that followed ships.

163

Full well he knew the water-world; he heard
A grander music there than we on land,
When organ shakes a church; swore he would
      make
The sea his home, though it was always roused
By such wild storms as never leave Cape Horn,
Happy to hear the tempest grunt and squeal
Like pigs heard dying in a slaughter-house.
A true-born mariner, and this his hope –
His coffin would be what his cradle was,
A boat to drown in and be sunk at sea;
To drown at sea and lie a dainty corpse
Salted and iced in Neptune's larder deep.
This man despised small coasters, fishing-smacks,
He scorned those sailors who at night and morn
Can see the coast, when in their little boats
They go a six days' voyage and are back
Home with their wives for every Sabbath day.
Much did he talk of tankards of old beer,
And bottled stuff he drank in other lands,
Which was a liquid fire like Hell to gulp,
But Paradise to sip.
                        And so he talked;
Nor did those people listen with more awe
To Lazarus – whom they had seen stone-dead –
Than did we urchins to that seaman's voice.
He many a tale of wonder told: of where,
At Argostoli, Cephalonia's sea
Ran over the earth's lip in heavy floods;
And then again of how the strange Chinese
Conversed much as our homely Blackbirds sing.
He told us how he sailed in one old ship
Near that volcano Martinique, whose power
Shook like dry leaves the whole Caribbean seas;

And made the Sun set in a sea of fire
Which only half was his; and dust was thick
On deck, and stones were pelted at the mast.
So, as we walked along, that seaman dropped
Into my greedy ears such words that sleep
Stood at my pillow half the night perplexed.
He told how isles sprang up and sank again,
Between short voyages, to his amaze;
How they did come and go, and cheated charts;
Told how a crew was cursed when one man killed
A bird that perched upon a moving barque;
And how the sea's sharp needles, firm and strong,
Ripped open the bellies of big, iron ships;
Of mighty icebergs in the Northern seas,
That haunt the far horizon like white ghosts.
He told of waves that lift a ship so high
That birds could pass from starboard unto port
Under her dripping keel.

          Oh, it was sweet
To hear that seaman tell such wondrous tales:
How deep the sea in parts, that drowned men
Must go a long way to their graves and sink
Day after day, and wander with the tides.
He spake of his own deeds; of how he sailed
One summer's night along the Bosphorus,
And he – who knew no music like the wash
Of waves against a ship, or wind in shrouds –
Heard then the music on that woody shore
Of nightingales, and feared to leave the deck,
He thought 'twas sailing into Paradise.
To hear these stories all we urchins placed
Our pennies in that seaman's ready hand;
Until one morn he signed for a long cruise,
And sailed away – we never saw him more.

Could such a man sink in the sea unknown?
Nay, he had found a land with something rich,
That kept his eyes turned inland for his life.
'A damn bad sailor and a landshark too,
No good in port or out' – my grandad said.

115. Thunderstorms

My mind has thunderstorms,
   That brood for heavy hours:
Until they rain me words,
   My thoughts are drooping flowers
And sulking, silent birds.

Yet come, dark thunderstorms,
   And brood your heavy hours;
For when you rain me words,
   My thoughts are dancing flowers
And joyful singing birds.

116. Strong Moments

Sometimes I hear fine ladies sing,
   Sometimes I smoke and drink with men;
Sometimes I play at games of cards –
   Judge me to be no strong man then.

The strongest moment of my life
　　Is when I think about the poor;
When, like a spring that rain has fed,
　　My pity rises more and more.

The flower that loves the warmth and light
　　Has all its mornings bathed in dew;
My heart has moments wet with tears,
　　My weakness is they are so few.

117.　A Greeting

Good morning, Life – and all
Things glad and beautiful.
My pockets nothing hold,
But he that owns the gold,
The Sun, is my great friend –
His spending has no end.

Hail to the morning sky,
Which bright clouds measure high;
Hail to you birds whose throats
Would number leaves by notes;
Hail to you shady bowers,
And you green fields of flowers.

Hail to you women fair,
That make a show so rare
In cloth as white as milk –
Be't calico or silk:
Good morning, Life – and all
Things glad and beautiful.

118. Sweet Stay-at-Home

Sweet Stay-at-Home, sweet Well-content,
Thou knowest of no strange continent:
Thou hast not felt thy bosom keep
A gentle motion with the deep;
Thou hast not sailed in Indian seas,
Where scent comes forth in every breeze.
Thou hast not seen the rich grape grow
For miles, as far as eyes can go;
Thou hast not seen a summer's night
When maids could sew by a worm's light;
Nor the North Sea in spring send out
Bright hues that like birds flit about
In solid cages of white ice –
Sweet Stay-at-Home, sweet Love-one-place.
Thou hast not seen black fingers pick
White cotton when the bloom is thick,
Nor heard black throats in harmony;
Nor hast thou sat on stones that lie
Flat on the earth, that once did rise
To hide proud kings from common eyes;
Thou hast not seen plains full of bloom
Where green things had such little room
They pleased the eye like fairer flowers –
Sweet Stay-at-Home, all these long hours.
Sweet Well-content, sweet Love-one-place,
Sweet, simple maid, bless thy dear face;
For thou hast made more homely stuff
Nurture thy gentle self enough;
I love thee for a heart that's kind –
Not for the knowledge in thy mind.

119. The Starved

My little Lamb, what is amiss?
If there was milk in mother's kiss,
You would not look as white as this.

The wolf of Hunger, it is he
That takes away thy milk from me,
And I have much to do for thee.

If thou couldst live on love, I know
No babe in all the land could show
More rosy cheeks and louder crow.

Thy father's dead, Alas for thee:
I cannot keep this wolf from me,
That takes thy milk so bold and free.

If thy dear father lived, he'd drive
Away this beast with whom I strive,
And thou, my pretty Lamb, wouldst thrive.

Ah, my poor babe, my love's so great
I'd swallow common rags for meat –
If they could make milk rich and sweet.

My little Lamb, what is amiss?
Come, I must wake thee with a kiss,
For Death would own a sleep like this.

120.   A May Morning

The sky is clear,
  The sun is bright:
The cows are red,
  The sheep are white;
Trees in the meadows
Make happy shadows.

Birds in the hedge
  Are perched and sing;
Swallows and larks
  Are on the wing:
Two merry cuckoos
Are making echoes.

Bird and the beast
  Have the dew yet;
My road shines dry,
  Theirs bright and wet;
Death gives no warning
On this May morning.

I see no Christ
  Nailed on a tree
Dying for sin;
  No sin I see:
No thoughts for sadness,
All thoughts for gladness.

121. The Lonely Dreamer

He lives his lonely life, and when he dies
A thousand hearts maybe will utter sighs;
Because they liked his songs, and now their bird
Sleeps with his head beneath his wing, unheard.

But what kind hand will tend his grave, and bring
Those blossoms there, of which he used to sing?
Who'll kiss his mound, and wish the time would come
To lie with him inside that silent tomb?

And who'll forget the dreamer's skill, and shed
A tear because a loving heart is dead?
Heigh ho for gossip then, and common sighs –
And let his death bring tears in no one's eyes.

122. Christmas

Christmas has come, let's eat and drink –
This is no time to sit and think;
Farewell to study, books and pen,
And welcome to all kinds of men.
Let all men now get rid of care,
And what one has let others share;
Then 'tis the same, no matter which
Of us is poor, or which is rich.
Let each man have enough this day,
Since those that can are glad to pay;
There's nothing now too rich or good
For poor men, not the King's own food.
Now like a singing bird my feet
Touch earth, and I must drink and eat.

Welcome to all men: I'll not care
What any of my fellows wear;
We'll not let cloth divide our souls,
They'll swim stark naked in the bowls.
Welcome, poor beggar: I'll not see
That hand of yours dislodge a flea, –
While you sit at my side and beg,
Or right foot scratching your left leg.
Farewell restraint: we will not now
Measure the ale our brains allow,
But drink as much as we can hold.
We'll count no change when we spend gold;
This is no time to save, but spend,
To give for nothing, not to lend.
Let foes make friends: let them forget
The mischief-making dead that fret
The living with complaint like this –
'He wronged us once, hate him and his.'
Christmas has come; let every man
Eat, drink, be merry all he can.
Ale's my best mark, but if port wine
Or whisky's yours – let it be mine;
No matter what lies in the bowls,
We'll make it rich with our own souls.
Farewell to study, books and pen,
And welcome to all kinds of men.

123. Laughing Rose

If I were gusty April now,
    How I would blow at laughing Rose;
I'd make her ribbons slip their knots,
    And all her hair come loose.

172

If I were merry April now,
  How I would pelt her cheeks with showers;
I'd make carnations, rich and warm,
  Of her vermilion flowers.

Since she will laugh in April's face,
  No matter how he rains or blows –
Then O that I wild April were,
  To play with laughing Rose.

124. Seeking Joy

Joy, how I sought thee!
Silver I spent and gold,
On the pleasures of this world,
  In splendid garments clad;
The wine I drank was sweet,
Rich morsels I did eat –
  Oh, but my life was sad!
Joy, how I sought thee!

Joy, I have found thee!
Far from the halls of Mirth,
Back to the soft green earth,
  Where people are not many;
I find thee, Joy, in hours
With clouds, and birds, and flowers
  Thou dost not charge one penny.
Joy, I have found thee!

125. The Old Oak Tree

I sit beneath your leaves, old oak,
  You mighty one of all the trees;
Within whose hollow trunk a man
  Could stable his big horse with ease.

I see your knuckles hard and strong,
  But have no fear they'll come to blows;
Your life is long, and mine is short,
  But which has known the greater woes?

Thou hast not seen starved women here,
  Or man gone mad because ill-fed –
Who stares at stones in city streets,
  Mistaking them for hunks of bread.

Thou hast not felt the shivering backs
  Of homeless children lying down
And sleeping in the cold, night air –
  Like doors and walls, in London town.

Knowing thou hast not known such shame,
  And only storms have come thy way,
Methinks I could in comfort spend
  My summer with thee, day by day.

To lie by day in thy green shade,
  And in thy hollow rest at night;
And through the open doorway see
  The stars turn over leaves of light.

126. Poor Kings

God's pity on poor kings,
  They know no gentle rest;
The North and South cry out,
  Cries come from East and West –
'Come, open this new Dock,
  Building, Bazaar, or Fair.'
Lord, what a wretched life
  Such men must bear.

They're followed, watched and spied,
  No liberty they know;
Some eye will watch them still,
  No matter where they go.
When in green lanes I muse,
  Alone, and hear birds sing,
God's pity then, say I,
  On some poor king.

127. Love and the Muse

My back is turned on Spring and all her flowers,
  The birds no longer charm from tree to tree;
The cuckoo had his home in this green world
  Ten days before his voice was heard by me.

Had I an answer from a dear one's lips,
  My love of life would soon regain its power;
And suckle my sweet dreams, that tug my heart,
  And whimper to be nourished every hour.

Give me that answer now, and then my Muse,
   That for my sweet life's sake must never die,
Will rise like that great wave that leaps and hangs
   The seaweed on a vessel's mast-top high.

128. My Youth

My youth was my old age,
   Weary and long;
It had too many cares
   To think of song;
My moulting days all came
   When I was young.

Now, in life's prime, my soul
   Comes out in flower;
Late, as with Robin, comes
   My singing power;
I was not born to joy
   Till this late hour.

129. Smiles

I saw a black girl once,
   As black as winter's night;
Till through her parted lips
   There came a flood of light;
It was the milky way
   Across her face so black:
Her two lips closed again,
   And night came back.

I see a maiden now,
  Fair as a summer's day;
Yet through her parted lips
  I see the milky way;
It makes the broad daylight
  In summer time look black:
Her two lips close again,
  And night comes back.

130. Mad Poll

There goes mad Poll, dressed in wild flowers,
  Poor, crazy Poll, now old and wan;
Her hair all down, like any child:
  She swings her two arms like a man.

Poor, crazy Poll is never sad,
  She never misses one that dies;
When neighbours show their new-born babes,
  They seem familiar to her eyes.

Her bonnet's always in her hand,
  Or on the ground, and lying near;
She thinks it is a thing for play,
  Or pretty show, and not to wear.

She gives the sick no sympathy,
  She never soothes a child that cries;
She never whimpers, night or day,
  She makes no moans, she makes no sighs.

She talks about some battle old,
　　Fought many a day from yesterday;
And when that war is done, her love –
　　'Ha, ha!' Poll laughs, and skips away.

131.　Joy Supreme

The birds are pirates of her notes,
　　The blossoms steal her face's light;
The stars in ambush lie all day,
　　To take her glances for the night.
Her voice can shame rain-pelted leaves;
　　Young robin has no notes as sweet
In autumn, when the air is still,
　　And all the other birds are mute.

When I set eyes on ripe, red plums
　　That seem a sin and shame to bite,
Such are her lips, which I would kiss,
　　And still would keep before my sight.
When I behold proud gossamer
　　Make silent billows in the air,
Then think I of her head's fine stuff,
　　Finer than gossamer's, I swear.

The miser has his joy, with gold
　　Beneath his pillow in the night;
My head shall lie on soft warm hair,
　　And misers know not that delight.
Captains that own their ships can boast
　　Their joy to feel the rolling brine –
But I shall lie near her, and feel
　　Her soft warm bosom swell on mine.

132. Francis Thompson

Thou hadst no home, and thou couldst see
   In every street the windows' light:
   Dragging thy limbs about all night,
No window kept a light for thee.

However much thou wert distressed,
   Or tired of moving, and felt sick,
   Thy life was on the open deck –
Thou hadst no cabin for thy rest.

Thy barque was helpless 'neath the sky,
   No pilot thought thee worth his pains
   To guide for love or money gains –
Like phantom ships the rich sailed by.

Thy shadow mocked thee night and day,
   Thy life's companion, it alone;
   It did not sigh, it did not moan,
But mocked thy moves in every way.

In spite of all, the mind had force,
   And, like a stream whose surface flows
   The wrong way when a strong wind blows,
It underneath maintained its course.

Oft didst thou think thy mind would flower
   Too late for good, as some bruised tree
   That blooms in Autumn, and we see
Fruit not worth picking, hard and sour.

Some poets *feign* their wounds and scars:
   If they had known real suffering hours,
   They'd show, in place of Fancy's flowers,
More of Imagination's stars.

So, if thy fruits of Poesy
  Are rich, it is at this dear cost –
  That they were nipt by Sorrow's frost,
In nights of homeless misery.

133. The Bird-Man

Man is a bird:
  He rises on fine wings
Into the Heaven's clear light;
  He flies away and sings –
There's music in his flight.

Man is a bird:
  In swiftest speed he burns,
With twist and dive and leap;
  A bird whose sudden turns
Can drive the frightened sheep.

Man is a bird:
  Over the mountain high,
Whose head is in the skies,
  Cut from its shoulder by
A cloud – the bird-man flies.

Man is a bird:
  Eagles from mountain crag
Swooped down to prove his worth;
  But *now* they *rise* to drag
Him down from Heaven to earth!

34. Winter's Beauty

Is it not fine to walk in spring,
When leaves are born, and hear birds sing?
And when they lose their singing powers,
In summer, watch the bees at flowers?
Is it not fine, when summer's past,
To have the leaves, no longer fast,
Biting my heel where'er I go,
Or dancing lightly on my toe?
Now winter's here and rivers freeze;
As I walk out I see the trees,
Wherein the pretty squirrels sleep,
All standing in the snow so deep:
And every twig, however small,
Is blossomed white and beautiful.
Then welcome, winter, with thy power
To make this tree a big white flower;
To make this tree a lovely sight,
With fifty brown arms draped in white,
While thousands of small fingers show
In soft white gloves of purest snow.

135. The Church Organ

The homeless man has heard thy voice,
  Its sound doth move his memory deep;
He stares bewildered, as a man
  That's shook by earthquake in his sleep.

Thy solemn voice doth bring to mind
  The days that are for ever gone:
Thou bringest to mind our early days,
  Ere we made second homes or none.

136. Night Wanderers

They hear the bell of midnight toll,
And shiver in their flesh and soul;
They lie on hard, cold wood or stone,
Iron, and ache in every bone;
They hate the night: they see no eyes
Of loved ones in the starlit skies.
They see the cold, dark water near;
They dare not take long looks for fear
They'll fall like those poor birds that see
A snake's eyes staring at their tree.
Some of them laugh, half-mad; and some
All through the chilly night are dumb;
Like poor, weak infants some converse,
And cough like giants, deep and hoarse.

137. Young Beauty

When at each door the ruffian winds
  Have laid a dying man to groan,
And filled the air on winter nights
  With cries of infants left alone;
And every thing that has a bed
  Will sigh for others that have none:

On such a night, when bitter cold,
  Young Beauty, full of love thoughts sweet,
Can redden in her looking-glass;
  With but one gown on, in bare feet,
She from her own reflected charms
  Can feel the joy of summer's heat.

138. The Two Lives

Now how could I, with gold to spare,
  Who know the harlot's arms, and wine,
Sit in this green field all alone,
  If Nature was not truly mine?

That Pleasure life wakes stale at morn,
  From heavy sleep that no rest brings:
This life of quiet joy wakes fresh,
  And claps its wings at morn, and sings.

So here sit I, alone till noon,
  In one long dream of quiet bliss;
I hear the lark and share his joy,
  With no more winedrops than were his.

Such, Nature, is thy charm and power –
  Since I have made the Muse my wife –
To keep me from the harlot's arms,
  And save me from a drunkard's life.

139. Hidden Love

The bird of Fortune sings when free,
But captured, soon grows dumb; and we,
To hear his fast declining powers,
Must soon forget that he is ours.

So, when I win that maid, no doubt
Love soon will seem to be half out;
Like blighted leaves drooped to the ground,
Whose roots are still untouched and sound,
So will our love's root still be strong
When others think the leaves go wrong.
Though we may quarrel, 'twill not prove
That she and I are less in love;
The parrot, though he mocked the dove,
Died when she died, and proved his love.
When merry springtime comes, we hear
How all things into love must stir;
How birds would rather sing than eat,
How joyful sheep would rather bleat:
And daffodils nod heads of gold,
And dance in April's sparkling cold.
So in our early love did we
Dance much and skip, and laugh with glee:
But let none think our love is flown
If, when we're married, little's shown:
E'en though our lips be dumb of song,
Our hearts can still be singing strong.

140. Life is Jolly

This life is jolly, O!
   I envy no man's lot;
My eyes can much admire,
   And still my heart crave not;
There's no true joy in gold,
   It breeds desire for more;
Whatever wealth man has,
   Desire can keep him poor.

This life is jolly, O!
  Power has his fawning slaves,
But if he rests his mind,
  Those wretches turn bold knaves.
Fame's field is full of flowers,
  It dazzles as we pass,
But men who walk that field
  Starve for the common grass.

This life is jolly, O!
  Let others know they die,
Enough to know I live,
  And make no question why;
I care not whence I came,
  Nor whither I shall go;
Let others think of these –
  This life is jolly, O!

141. The Fog

I saw the fog grow thick,
  Which soon made blind my ken;
It made tall men of boys,
  And giants of tall men.

It clutched my throat, I coughed;
  Nothing was in my head
Except two heavy eyes
  Like balls of burning lead.

And when it grew so black
    That I could know no place,
I lost all judgment then,
    Of distance and of space.

The street lamps, and the lights
    Upon the halted cars,
Could either be on earth
    Or be the heavenly stars.

A man passed by me close,
    I asked my way, he said,
'Come, follow me, my friend' –
    I followed where he led.

He rapped the stones in front,
    'Trust me,' he said, 'and come';
I followed like a child –
    A blind man led me home.

142. A Woman's Charms

My purse is yours, Sweet Heart, for I
Can count no coins with you close by;
I scorn like sailors them, when they
Have drawn on shore their deep-sea pay;
Only my thoughts I value now,
Which, like the simple glow-worms, throw
Their beams to greet thee bravely, Love –
Their glorious light in Heaven above.

Since I have felt thy waves of light,
Beating against my soul, the sight
Of gems from Afric's continent
Moves me to no great wonderment.
Since I, Sweet Heart, have known thine hair,
The fur of ermine, sable, bear,
Or silver fox, for me can keep
No more to praise than common sheep.
Though ten Isaiahs' souls were mine,
They could not sing such charms as thine.
Two little hands that show with pride,
Two timid, little feet that hide;
Two eyes no dark Señoras show
Their burning like in Mexico;
Two coral gates wherein is shown
Your queen of charms, on a white throne;
Your queen of charms, the lovely smile
That on its white throne could beguile
The mastiff from his gates in hell;
Who by no whine or bark could tell
His masters what thing made him go –
And countless other charms I know.
October's hedge has far less hues
Than thou hast charms from which to choose.

143. Dreams of the Sea

I know not why I yearn for thee again,
    To sail once more upon thy fickle flood;
I'll hear thy waves wash under my death-bed,
    Thy salt is lodged for ever in my blood.

Yet I have seen thee lash the vessel's sides
   In fury, with thy many tailèd whip;
And I have seen thee, too, like Galilee,
   When Jesus walked in peace to Simon's ship.

And I have seen thy gentle breeze as soft
   As summer's, when it makes the cornfields run;
And I have seen thy rude and lusty gale
   Make ships show half their bellies to the sun.

Thou knowest the way to tame the wildest life,
   Thou knowest the way to bend the great and proud.
I think of that Armada whose puffed sails,
   Greedy and large, came swallowing every cloud.

But I have seen the sea-boy, young and drowned,
   Lying on shore and, by thy cruel hand,
A seaweed beard was on his tender chin,
   His heaven-blue eyes were filled with common
     sand.

And yet, for all, I yearn for thee again,
   To sail once more upon thy fickle flood:
I'll hear thy waves wash under my death-bed,
   Thy salt is lodged for ever in my blood.

144. The Wonder-Maker

Come, if thou'rt cold to Summer's charms,
   Her clouds of green, her starry flowers,
And let this bird, this wandering bird,
   Make his fine wonder yours.

He, hiding in the leaves so green,
    When sampling this fair world of ours,
Cries Cuckoo, clear; and like Lot's wife,
I look, though it should cost my life.

When I can hear the charmed one's voice,
    I taste of immortality;
My joy's so great that on my heart
    Doth lie eternity,
As light as any little flower –
    So strong a wonder works in me;
Cuckoo! he cries, and fills my soul
With all that's rich and beautiful.

145. An Early Love

Ah, sweet young blood, that makes the heart
    So full of joy, and light,
That dying children dance with it
    From early morn till night.

My dreams were blossoms, hers the fruit,
    She was my dearest care;
With gentle hand, and for it, I
    Made playthings of her hair.

I made my fingers rings of gold,
    And bangles for my wrist;
You should have felt the soft, warm thing
    I made to glove my fist.

189

And she should have a crown, I swore,
  With only gold enough
To keep together stones more rich
  Than that fine metal stuff.

Her golden hair gave me more joy
  Than Jason's heart could hold,
When all his men cried out – Ah, look!
  He has the Fleece of Gold!

146. Dream Tragedies

Thou art not always kind, O sleep:
What awful secrets thou dost keep
In store, and ofttimes make us know;
What hero has not fallen low
In sleep before a monster grim,
And whined for mercy unto him;
Knights, constables, and men-at-arms
Have quailed and whined in sleep's alarms.
Thou wert not kind last night to make
Me like a very coward shake –
Shake like a thin red-currant bush
Robbed of its fruit by a strong thrush.
I felt this earth did move; more slow,
And slower yet began to go;
And not a bird was heard to sing,
Men and great beasts were shivering;
All living things knew well that when
This earth stood still, destruction then
Would follow with a mighty crash.
'Twas then I broke that awful hush:

E'en as a mother, who does come
Running in haste back to her home,
And looks at once, and lo, the child
She left asleep is gone; and wild
She shrieks and loud – so did I break
With a mad cry that dream, and wake

147. Children at Play

I hear a merry noise indeed:
  Is it the geese and ducks that take
Their first plunge in a quiet pond
  That into scores of ripples break –
Or children make this merry sound?

I see an oak tree, its strong back
  Could not be bent an inch though all
Its leaves were stone, or iron even:
  A boy, with many a lusty call,
Rides on a bough bareback through Heaven.

I see two children dig a hole
  And plant in it a cherry-stone:
'We'll come to-morrow,' one child said –
  'And then the tree will be full-grown,
And all its boughs have cherries red.'

Ah, children, what a life to lead:
  You love the flowers, but when they're past
No flowers are missed by your bright eyes;
  And when cold winter comes at last,
Snowflakes shall be your butterflies.

148. Return to Nature

My song is of that city which
Has men too poor and men too rich;
Where some are sick, too richly fed,
While others take the sparrows' bread:
Where some have beds to warm their bones,
While others sleep on hard, cold stones
That suck away their bodies' heat.
Where men are drunk in every street;
Men full of poison, like those flies
That still attack the horses' eyes.
Where some men freeze for want of cloth,
While others show their jewels' worth
And dress in satin, fur or silk;
Where fine rich ladies wash in milk,
While starving mothers have no food
To make them fit in flesh and blood;
So that their watery breasts can give
Their babies milk and make them live.
Where one man does the work of four,
And dies worn out before his hour;
While some seek work in vain, and grief
Doth make their fretful lives as brief.
Where ragged men are seen to wait
For charity that's small and late;
While others haunt in idle leisure,
Theatre doors to pay for pleasure.
No more I'll walk those crowded places
And take hot dreams from harlots' faces;
I'll know no more those passions' dreams,
While musing near these quiet streams;
That biting state of savage lust
Which, true love absent, burns to dust.

Gold's rattle shall not rob my ears
Of this sweet music of the spheres.
I'll walk abroad with fancy free;
Each leafy summer's morn I'll see
The trees, all legs or bodies, when
They vary in their shapes like men.
I'll walk abroad and see again
How quiet pools are pricked by rain;
And you shall hear a song as sweet
As when green leaves and raindrops meet.
I'll hear the Nightingale's fine mood,
Rattling with thunder in the wood,
Made bolder by each mighty crash;
Who drives her notes with every flash
Of lightning through the summer's night.
No more I'll walk in that pale light
That shows the homeless man awake,
Ragged and cold; harlot and rake
That have their hearts in rags, and die
Before that poor wretch they pass by.
Nay, I have found a life so fine
That every moment seems divine;
By shunning all those pleasures full,
That bring repentance cold and dull
Such misery seen in days gone by,
That, made a coward, now I fly
To green things, like a bird. Alas!
In days gone by I could not pass
Ten men but what the eyes of one
Would burn me for no kindness done;
And wretched women I passed by
Sent after me a moan or sigh.
Ah, wretched days: for in that place
My soul's leaves sought the human face,

And not the Sun's for warmth and light –
And so was never free from blight.
But seek me now, and you will find
Me on some soft green bank reclined;
Watching the stately deer close by,
That in a great deep hollow lie
Shaking their tails with all the ease
That lambs can. First, look for the trees,
Then, if you seek me, find me quick.
Seek me no more where men are thick,
But in green lanes where I can walk
A mile, and still no human folk
Tread on my shadow. Seek me where
The strange oak tree is, that can bear
One white-leaved branch among the
     green –
Which many a woodman has not seen.
If you would find me, go where cows
And sheep stand under shady boughs;
Where furious squirrels shake a tree
As though they'd like to bury me
Under a leaf shower heavy, and
I laugh at them for spite, and stand.
Seek me no more in human ways –
Who am a coward since those days
My mind was burned by poor men's eyes,
And frozen by poor women's sighs.
Then send your pearls across the sea,
Your feathers, scent and ivory,
You distant lands – but let my bales
Be brought by Cuckoos, Nightingales,
That come in spring from your far shores;
Sweet birds that carry richer stores
Than men can dream of, when they prize

Fine silks and pearls for merchandise;
And dream of ships that take the floods
Sunk to their decks with such vain goods;
Bringing that traitor silk, whose soft
Smooth tongue persuades the poor too oft
From sweet content; and pearls, whose
    fires
Make ashes of our best desires.
For I have heard the sighs and whines
Of rich men that drink costly wines
And eat the best of fish and fowl;
Men that have plenty, and still growl
Because they cannot like kings live –
'Alas!' they whine, 'we cannot save.'
Since I have heard those rich ones sigh,
Made poor by their desires so high,
I cherish more a simple mind;
That I am well content to find
My pictures in the open air,
And let my walls and floors go bare;
That I with lovely things can fill
My rooms, whene'er sweet Fancy will.
I make a fallen tree my chair,
And soon forget no cushion's there;
I lie upon the grass or straw,
And no soft down do I sigh for;
For with me all the time I keep
Sweet dreams that, do I wake or sleep,
Shed on me still their kindly beams;
Aye, I am richer with my dreams
Than banks where men dull-eyed and cold
Without a tremble shovel gold.
A happy life is this. I walk
And hear more birds than people talk;

I hear the birds that sing unseen,
On boughs now smothered with leaves green;
I sit and watch the swallows there,
Making a circus in the air;
That speed around straight-going crow,
As sharks around a ship can go;
I hear the skylark out of sight,
Hid perfectly in all this light.
The dappled cows in fields I pass,
Up to their bosoms in deep grass;
Old oak trees, with their bowels gone,
I see with spring's green finery on.
I watch the buzzing bees for hours,
To see them rush at laughing flowers –
And butterflies that lie so still.
I see great houses on the hill,
With shining roofs; and there shines one,
It seems that heaven has dropped the sun.
I see yon cloudlet sail the skies,
Racing with clouds ten times its size.
I walk green pathways, where love waits
To talk in whispers at old gates;
Past stiles – on which I lean, alone –
Carved with the names of lovers gone;
I stand on arches whose dark stones
Can turn the wind's soft sighs to groans.
I hear the Cuckoo when first he
Makes this green world's discovery,
And re-creates it in my mind,
Proving my eyes were growing blind.
I see the rainbow come forth clear
And wave her coloured scarf to cheer
The sun long swallowed by a flood –
So do I live in lane and wood.

Let me look forward to each spring
As eager as the birds that sing;
And feed my eyes on spring's young flowers
Before the bees by many hours,
My heart to leap and sing her praise
Before the birds by many days.
Go white my hair and skin go dry –
But let my heart a dewdrop lie
Inside those leaves when they go wrong,
As fresh as when my life was young.

149. A Strange City

A wondrous city, that had temples there
More rich than that one built by David's son,
Which called forth Ophir's gold, when Israel
Made Lebanon half naked for her sake.
I saw white towers where so-called traitors died –
True men whose tongues were bells to honest hearts,
And rang out boldly in false monarchs' ears.
Saw old black gateways, on whose arches crouched
Stone lions with their bodies gnawed by age.
I looked with awe on iron gates that could
Tell bloody stories if they had our tongues.
I saw tall mounted spires shine in the sun,
That stood amidst their army of low streets.
I saw in buildings pictures, statues rare,
Made in those days when Rome was young, and new
In marble quarried from Carrara's hills;

Statues by sculptors that could almost make
Fine cobwebs out of stone – so light they worked.
Pictures that breathe in us a living soul,
Such as we seldom feel come from that life
The artist copies. Many a lovely sight –
Such as the half-sunk barge with bales of hay,
Or sparkling coals – employed my wondering eyes.
I saw old Thames, whose ripples swarmed with
      stars
Bred by the sun on that fine summer's day;
I saw in fancy fowl and green banks there,
And Liza's barge rowed past a thousand swans.
I walked in parks and heard sweet music cry
In solemn courtyards, midst the men-at-arms;
Which suddenly would leap those stony walls
And spring up with loud laughter into trees.
I walked in busy streets where music oft
Went on the march with men; and ofttimes heard
The organ in cathedral, when the boys
Like nightingales sang in that thunderstorm;
The organ, with its rich and solemn tones –
As near a God's voice as a man conceives;
Nor ever dreamt the silent misery
That solemn organ brought to homeless men.
I heard the drums and soft brass instruments,
Led by the silver cornets clear and high –
Whose sounds turned playing children into stones.
I saw at night the City's lights shine bright,
A greater milky way; how in its spell
It fascinated with ten thousand eyes;
Like those sweet wiles of an enchantress who
Would still detain her knight gone cold in love;
It was an iceberg with long arms unseen,
That felt the deep for vessels far away.

All things seemed strange, I stared like any child
That pores on some old face and sees a world
Which its familiar grandad and his dame
Hid with their love and laughter until then.
My feet had not yet felt the cruel rocks
Beneath the pleasant moss I seemed to tread.
But soon my ears grew weary of that din,
My eyes grew tired of all that flesh and stone;
And, as a snail that crawls on a smooth stalk,
Will reach the end and find a sharpened thorn –
So did I reach the cruel end at last.
I saw the starving mother and her child,
Who feared that Death would surely end its sleep,
And cursed the wolf of Hunger with her moans.
And yet, methought, when first I entered there,
Into that city with my wondering mind,
How marvellous its many sights and sounds;
The traffic with its sound of heavy seas
That have and would again unseat the rocks.
How common then seemed Nature's hills and fields
Compared with these high domes and even streets,
And churches with white towers and bodies black.
The traffic's sound was music to my ears;
A sound of where the white waves, hour by hour,
Attack a reef of coral rising yet;
Or where a mighty warship in a fog,
Steams into a large fleet of little boats.
Aye, and that fog was strange and wonderful,
That made men blind and grope their way at noon.
I saw that City with fierce human surge,
With millions of dark waves that still spread out
To swallow more of their green boundaries.
Then came a day that noise so stirred my soul,
I called them hellish sounds, and thought red war

Was better far than peace in such a town.
To hear that din all day, sometimes my mind
Went crazed, and it seemed strange, as I were lost
In some vast forest full of chattering apes.
How sick I grew to hear that lasting noise,
And all those people forced across my sight,
Knowing the acres of green fields and woods
That in some country parts outnumbered men;
In half an hour ten thousand men I passed –
More than nine thousand should have been green trees.
There on a summer's day I saw such crowds
That where there was no man man's shadow was;
Millions all cramped together in one hive,
Storing, methought, more bitter stuff than sweet.
The air was foul and stale; from their green homes
Young blood had brought its fresh and rosy cheeks,
Which soon turned colour, like blue streams in flood.
Aye, solitude, black solitude indeed,
To meet a million souls and know not one;
This world must soon grow stale to one compelled
To look all day at faces strange and cold.
Oft full of smoke that town; its summer's day
Was darker than a summer's night at sea;
Poison was there, and still men rushed for it,
Like cows for acorns that have made them sick.
That town was rich and old; man's flesh was cheap,
But common earth was dear to buy one foot.
If I must be fenced in, then let my fence
Be some green hedgerow; under its green sprays,
That shake suspended, let me walk in joy –
As I do now, in these dear months I love.

150. When I am Old

When I am old, and it is spring,
   And joy leaps dancing wild and free,
Clear out of every living thing,
   While I command no ecstasy;
And to translate the songs of birds
Will be beyond my power in words:

When Time serves notice on my Muse
   To leave at last her lyric home,
With no extension of her lease –
   Then to the blackest pits I come,
To see by day the stars' cold light,
And in my coffin sleep at night.

For when these little songs shall fail,
   These happy notes that to the world
Are puny mole-hills, nothing more,
   That unto me are Alps of gold –
That toad's dark life must be my own,
Buried alive inside a stone.

151. From France

What little bird is this that sings?
   I wonder if he comes from France:
Lord, how he sings, and makes our leaves
   In happy England dance!
What's in his song; is it sweet laughter,
Or anger that he crossed the water?

A song of roses, apples, corn,
　　Seen here in England – not his home;
Or lilies, olives, and the grapes
　　In France, across the foam?
No matter, little friend from France –
Sing till our leaves in England dance.

152.　Starers

'he small birds peck at apples ripe,
　　And twice as big as them in size;
The wind doth make the hedge's leaves
　　Shiver with joy, until it dies.
Young Gossamer is in the field;
　　He holds the flowers with silver line –
They nod their heads as horses should.
　　And there are forty dappled kine
As fat as snails in deep, dark wells,
　　And just as shiny too – as they
Lie in a green field, motionless,
　　And everyone now stares my way.
I must become a starer too:
　　I stare at them as urchins can
When seamen talk, or any child
　　That sees by chance its first black man.
I stare at drops of rain that shine
　　Like glow-worms, when the time is noon
I stare at little stars in Heaven,
　　That try to stare like the big Moon.

153. The Best Friend

Now shall I walk,
　　Or shall I ride?
'Ride,' Pleasure said;
　　'Walk,' Joy replied.

Now what shall I –
　　Stay home or roam?
'Roam,' Pleasure said;
　　And Joy – 'Stay home.'

Now shall I dance,
　　Or sit for dreams?
'Sit,' answers Joy;
　　'Dance,' Pleasure screams.

Which of ye two
　　Will kindest be?
Pleasure laughed sweet,
　　But Joy kissed me.

154. Heaven

That paradise the Arab dreams,
Is far less sand and more fresh streams.
The only heaven an Indian knows,
Is hunting deer and buffaloes.
The Yankee heaven – to bring Fame forth
By some freak show of what he's worth.
The heaven that fills an English heart,
Is Union Jacks in every part.

The Irish heaven is heaven of old,
When Satan cracked skulls manifold.
The Scotsman has his heaven to come –
To argue his Creator dumb.
The Welshman's heaven is singing airs –
No matter who feels sick and swears.

155. Sweet Night

Sweet Night, that like an angel comes
   To take this bright and happy Day,
A lover gives his grateful heart,
   For starlight on his way.

Lord, how my heart goes forth in joy,
   How my brave spirits soar and rise
To think how Love's advancing lips
   Will shut Love's joyful eyes.

What loving looks of serious care,
   What tender sweetness she will give!
Such love a mother gives that child
   She fears she will outlive.

156. Early Spring

How sweet this morning air in spring,
   When tender is the grass, and wet!
I see some little leaves have not
   Outgrown their curly childhood yet;
And cows no longer hurry home,
However sweet a voice cries 'Come.'

Here, with green Nature all around,
   While that fine bird the skylark sings;
Who now in such a passion is,
   He flies by it, and not his wings;
And many a blackbird, thrush and sparrow
Sing sweeter songs than I may borrow.

157. The Mind's Liberty

The mind, with its own eyes and ears,
   May for these others have no care;
No matter where this body is,
   The mind is free to go elsewhere.
My mind can be a sailor, when
   This body's still confined to land;
And turn these mortals into trees,
   That walk in Fleet Street or the Strand.

So, when I'm passing Charing Cross,
   Where porters work both night and day,
I ofttimes hear sweet Malpas Brook,
   That flows thrice fifty miles away.
And when I'm passing near St. Paul's,
   I see, beyond the dome and crowd,
Twm Barlum, that green pap in Gwent,
   With its dark nipple in a cloud.

158. When on a Summer's Morn

When on a summer's morn I wake,
   And open my two eyes,
Out to the clear, born-singing rills
   My bird-like spirit flies.

To hear the Blackbird, Cuckoo, Thrush,
  Or any bird in song;
And common leaves that hum all day,
  Without a throat or tongue.

And when Time strikes the hour for sleep,
  Back in my room alone,
My heart has many a sweet bird's song –
  And one that's all my own.

159. Again I Sing

Again I sing of thee, sweet youth:
  Thy hours are minutes, they can hear
No challenge from stern sentinels,
  To wake their fear;
You love the flowers, but feel no grief
Because their pretty lives are brief.

Nature sets no conspirators
  Of withered things to lie in wait
And show thee with their faded charms
  Thy coming state;
No dread example she sets thee
In dead things falling off a tree.

Thou seest no bones inside the earth,
  Thy sweat comes not of toil, but play;
On thy red blossom no pale worm
  Can work decay;
No toad can muddy thy clear spring –
Time is thy subject, thou his king!

160. The Dumb World

Shall I collect for this world's eyes
My sins in birds or butterflies;
Shall I keep useless things around,
For ornament, and sell my hound?
When I give poor dumb things my cares,
Let all men know I've said my prayers.
That man who sells for gain his hound,
May he be robbed and beaten found;
May men that shoot sweet singing-birds
Be robbed of power to utter words;
May men that torture things alive
Live for a hundred years, and have
Their wretched bodies stabbed with pains,
Until their toe-nails pierce their brains.
My love for dumb things is intense:
I cannot walk beside a fence
And see the horses in a row,
Staring, but I must say Hallo!
And when I see two horses lean
Across a gate that stands between
Them as they kiss each other there –
For no man's company I care.
I hate to leave the calf when he,
Licking his tongue, still follows me,
To lick again at my old clothes.
A lamb that lets me stroke his nose
Can make me feel a battle won
That had ten soldiers to my one.
I'd rather see the sheep and kine
Than any troops that march in line,
With all their colours in the light,
Helmets and scabbards shining bright.

When I give robins cheerful words,
I'm pleased to see those grateful birds
Try on their little feet to dance,
And eyeing me with consequence.
Had I at home a talking bird
That would repeat a wicked word,
I would not care a fig or apple
For my own hymns in church or chapel.
Had I a monkey that would drink
My ale and, when I sit to think,
Would mock me with his scornful cries –
I, thinking less, would grow more wise;
With him I'd sit and drink and play,
And save the world this worthless lay.

161. The Weeping Child

What makes thee weep so, little child,
　　What cause hast thou for all this grief?
When thou art old much cause may be,
　　And tears will bring thee no relief.

Thou dost not know thy mother yet,
　　Thou'dst sleep on any bosom near;
Thou dost not see a daughter dying,
　　No son is coughing in thy ear.

Thy father is a bearded man,
　　Yet any bearded man could take
Thee in his arms, and thou not know
　　Which man would die for thy sweet sake.

What makes thee weep then, little child,
    What cause hast thou for all this bother;
Whose father could be any man,
    And any woman be thy mother?

162. The Den

They sleep together in one den,
Ten in a row – ten beds, ten men;
Three dying men are in that room,
Whose coughs at night will soon become
Death's rattle: drunkards in bed
Sound as they worried things half dead.

Jim Lasker dreamt, when in that den,
He saw ten beds that had ten men;
One sleeper in a sack was sewn,
With nothing of his features shown:
Jim felt that face he could not see –
'This face is mine, I'm dead,' said he.

.   .   .   .   .

'James Lasker, you're the last to rise;
Wake up, wake up!' the master cries.
'You've not paid me for daylight's sleep –
Suppose you had some kids to keep?
Ah, now I see: this man of mine
Came here to die, not sleep – the swine!'

163. This World

Who dreams a sweeter life than this,
  To stand and stare, when at this fence,
Back into those dumb creatures' eyes,
  And think we have their innocence –
Our looks as open as the skies.

Lambs with their legs and noses black,
  Whose woolly necks, so soft and white,
Can take away the children's breath;
  Who'd strangle them in their delight –
And calves they'd worry half to death.

This world's too full of those dull men
  Who ne'er advance from that first state
Which opens mouth before the eye;
  Who, when they think of dumb things, rate
Them by the body's gluttony.

164. A Fleeting Passion

Thou shalt not laugh, thou shalt not romp,
  Let's grimly kiss with bated breath;
As quietly and solemnly
  As Life when it is kissing Death.
Now in the silence of the grave,
  My hand is squeezing that soft breast;
While thou dost in such passion lie,
  It mocks me with its look of rest.

But when the morning comes at last,
    And we must part, our passions cold,
You'll think of some new feather, scarf
    To buy with my small piece of gold;
And I'll be dreaming of green lanes,
    Where little things with beating hearts
Hold shining eyes between the leaves,
    Till men with horses pass, and carts.

165. Plants and Men

You berries once,
    In early hours,
Were pretty buds,
    And then fair flowers.

Drop, drop at once,
    Your life is done;
You cannot feel
    The dew or sun.

We are the same,
    First buds, then flowers;
Hard berries then,
    In our last hours.

Sweet buds, fair flowers,
    Hard berries then –
Such is the life
    Of plants and men.

166. A Midsummer's Night's Storm

Night, Lightning, Thunder, Rain.
  I see black Night
Open her lips;
  Her teeth gleam bright,
A moment seen;
  Then comes rich laughter;
And happy tears,
  That follow after,
Fall on the bosoms
Of birds and blossoms.

167. The Dreaming Boy

Sweet are thy dreams, thou happy, careless boy;
Thou know'st the taste of immortality;
No weary limbs can rest upon thy heart;
Sleep has no care to ease thee of at night;
The same move shuts together eye and mind,
And in the morning one move opens both.
Life lies before thee, hardly stepped on yet,
Like a green prairie, fresh, and full of flowers.
Life lies before thee for experiment,
Until old age comes, whose sad eyes can trace
A better path he missed, with fairer flowers,
Which other men have walked in misery.
Thou hast no knowledge of a life of toil,
How hard Necessity destroys our dreams,
And castles-in-the-air must pay him tithes
So heavy that no tenants keep them long.
To thee the world is still unknown and strange;

Still full of wild romance, as in those days
Ere England launched her forests on the sea.
Thou wilt discover in far mountains caves
Deserted, lamps left burning for thy feet,
And comfort in them more than kings are worth.
Aye, many a gate will open at thy call,
And wise men will come forth to welcome thee,
And bells will ring for pleasure in thy ear.
Great monsters in dark woods, with mighty
      mouths
That swallow their own faces when they yawn,
And mountain bears that carry on their backs
Rough, shaggy coats whose price compares with
      silk —
Will fall by thy strong, right, all-conquering arm.
And who can stop thee; who can turn thee back?
Not giants, though they stand full twenty feet,
And sit too tall for common men to stand.
Oh, that sweet magic in thee, happy boy!
It makes a golden world for all things young.
Thou with an iron ring, a piece of bone,
A rusty blade, or half a yard of rope,
Art richer than a man with mines and ships.
The child's fresh mind makes honey out of soot,
Sweeter than age can make on banks of flowers;
He needs but cross a bridge, that happy boy,
And he can breathe the air of a new world.
Sweet children, with your trust in this hard life —
Like little birds that ope their mouths for food
From hands that come to cage them till they die.

168. The Hawk

Thou dost not fly, thou art not perched,
    The air is all around:
What is it that can keep thee set,
    From falling to the ground?
The concentration of thy mind
    Supports thee in the air;
As thou dost watch the small young birds,
    With such a deadly care.

My mind has such a hawk as thou,
    It is an evil mood;
It comes when there's no cause for grief,
    And on my joys doth brood.
Then do I see my life in parts;
    The earth receives my bones,
The common air absorbs my mind –
    It knows not flowers from stones.

169. The Signs

Flowers white and red my garden has;
    So, when I miss her from my place,
I see a colour through the leaves,
    And think it is her frock or face.

Here, while I sit and read old tales,
    She comes to knit with needles bright;
She shows, by how she stabs with them,
    How she would punish a false knight.

And though she speaks not any word,
  I see, by how she smooths the cloth –
That's stretched across from knee to knee –
  She binds his wounds who bleeds for truth.

170. The Moon

Thy beauty haunts me heart and soul,
  Oh thou fair Moon, so close and bright;
Thy beauty makes me like the child,
  That cries aloud to own thy light:
The little child that lifts each arm,
To press thee to her bosom warm.

Though there are birds that sing this night
  With thy white beams across their throats,
Let my deep silence speak for me
  More than for them their sweetest notes:
Who worships thee till music fails,
Is greater than thy nightingales.

171. A Great Time

Sweet Chance, that led my steps abroad,
  Beyond the town, where wild flowers grow –
A rainbow and a cuckoo, Lord,
  How rich and great the times are now!
      Know, all ye sheep
      And cows, that keep

On staring that I stand so long
   In grass that's wet from heavy rain –
A rainbow and a cuckoo's song
   May never come together again;
      May never come
      This side the tomb.

172. Her Absence

How rich hath Time become through her,
   His sands are turned to purest gold!
And yet it grieves my heart full sore
   To see them slipping from my hold.
How precious now each moment is,
   Which I must cast like dirt away!
My only hope and comfort this –
   Each moment will return that day,
On that sweet day, that joyful hour
When she lies willing in my power.

Nay, these rich moments are not lost,
   But, like the morning's dewdrops, which
Into the sun their sweet lives cast,
   To make his body far more rich –
So do these precious moments glide
   Into her being, where they store;
Until I clasp her as my bride,
   And get them back with thousands more;
Where they have banked in her sweet breast,
And saved themselves with interest.

173. The Wanderer

No morning breaks but he would pack,
With knapsack flung across his back,
And farther than the cuckoo roam,
Who makes no nest, and he no home.
And who he is, or where shall go,
No woman and no man shall know;
And where he sleeps a secret is,
Only the harvest moon's and his.
And long before his meal is done,
A wandering dog shall have his bone;
Beneath the trees, what birds are there
Shall have without a song their share.
And those that ride in coach or car,
While he's afoot, where towns are far,
Will point and say – 'A beggar, he!'
But where he shows his money free,
For ale the best – not begs for water –
He'll hear the landlord's smiling daughter
Go whispering to her room, surprised –
'He's some big man come here disguised!'
And everywhere he goes he'll be,
To young and old, a mystery;
And laughing in his heart, will sow
His wonder-seeds where he shall go.
For, free, he lives his simple life,
And has not risked it with a wife.
Prefers tobacco's quiet blisses
To Love's breath-mixture sealed by kisses.
Can drink his ale, for days and days,
With no one to upbraid his ways.
Has studied his own self, to find
His best friends fancies of the mind;

More faithful friends by far than he
Shall find in human company.
Has forced his presence in no place,
To meet at last declining grace;
Has always waited others' greeting,
Before he ventured on their meeting.
Since all his life has been like this,
Retiring into dreams of bliss,
Write these true words above his dust:
'He died because Age said he must;
He gave no man or woman power
To change him from sweet looks to sour;
Society never gave him pain,
No woman broke his heart in twain;
His body perished when his heart
Had no foul blight in any part;
From day to day, from birth to death,
He took in joy at every breath.'

174. The Black Cloud

Little flocks of peaceful clouds,
   Lying in your fields so blue,
While my eyes look up they see
   A black Ram coming close to you.

He will scatter you poor flocks,
   He will tear up north and south;
Lightning will come from his eye,
   And fierce thunder from his mouth.

Little flocks of peaceful clouds,
  Soon there'll be a dreadful rout,
That Ram's horns can toss big ships,
  Tear an oak tree's bowels out.

175. When I in Praise

When I in praise of babies speak,
  She coldly smiles like winter's snow,
And looks on me with no soft eye:
  Yet I have seen her kiss them so,
Her wealth of rapture made them cry.

Sometimes it seems her blood's too cold
  For Love to even wet his toes,
Much less to paddle all about;
  But when she's kissed till her eyes close,
That god is warmer in than out.

I laugh, when she for other men
  Confesses love; but when she says
She hated one man she could kill,
  My heart is all one jealous blaze,
For, pity me, she hates him still!

176. Sweet Child

Sweet child, thou wast my bird by day,
  My bird that never failed in song;
That on my bosom wast a bee,
  And layst there all night long:

No more I'll hear thy voice at noon,
　For Death has pierced thee with a thorn;
No more thou'lt sleep upon my breast,
　And trample it at morn.

Then break, oh break, poor empty cage,
　The bird is dead, thy use is done;
And die, poor plant, for your sweet bee
　Is gone, for ever gone.

177.　The Life Divine

Give me the poet's life divine,
　For ever fresh and young;
The only hours that vex his soul
　Are hours that give no song;
　　If he but can,
　　A homeless man,
Turn suffering into songs divine –
　That poet's life is still divine,
　　His life is still divine.

If but the Muse will help his soul
　To sing a grief that's wild,
No faithless spouse can pull him down,
　Nor disobedient child;
　　Let her but prove
　　His faithful love,
To sing his cares in songs divine –
　That poet's life is still divine,
　　His life is still divine.

178. Love's Youth

Not only is my love a flower
    That blooms in broad daylight,
But, like the Evening Primrose, it
    Can bloom again at night.

My heart, though I have reached my prime,
    It still beats fresh and young;
I tremble at sweet Beauty's glance,
    And Love is still my song.

At thy bright smile I burn and shake,
    Though treated as thy brother:
Canst thou not see my eyes have twins
    That laugh and call thee mother?

179. Rich Days

Welcome to you rich Autumn days,
    Ere comes the cold, leaf-picking wind,
When golden stooks are seen in fields,
    All standing arm-in-arm entwined;
And gallons of sweet cider seen
On trees in apples red and green.

With mellow pears that cheat our teeth,
    Which melt that tongues may suck them in;
With blue-black damsons, yellow plums,
    Now sweet and soft from stone to skin;
And woodnuts rich, to make us go
Into the loneliest lanes we know.

180. Near a Quiet Stream

When musing near a quiet stream,
  Of how true, happy minds are rare;
How some men mourn their fleeting days,
  And still unhappy thoughts they bear;
How others fear the loss of wealth,
  Though much they have above their share;
While some men strive in vain for fame,
  Till pale and lean, and white their hair:
'Poor fools,' thought I, amazed at this –
  'Why should true happy minds be rare?
If on these things we set no price,
  Where is their power to *make* us care?
Such cares, invented by ourselves,
  Have no wise substance anywhere.'

181. The Hermit

What moves that lonely man is not the boom
  Of waves that break against the cliff so strong;
Nor roar of thunder, when that travelling voice
  Is caught by rocks that carry far along.

'Tis not the groan of oak tree in its prime,
  When lightning strikes its solid heart to dust;
Nor frozen pond when, melted by the sun,
  It suddenly doth break its sparkling crust.

What moves that man is when the blind bat taps
  His window when he sits alone at night;
Or when the small bird sounds like some great beast
  Among the dead, dry leaves so frail and light;

Or when the moths on his night-pillow beat
    Such heavy blows he fears they'll break his bones;
Or when a mouse inside the papered walls,
    Comes like a tiger crunching through the stones.

182. In the End

With all thy gold, thou canst not make
    Time sell his sand;
With all thy cloth, a thin white shroud
    Is Death's command;
Death gives thee but a poor man's space,
    With all thy land.

The beggar in his grave and thou
    Must be the same;
For neither thou nor he shall hear
    Men's praise or blame;
Though thunder and a thousand rocks
    Should call thy name.

183. On the Mountain

When from this mighty mountain's top
    My wandering eyes go forth,
Trees look like bonnets, fields like flags
    In all those miles of earth.
I see afar big towns look now
    Like flocks of sheep washed white;
And villages – their straggling lambs –
    May never meet my sight.

Windows – no more than drops of dew –
　　Are sparkling in the green;
The sun in heaven seems small indeed,
　　To light so vast a scene.
A mighty stretch of land like this,
　　Doth make me shut my eyes;
For when I look I fear to see
　　Its sudden fall or rise.

184.　Infancy

Born to the world with my hands clenched,
　　I wept and shut my eyes;
Into my mouth a breast was forced,
　　To stop my bitter cries.
I did not know – nor cared to know –
　　A woman from a man;
Until I saw a sudden light,
　　And all my joys began.

From that great hour my hands went forth,
　　And I began to prove
That many a thing my two eyes saw
　　My hands had power to move:
My fingers now began to work,
　　And all my toes likewise;
And reaching out with fingers stretched,
　　I laughed, with open eyes.

185. Nell Barnes

They lived apart for three long years,
    Bill Barnes and Nell, his wife;
He took his joy from other girls,
    She led a wicked life.

Yet ofttimes she would pass his shop,
    With some strange man awhile;
And, looking, meet her husband's frown
    With her malicious smile.

Until one day, when passing there,
    She saw her man had gone;
And when she saw the empty shop,
    She fell down with a moan.

And when she heard that he had gone
    Five thousand miles away,
And that she'd see his face no more,
    She sickened from that day.

To see his face was health and life,
    And when it was denied,
She could not eat, and broke her heart –
    It was for love she died.

186. The Bird of Paradise

Here comes Kate Summers who, for gold,
    Takes any man to bed:
'You knew my friend, Nell Barnes,' said she;
    'You knew Nell Barnes – she's dead.

'Nell Barnes was bad on all you men,
    Unclean, a thief as well;
Yet all my life I have not found
    A better friend than Nell.

'So I sat at her side at last,
    For hours, till she was dead;
And yet she had no sense at all
    Of any word I said.

'For all her cry but came to this –
    "Not for the world! Take care:
Don't touch that bird of paradise,
    Perched on the bedpost there!"

'I asked her would she like some grapes,
    Some damsons ripe and sweet;
A custard made with new-laid eggs,
    Or tender fowl to eat.

'I promised I would follow her,
    To see her in her grave;
And buy a wreath with borrowed pence,
    If nothing I could save.

'Yet still her cry but came to this –
    "Not for the world! Take care:
Don't touch that bird of paradise,
    Perched on the bedpost there!" '

187. The Inexpressible

Thinking of my caged birds indoors,
    My books, whose music serves my will;
Which, when I bid them sing, will sing,
    And when I sing myself are still;

And that my scent is drops of ink,
    Which, were my song as great as I,
Would sweeten man till he was dust,
    And make the world one Araby;
Thinking how my hot passions make
    Strong floods of shallows that run cold –
Oh how I burn to make my dreams
    Lighten and thunder through the world!

188. This Night

This night, as I sit here alone,
And brood on what is dead and gone,
The owl that's in this Highgate Wood
Has found his fellow in my mood;
To every star, as it doth rise –
Oh-o-o! Oh-o-o! he shivering cries.

And, looking at the Moon this night,
There's that dark shadow in her light.
Ah! Life and Death, my fairest one,
Thy lover is a skeleton!
'And why is that?' I question – 'why?'
Oh-o-o! oh-o-o! the owl doth cry.

189. The Visitor

She brings that breath, and music too,
    That comes when April's days begin;
And sweetness Autumn never had
    In any bursting skin.

She's big with laughter at the breasts,
    Like netted fish they leap:
Oh God, that I were far from here,
    Or lying fast asleep!

190. April's Charms

When April scatters coins of primrose gold
Among the copper leaves in thickets old,
And singing skylarks from the meadows rise,
To twinkle like black stars in sunny skies;

When I can hear the small woodpecker ring
Time on a tree for all the birds that sing;
And hear the pleasant cuckoo, loud and long –
The simple bird that thinks two notes a song;

When I can hear the woodland brook, that could
Not drown a babe, with all his threatening mood;
Upon whose banks the violets make their home,
And let a few small strawberry blossoms come:

When I go forth on such a pleasant day,
One breath outdoors takes all my care away;
It goes like heavy smoke, when flames take hold
Of wood that's green and fill a grate with gold.

191. Kitty and I

The gentle wind that waves
    The green boughs here and there,
Is showing how my hand
    Waved Kitty's finer hair.

The Bee, when all his joints
    Are clinging to a Blossom,
Is showing how I clung
    To Kitty's softer bosom.

The Rill, when his sweet voice
    Is hushed by water-cresses,
Is Kitty's sweeter voice
    Subdued by my long kisses.

Those little stars that shine
    So happy in the skies,
Are those sweet babes I saw,
    Whose heaven was Kitty's eyes.

The Moon, that casts her beam
    Upon the hill's dark crest,
Is Kitty's whiter arm
    Across my hairy breast.

The hazel nuts, when paired
    Unseen beneath the boughs,
Are Kitty and myself,
    Whenever Chance allows.

192. Thou Comest, May

Thou comest, May, with leaves and flowers,
   And nights grow short, and days grow long;
And for thy sake in bush and tree,
   The small birds sing, both old and young;
And only I am dumb and wait
The passing of a fish-like state.

You birds, you old grandfathers now,
   That have such power to welcome spring,
I, but a father in my years,
   Have nothing in my mind to sing;
My lips, like gills in deep-sea homes,
Beat time, and still no music comes.

193. The Hospital Waiting-Room

We wait our turn, as still as mice,
For medicine free, and free advice:
Two mothers, and their little girls
So small – each one with flaxen curls –
And I myself, the last to come.
Now as I entered that bare room,
I was not seen or heard; for both
The mothers – one in finest cloth,
With velvet blouse and crocheted lace,
Lips painted red, and powdered face;
The other ragged, whose face took
Its own dull, white, and wormy look –
Exchanged a hard and bitter stare.
And both the children, sitting there,

Taking example from that sight,
Made ugly faces, full of spite.
This woman said, though not a word
From her red painted lips was heard –
'Why have I come to this, to be
In such a slattern's company?'
The ragged woman's look replied –
'If you can dress with so much pride,
Why are you here, so neat, and nice,
For medicine free, and free advice?'
And I, who needed richer food,
Not medicine, to help my blood;
Who could have swallowed then a horse,
And chased its rider round the course,
Sat looking on, ashamed, perplexed,
Until a welcome voice cried – 'Next!'

194. The White Cascade

What happy mortal sees that mountain now,
The white cascade that's shining on its brow;

The white cascade that's both a bird and star,
That has a ten-mile voice and shines as far?

Though I may never leave this land again,
Yet every spring my mind must cross the main

To hear and see that water-bird and star
That on the mountain sings, and shines so far.

195. The One Singer

Dead leaves from off the tree
   Make whirlpools on the ground;
Like dogs that chase their tails,
   Those leaves go round and round;
Like birds unfledged and young,
   The old bare branches cry;
Branches that shake and bend
   To feel the winds go by.

No other sound is heard,
   Save from those boughs so bare –
Hark! who sings that one song?
   'Tis Robin sings so rare.
How sweet! like those sad tunes
   In homes where grief's not known;
Or that a blind girl sings
   When she is left alone.

196. The Inquest

I took my oath I would inquire,
   Without affection, hate, or wrath,
Into the death of Ada Wright –
   So help me God! I took that oath.

When I went out to see the corpse,
   The four months' babe that died so young,
I judged it was seven pounds in weight,
   And little more than one foot long.

One eye, that had a yellow lid,
  Was shut – so was the mouth, that smiled;
The left eye open, shining bright –
  It seemed a knowing little child.

For as I looked at that one eye,
  It seemed to laugh, and say with glee:
'What caused my death you'll never know –
  Perhaps my mother murdered me.'

When I went into court again,
  To hear the mother's evidence –
It was a love-child, she explained.
  And smiled, for our intelligence.

'Now, Gentlemen of the Jury,' said
  The coroner – 'this woman's child
By misadventure met its death.'
  'Aye, aye,' said we.   The mother smiled.

And I could see that child's one eye
  Which seemed to laugh, and say with glee:
'What caused my death you'll never know –
  Perhaps my mother murdered me.'

197. The Two Children

'Ah, little boy! I see
  You have a wooden spade.
Into this sand you dig
  So deep – for what?' I said.

'There's more rich gold,' said he,
  'Down under where I stand,
Than twenty elephants
  Could move across the land.'

'Ah, little girl with wool! –
  What are you making now?'
'Some stockings for a bird,
  To keep his legs from snow.'
And there those children are,
  So happy, small, and proud:
The boy that digs his grave,
  The girl that knits her shroud.

198. Come, thou Sweet Wonder

Come, thou sweet Wonder, by whose power
  We more or less enjoy our years;
That mak'st a child forget the breast,
  And dry'st at once the children's tears,
Till sleep shall bring their minds more rest.

Come to my heavy rain of care,
  And make it weigh like dew; charm me
With Beauty's hair, her eyes or lips;
  With mountain dawn, or sunset sea
That's like a thousand burning ships.

199. Charms

She walks as lightly as the fly
Skates on the water in July.

To hear her moving petticoat,
For me is music's highest note.

Stones are not heard, when her feet pass,
No more than tumps of moss or grass.

When she sits still, she's like the flower
To be a butterfly next hour.

The brook laughs not more sweet, when he
Trips over pebbles suddenly.

My Love, like him, can whisper low –
When he comes where green cresses grow.

She rises like the lark, that hour
He goes half-way to meet a shower.

A fresher drink is in her looks
Than Nature gives me, or old books.

When I in my Love's shadow sit,
I do not miss the sun one bit.

When she is near, my arms can hold
All that's worth having in this world.

And when I know not where she is,
Nothing can come but comes amiss.

200. Friends

They're creeping on the stairs outside,
    They're whispering soft and low;
Now up, now down, I hear his friends,
    And still they come and go.

The sweat that runs my side, from that
    Hot pit beneath my shoulder,
Is not so cold as he will be,
    Before the night's much older.

My fire I feed with naked hands,
    No sound shall reach their ears;
I'm moving like the careful cat,
    That stalks a rat it fears.

And as his friends still come and go,
    A thoughtful head is mine:
Had Life as many friends as Death,
    Lord, how this world would shine.

And since I'll have so many friends,
    When on my death-bed lying –
I wish my life had more love now,
    And less when I am dying.

201. The Power of Silence

And will she never hold her tongue,
    About that feather in her hat;
Her scarf, when she has done with that,

And then the bangle on her wrist;
   And is my silence meant to make
Her talk the more – the more she's kissed?

At last, with silence matching mine,
   She feels the passion deep and strong,
   That fears to trust a timid tongue.
Say, Love – that draws us close together –
   Isn't she the very life of Death?
No more of bangle, scarf or feather.

202. A Mother to her Sick Child

Thou canst not understand my words,
   No love for me was meant;
The smile that lately crossed thy face
   Was but an accident.

The music's thine, but mine the tears
   That make thy lullaby;
To-day I'll rock thee into sleep,
   To-morrow thou must die.

And when our babies sleep their last,
   Like agèd dames or men,
They need nor mother's lullaby,
   Nor any rocking then.

203. The White Monster

Last night I saw the monster near; the big
White monster that was like a lazy slug,
That hovered in the air, not far away,
As quiet as the black hawk seen by day.
I saw it turn its body round about,
And look my way; I saw its big, fat snout
Turn straight towards my face, till I was one
In coldness with that statue made of stone,
The one-armed sailor seen upon my right –
With no more power than he to offer fight;
The great white monster slug that, even then,
Killed women, children, and defenceless men.
But soon its venom was discharged, and it,
Knowing it had no more the power to spit
Death on the most defenceless English folk,
Let out a large, thick cloud of its own smoke;
And when the smoke had cleared away from
      there,
I saw no sign of any monster near;
And nothing but the stars to give alarm –
That never did the earth a moment's harm.
Oh, it was strange to see a thing like jelly,
An ugly, boneless thing all back and belly,
Among the peaceful stars – that should have
      been
A mile deep in the sea, and never seen:
A big, fat, lazy slug that, even then,
Killed women, children, and defenceless men.

204. Child Lovers

Six summers old was she, and when she came
Her head was in an everlasting flame;
The golden fire it licked her neck and face,
But left no mark of soot in any place.

When this young thing had seen her lover boy,
She threw her arms around his neck for joy;
Then, paired like hazel nuts, those two were seen
To make their way towards the meadows green.

Now, to a field they came at last, which was
So full of buttercups they hid the grass;
'Twas fit for kings to meet, and councils hold –
You never saw so fine a cloth of gold.

Then in a while they to a green park came,
A captain owned it, and they knew his name;
And what think you those happy children saw?
The big, black horse that once was in a war.

Now soon she tied her lover with some string,
And laughed, and danced around him in a ring;
He, like a flower that gossamer has tied,
Stood standing quiet there, and full of pride.

Lord, how she laughed! Her golden ringlets shook
As fast as lambs' tails, when those youngsters suck;
Sweeter than that enchantress laughed, when she
Shut Merlin fast for ever in a tree.

As they went home, that little boy began;
'Love me and, when I'm a big sailor-man,
I'll bring you home more coral, silk, and gold,
Than twenty-five four-funnelled ships could hold.

'And fifty coffins carried to their grave,
Will not have half the lilies you shall have:
Now say at once that you will be my love –
And have a pearl ten stallions could not move.'

205. Body and Spirit

Who stands before me on the stairs:
    Ah, is it you, my love?
My candle-light burns through your arm,
    And still thou dost not move;
Thy body's dead, this is not you –
It is thy ghost my light burns through.

Thy spirit this: I leap the stairs,
    To reach thy body's place;
I kiss and kiss, and still there comes
    No colour to thy face;
I hug thee for one little breath –
For this is sleep, it is not death!

.   .   .   .   .

The first night she was in her grave,
    And I looked in the glass,
I saw her sit upright in bed –
    Without a sound it was;
I saw her hand feel in the cloth,
To fetch a box of powder forth.

She sat and watched me all the while,
  For fear I looked her way;
I saw her powder cheek and chin,
  Her fast corrupting clay;
Then down my lady lay, and smiled –
She thought her beauty saved, poor child.

Now down the stairs I leap half-mad,
  And up the street I start;
I still can see her hand at work,
  And Oh, it breaks my heart:
All night behind my back I see
Her powdering, with her eyes on me.

206. Raptures

Sing for the sun your lyric, lark,
  Of twice ten thousand notes;
Sing for the moon, you nightingales,
  Whose light shall kiss your throats;
Sing, sparrows, for the soft, warm rain,
  To wet your feathers through;
And, when a rainbow's in the sky,
  Sing you, cuckoo – 'Cuckoo!'

Sing for your five blue eggs, fond thrush,
  By many a leaf concealed;
You starlings, wrens, and blackbirds sing
  In every wood and field;
While I, who fail to give my love
  Long raptures twice as fine,
Will for her beauty breathe this one
  A sigh, that's more divine.

241

207. The Voice

The nightingale I had not heard,
Though charmed by many another bird;
If no one tells me it is her,
How shall I know whose voice is near?
She sings, I'm told, in some dark wood,
Ten yards of moonlight from the road.

This night, as I go forth alone,
Before the month of June has gone,
What voice is this among the trees,
So startling sweet? The matchless ease,
The passion, power that will not fail –
The nightingale! The nightingale!

I ask no man what bird is this,
The singer of such pain and bliss;
All other birds sing from their throats,
But from her heart come this bird's notes:
To them I give my common cheers,
But you, my love, I thank with tears.

208. Confession

One hour in every hundred hours
I sing of childhood, birds and flowers;
Who reads my character in song
Will not see much in me that's wrong.

But in my ninety hours and nine
I would not tell what thoughts are mine:
They're not so pure as find their words
In songs of childhood, flowers and birds.

209. Easter

What exultations in my mind
From the love-bite of this Easter wind!
My head thrown back, my face doth shine
Like yonder Sun's, but warmer mine.
A butterfly – from who knows where? –
Comes with a stagger through the air,
And, lying down, doth ope and close
His wings, as babies work their toes;
Perhaps he thinks of pressing tight
Into his wings a little light!
And many a bird hops in between
The leaves he dreams of, long and green,
And sings for nipple-buds that show
Where the full-breasted leaves must grow.
Winter is dead, and now we sing
This welcome to the new-born Spring.

210. My Love could Walk

My Love could walk in richer hues
    Than any bird of paradise,
And no one envy her her dress:
    Since in her looks the world would see
A robin's love and friendliness.

And she could be the lily fair,
    More richly dressed than all her kind,
And no one envy her her gain:
    Since in her looks the world would see
A daisy that was sweet and plain.

Oh, she could sit like any queen
  That's nailed by diamonds to a throne,
Her splendour envied by not one:
  Since in her looks the world would see
A queen that's more than half a nun.

211. My Old Acquaintance

Working her toothless gums till her sharp chin
Could almost reach and touch her sharper nose,
These are the words my old acquaintance said:
'I have four children, all alive and well;
My eldest girl was seventy years in March,
And though when she was born her body was
Covered all over with black hair, and long,
Which when I saw at first made me cry out,
'Take it away, it is a monkey – ugh!'
Yet she's as smooth and fair as any, now.
And I, who sit for hours in this green space
That has seven currents of good air, and pray
At night to Jesus and His Mother, live
In hopes to reach my ninetieth year in June.
But ere it pleases God to take my soul,
I'll sell my fine false teeth, which cost five pounds,
Preserved in water now for twenty years,
For well I know those girls will fight for them
As soon as I am near my death; before
My skin's too cold to feel the feet of flies.
God bless you and good day – I wish you well.
For me, I cannot relish food, or sleep,

Till God sees fit to hold the Kaiser fast,
Stabbed, shot, or hanged – and his black soul
Sent into hell, to bubble, burn and squeal;
Think of the price of fish – and look at bacon!'

212. A Winter's Night

It is a winter's night and cold,
    The wind is blowing half a gale;
I, with a red-hot poker, stir
    To take the chill off my old ale.

I drink my ale, I smoke my pipe,
    While fire-flames leap to fight the cold;
And yet, before my bedtime comes,
    I must look out on the wide world.

And what strange beauty I behold:
    The wild fast-driven clouds this night
Hurled at the moon, whose smiling face
    Still shines with undiminished light.

213. Birds

When our two souls have left this mortal clay,
    And, seeking mine, you think that mine is lost –
Look for me first in that Elysian glade
    Where Lesbia is, for whom the birds sing most.

What happy hearts those feathered mortals have,
　　That sing so sweet when they're wet through in
　　　spring!
For in that month of May when leaves are young,
　　Birds dream of song, and in their sleep they sing.

And when the spring has gone and they are dumb,
　　Is it not fine to watch them at their play:
Is it not fine to see a bird that tries
　　To stand upon the end of every spray?

See how they tilt their pretty heads aside:
　　When women make that move they always please.
What cosy homes birds make in leafy walls
　　That Nature's love has ruined – and the trees.

Oft have I seen in fields the little birds
　　Go in between a bullock's legs to eat;
But what gives me most joy is when I see
　　Snow on my doorstep, printed by their feet.

214. Jove Warns Us

Jove warns us with his lightning first,
　　Before he sends his thunder;
Before the cock begins to crow,
　　He claps his wings down under.
But I, who go to see a maid,
　　This springtime in the morning,
Fall under every spell she has,
　　Without a word of warning.

She little thinks what charms her breath
    To cunning eyes reveal;
The waves that down her body glide,
    That from her bosom steal.
Her moth-like plumpness caught my eye,
    I watched it like a spider;
By her own hair my web is made,
    To fasten me beside her.

215. The Excuse

'Why did you kill that harmless frog?
    Tell me, my little boy.'
He hung his head for shame, and gone
    Was all his joy.

But now a thought comes to his mind,
    He lifts his head with pride:
'I only *half*-killed it,' he said –
    'And then it died.'

216. In the Snow

Hear how my friend the robin sings!
    That little hunchback in the snow,
As it comes down as fast as rain.
    The air is cold, the wind doth blow,
And still his heart can feel no pain.

And I, with heart as light as his,
    And to my ankles deep in snow,
Hold up a fist as cold as Death's,
    And into it I laugh and blow –
I laugh and blow my life's warm breath.

217. Molly

Molly, with hips and ankles plump,
   With hands and feet and waist so small,
Whose breasts could carry flowers unpinned,
   And not one blossom fall —
Give me your answer plain and true,
Do you love me as I love you?

Molly, as timid as a sheep
   That trembles at the shadow
Of any harmless little bird
   That flies across its meadow,
Are you a sweet good-tempered maid?
'Sometimes I'd crush a grape!' she said.

Molly, as gentle as the sun
   That lifts the dew to Heaven's breast,
Of all the lovers you have had,
   Am I the one that's loved the best?
'By all the men betrayed by me,
I swear I love you true,' said she.

218. Killed in Action

(EDWARD THOMAS)

Happy the man whose home is still
   In Nature's green and peaceful ways;
To wake and hear the birds so loud,
   That scream for joy to see the sun
Is shouldering past a sullen cloud.

And we have known those days, when we
    Would wait to hear the cuckoo first;
When you and I, with thoughtful mind,
    Would help a bird to hide her nest,
For fear of other hands less kind.

But thou, my friend, art lying dead:
    War, with its hell-born childishness,
Has claimed thy life, with many more:
    The man that loved this England well,
And never left it once before.

219. Lovely Dames

Few are my books, but my small few have told
Of many a lovely dame that lived of old;
And they have made me see those fatal charms
Of Helen, which brought Troy so many harms;
And lovely Venus, when she stood so white
Close to her husband's forge in its red light.
I have seen Dian's beauty in my dreams,
When she had trained her looks in all the streams
She crossed to Latmos and Endymion;
And Cleopatra's eyes, that hour they shone
The brighter for a pearl she drank to prove
How poor it was compared to her rich love:
But when I look on thee, love, thou dost give
Substance to those fine ghosts, and make them live.

220. Cowslips and Larks

I hear it said yon land is poor,
In spite of those rich cowslips there –
And all the singing larks it shoots
To heaven from the cowslips' roots.
But I, with eyes that beauty find,
And music ever in my mind,
Feed my thoughts well upon that grass
Which starves the horse, the ox, and ass.
So here I stand, two miles to come
To Shapwick and my ten-days-home,
Taking my summer's joy, although
The distant clouds are dark and low,
And comes a storm that, fierce and strong,
Has brought the Mendip Hills along:
Those hills that, when the light is there,
Are many a sunny mile from here.

221. Forgiveness

Stung by a spiteful wasp,
  I let him go life free;
That proved the difference
  In him and me.

For, had I killed my foe,
  It had proved me at once
The stronger wasp, and no
  More difference.

222. That Day She Seized

That day she seized me like a bee,
  To make me her weak blossom,
I felt her arms so strong that I
  Lay helpless on her bosom.
But cunning I, by artful moves,
  Soon had her in my power:
'Ah, Molly, who's the strong bee now –
  And who's the poor weak flower?'

That time she thought I was a fly,
  And she a great big spider,
She held me fast, my breath was gone,
  As I lay bound beside her.
But cunning I, by artful moves,
  Could laugh at last and cry:
'Ah, Molly, who's the spider now –
  And who's the poor weak fly?'

223. The Bell

It is the bell of death I hear,
Which tells me my own time is near,
When I must join those quiet souls
Where nothing lives but worms and moles;
And not come through the grass again,
Like worms and moles, for breath or rain;
Yet let none weep when my life's through,
For I myself have wept for few.

The only things that knew me well
Were children, dogs, and girls that fell;
I bought poor children cakes and sweets,
Dogs heard my voice and danced the streets,
And, gentle to a fallen lass,
I made her weep for what she was.
Good men and women know not me,
Nor love nor hate the mystery.

224. A Strange Meeting

The moon is full, and so am I;
   The night is late, the ale was good;
And I must go two miles and more
   Along a country road.

Now what is this that's drawing near?
   It seems a man, and tall;
But where the face should show its white
   I see no white at all.

Where is his face: or do I see
   The back part of his head,
And, with his face turned round about,
   He walks this way? I said.

He's close at hand, but where's the face?
   What devil is this I see?
I'm glad my body's warm with ale,
   There's trouble here for me.

I clutch my staff, I make a halt,
  'His blood or mine,' said I.
'Good-night,' the black man said to me,
  As he went passing by.

225. When Yon Full Moon

When yon full moon's with her white fleet of stars,
  And but one bird makes music in the grove;
When you and I are breathing side by side,
  Where our two bodies make one shadow, love;

Not for her beauty will I praise the moon,
  But that she lights thy purer face and throat;
The only praise I'll give the nightingale
  Is that she draws from thee a richer note.

For, blinded with thy beauty, I am filled,
  Like Saul of Tarsus, with a greater light;
When he had heard that warning voice in Heaven,
  And lost his eyes to find a deeper sight.

Come, let us sit in that deep silence then,
  Launched on love's rapids, with our passions proud,
That makes all music hollow – though the lark
  Raves in his windy heights above a cloud.

226. Till I Went Out

Till I went out of doors to prove
What through my window I saw move;
To see if grass was brighter yet,
And if the stones were dark and wet;

Till I went out to see a sign –
That slanted rain, so light and fine,
Had almost settled in my mind
That I at last could see the wind.

227. The Soul's Companions

Though floods shall fail, and empty holes
  Gape for the great bright eyes of seas,
  And fires devour stone walls and trees –
Thou, soul of mine, dost think to live
  Safe in thy light, and laugh at these?

Thy bravery outwears all heat
  And cold, all steel, all brass and stone;
  When Time has mixed my flesh and bone
With rocks and roots of common plants –
  Thy shining life will not be done.

Thou hast two children: one called Hope,
  The other Doubt, who will not play,
  And drives that brighter child away:
How sweet this life, if Hope alone
  Would walk with me from day to day!

228. The Holly on the Wall

Play, little children, one and all,
For holly, holly on the wall.
You do not know that millions are
This moment in a deadly war;

Millions of men whose Christmas bells
Are guns' reports and bursting shells;
Whose holly berries, made of lead,
Take human blood to stain them red;
Whose leaves are swords, and bayonets too,
To pierce their fellow-mortals through.
For now the war is here, and men –
Like cats that stretch their bodies when
The light has gone and darkness comes –
Have armed and left their peaceful homes:
But men will be, when there's no war,
As gentle as you children are.
Play, little children, one and all,
For holly, holly on the wall.

229. Exalted Flower

No more of that, you butterfly,
    That lie so still on this green leaf,
Pretending you're a flower again,
    And wings but bring you grief:
You have no cause, exalted flower,
    To doubt your flying power.

No more of that! You with a gift
    Not granted yet to any bee
Or bird that's flying in the air:
    The precious gift to see
Dark tunnels in this open light,
    And vanish out of sight.

230. What Thoughts are Mine

What thoughts are mine when she is gone,
And I sit dreaming here, alone;
My fingers are the little people
That climb her breast to its red steeple;
And, there arrived, they play until
She wakes and murmurs – 'Love, be still'.

She is the patient, loving mare,
And I the colt to pull her hair;
She is the deer, and my desire
Pursues her like a forest fire;
She is the child, and does not know
What a fierce bear she calls 'Bow-wow'.

But, Lord, when her sweet self is near,
These very thoughts cause all my fear.
I sit beneath her quiet sense,
And each word fears its consequence;
So 'Puss, Puss, Puss!' I cry. At that
I hang my head and stroke the cat.

231. Angel and Mystery

Lo, I, that once was Fear, that hears
His own forgotten breath, and fears
The breath of something else is heard –
Am now bold Love, to dare the word;
No timid mouse am I, before
He'll cross a moonbeam on the floor.

So sit thou close, and I will pour
Into that rosy shell, thy ear,
My deep-sea passion; let me swear
There's nothing in the world so fair
As thy sweet face that does, and will,
Retain its baby roundness still:
With those two suns, thine eyes, that keep
Their light from clouds till Night brings sleep.
Forget my features, only see
The soul in them that burns for thee;
And never let it cross thy mind
That I am ugly for my kind.
Although the world may well declare,
'One is an angel sweet and fair,
But what it is that sits so close
Must rest with God – He only knows.'

232. They're Taxing Ale again

Ale's no false liar; though his mind
    Has thoughts that are not clear,
His honest heart speaks boldly out,
    Without reserve or fear.
Though shaky as that bird the bat,
    In its first flight at night,
Yet still old Ale will stand his ground
    For either wrong or right.

Though Ale is poor, he's no man's slave,
    He'll neither fawn nor lick;
He'd clap proud monarchs on the back,
    And call them Ned or Dick.

They're taxing Ale again, I hear,
  A penny more the can:
They're taxing poor old Ale again,
  The only honest man.

233. In Time of War

As I go walking down the street
Many's the lad and lass I meet;
There's many a soldier I see pass,
And every soldier has his lass.

But when I saw the others there,
The women that black mourning wear,
'Judged by the looks of these,' I said,
'The lads those lassies court are dead.'

234. England

We have no grass locked up in ice so fast
That cattle cut their faces and at last,
When it is reached, must lie them down and starve,
With bleeding mouths that freeze too hard to move.
We have not that delirious state of cold
That makes men warm and sing when in Death's hold.
We have no roaring floods whose angry shocks
Can kill the fishes dashed against their rocks.
We have no winds that cut down street by street,
As easy as our scythes can cut down wheat.
No mountains here to spew their burning hearts
Into the valleys, on our human parts.

No earthquakes here, that ring church bells afar,
A hundred miles from where those earthquakes are.
We have no cause to set our dreaming eyes,
Like Arabs, on fresh streams in Paradise.
We have no wilds to harbour men that tell
More murders than they can remember well.
No woman here shall wake from her night's rest,
To find a snake is sucking at her breast.
Though I have travelled many and many a mile,
And had a man to clean my boots and smile
With teeth that had less bone in them than gold –
Give me this England now for all my world.

235. Come, let us Find

Come, let us find a cottage, love,
   That's green for half a mile around;
To laugh at every grumbling bee,
   Whose sweetest blossom's not yet found.
Where many a bird shall sing for you,
   And in our garden build its nest:
They'll sing for you as though their eggs
   Were lying in your breast,
      My love –
Were lying warm in your soft breast.

'Tis strange how men find time to hate,
   When life is all too short for love;
But we, away from our own kind,
   A different life can live and prove.

And early on a summer's morn,
  As I go walking out with you,
We'll help the sun with our warm breath
  To clear away the dew,
      My love,
  To clear away the morning dew.

236. The Birds of Steel

This apple-tree, that once was green,
  Is now a thousand flowers in one!
And, with their bags strapped to their thighs,
  There's many a bee that comes for sweets,
To stretch each bag to its full size.

And when the night has grown a moon,
  And I lie half-asleep in bed,
I hear those bees again – ah no,
  It is the birds of steel, instead,
Seeking their innocent prey below.

Man-ridden birds of steel, unseen,
  That come to drop their murdering lime
On any child or harmless thing
  Before the early morning time:
Up, nearer to God, they fly and sing.

237. Rags and Bones

This morning, as I wandered forth,
　I heard a man cry, 'Rags and Bones!'
And little children in the streets
　Went home for bottles, bones and rags,
To barter for his toys and sweets.

And then I thought of grown-up man,
　That in our dreams we trust a God
Will think our rags and bones a boon,
　And give us His immortal sweets
For these poor lives cast off so soon.

The mind, they say, will gather strength
　That broods on what is hard to know:
The fear of unfamiliar things
　Is better than their parents' love,
To teach young birds to use their wings.

But riddles are not made for me,
　My joy's in beauty, not its cause:
Then give me but the open skies,
　And birds that sing in a green wood
That's snow-bound by anemones.

238. The Dancer

The great white Moon is not so fair –
When not one trembling star will dare
To shine within her zone of air.

And lo, this blue-eyed maiden soon
Moves lightly to the music's tune –
Light as a water-fly in June.

As she goes spinning round and round,
Her nimble toes, without a sound,
Sip honey from the common ground.

Like the humming-bird that, swift and strong,
Will never suck but, flying along,
Just lick the blossoms with his tongue.

Dance, dance, thou blue-eyed wonder, dance!
I still believe there's one small chance
Thou'lt fall into my arms in a trance.

239. On hearing Mrs. Woodhouse play the Harpsichord

We poets pride ourselves on what
    We feel, and not what we achieve;
The world may call our children fools,
    Enough for us that we conceive.
A little wren that loves the grass
Can be as proud as any lark
    That tumbles in a cloudless sky,
Up near the sun, till he becomes
    The apple of that shining eye.

So, lady, I would never dare
    To hear your music ev'ry day;
With those great bursts that send my nerves
    In waves to pound my heart away;

And those small notes that run like mice
Bewitched by light; else on those keys –
    My tombs of song – you should engrave:
'My music, stronger than his own,
    Has made this poet my dumb slave.'

240. Late Singers

The Spring was late in coming, so,
    Sweet bird, your songs are late:
Have you a certain number, then,
    Of verses to create?
If late to start means late to end,
You comfort me, sweet friend.

It was the summer of my life
    Ere I began to sing:
Will winter be my summer, then,
    As summer was my spring?
No matter how things change their hue,
We'll sing our number through.

241. The Start

When dogs play in the sun outdoors,
    And cats chase sunbeams on the mat;
When merry maidens laugh for joy,
    And young men cock their ears at that;
And babes can see in panes of glass
A better light than fire-grate has;

When to my teeth ale is not cold,
　And sweeter than hot toast is bread;
When I, no longer charmed by books,
　Seek human faces in their stead;
And every stranger that I meet
Will seem a friend whom I must greet;

When I no sooner up at morn,
　Must like a turkey bolt my food,
To tramp the white green-bordered roads,
　And hear birds sing in many a wood:
When such a time of year has come,
The whole wide world can be my home.

242. Old Sailors

I loved a ship from early boyhood days;
It seemed to me a thing that lived and felt,
To pet and coax, that knew the captain's voice.
I heard the captain shouting to his men,
And, as that voice which calleth home the cows
Will make the far-off sheep look up and bleat,
So in my heart that captain's voice found ears,
Meant for his men. Oh, what a joy was mine
To see in dock the little boat that sailed
Across the deep Atlantic with one man!
I saw the two old warships made of oak,
That in days gone had spake out fierce and loud
With iron tongues in bodies of hard wood.
I saw the steamship that could go its way
Without consulting any wind or tide;

That ship of steam, and its propeller with
Four mighty arms of iron that could churn
The sea for miles when it lay calm and blue.
I watched the sailors, every move they made;
Those sailors true, whose eyes would grow more
    bright,
Like glow-worms, when they saw a coming storm
This world on which we live is but a ship
Without a port on an eternal cruise;
Oft taking fire, it burns its living crew,
Then sailing into a cold void, its hull,
Encased in ice, takes a warm current back,
And a new crew is born for æons more.

243. The Lost Sex

What, still another woman false,
    Another honest man betrayed:
Then Heaven is made for only men,
    And Hell for women made.

Now, with that false deceitful sex,
    Henceforth I have for ever done;
Only one Judas lived a man,
    But every woman's one.

Send down, O Lord, ten thousand Christs,
    Each one as great as Christ Thy Son;
Not for all men, but just to make
    One woman true, just one.

244. In Neath Valley

Between two rows of trees,
Here let me take my ease;

To see the light afar,
Shining like one big star.

Is it not fine to lie
With boughs to change my sky;

Alone in this green way,
And let my fancies play?

Now as a growing boy
Will sometimes stand for joy

Tiptoe behind men small,
And raise himself as tall —

So shall my fancy's eye
See none more great than I.

245. The Blind Boxer

He goes with basket and slow feet,
To sell his nuts from street to street;
The very terror of his kind,
Till blackened eyes had made him blind.
For this is Boxer Bob, the man
That had hard muscles, harder than
A schoolboy's bones; who held his ground
When six tall bullies sparred around.

Small children now, that have no grace,
Can steal his nuts before his face;
And when he threatens with his hands,
Mock him two feet from where he stands;
Mock him who could some years ago
Have leapt five feet to strike a blow.
Poor Bobby, I remember when
Thou wert a god to drunken men;
But now they push thee off, or crack
Thy nuts and give no money back.
They swear they'll strike thee in the face,
Dost thou not hurry from that place.
Such are the men that once would pay
To keep thee drunk from day to day.
With all thy strength and cunning skill,
Thy courage, lasting breath and will,
Thou'rt helpless now; a little ball,
No bigger than a cherry small,
Has now refused to guide and lead
Twelve stone of strong hard flesh that need
But that ball's light to make thee leap
And strike these cowards down like sheep.
Poor helpless Bobby, blind; I see
Thy working face and pity thee.

246. Old Acquaintance

Thy water, Alteryn,
Shines brighter through my tears,
With childhood in my mind:
So will it shine when age
Has made me almost blind.

How canst thou look so young
On my fast changing flesh
And brooding cares that kill –
Oh, you sweet witch as fresh
And fair as childhood – still?

247. I am the Poet Davies, William

I am the Poet Davies, William,
    I sin without a blush or blink:
I am a man that lives to eat;
    I am a man that lives to drink.

My face is large, my lips are thick,
    My skin is coarse and black almost;
But the ugliest feature is my verse,
    Which proves my soul is black and lost.

Thank heaven thou didst not marry me,
    A poet full of blackest evil;
For how to manage my damned soul
    Will puzzle many a flaming devil.

248. The Moon and a Cloud

Sometimes I watch the moon at night,
    No matter be she near or far;
Up high, or in a leafy tree
    Caught laughing like a bigger star.

To-night the west is full of clouds;
  The east is full of stars that fly
Into the cloud's dark foliage,
  And the moon will follow by and by.

I see a dark brown shabby cloud –
  The moon has gone behind its back;
I looked to see her turn it white –
  She turned it to a lovely black.

A lovely cloud, a jet-black cloud;
  It shines with such a glorious light,
That I am glad with all my heart
  She turned it black instead of white.

249. The Hunt

We have no mind to reach that Pole
  Where monarchs keep their icy courts,
Where lords and ladies, proud and cold,
  May do no more than smile at sports;
Nay, laughing, lying at our ease
We keep our court beneath green trees.

Kings' beds are soft and silvery white,
  While ours are golden straw or hay:
So let kings lie, while gentle sleep
  Attends our harder beds, when they,
Inside their soft white bedclothes, yell
That nightmares ride them down to hell.

Poor lords and ladies, what tame sport
    To hunt a fox or stag, while we
Sit on a green bank in the sun
    And chase for hours a faster flea;
Which blesses us from day to day,
With all our faculties in play.

250. No Idle Gold

No idle gold – since this fine sun, my friend,
Is no mean miser, but doth freely spend.

No precious stones – since these green mornings show,
Without a charge, their pearls where'er I go.

No lifeless books – since birds with their sweet tongues
Will read aloud to me their happier songs.

No painted scenes – since clouds can change my skies
A hundred times a day to please my eyes.

No headstrong wine – since while I drink the spring
Into my eager ears will softly sing.

No surplus clothes – since every simple beast
Can teach me to be happy with the least.

251. Oh, Sweet Content!

Oh, sweet content, that turns the labourer's sweat
    To tears of joy, and shines the roughest face;
How often have I sought you high and low,
    And found you still in some lone quiet place.

Here, in my room, when full of happy dreams,
  With no life heard beyond that merry sound
Of moths that on my lighted ceiling kiss
  Their shadows as they dance and dance around.

Or in a garden, on a summer's night
  When I have seen the dark and solemn air
Blink with the blind bat's wings, and heaven's bright
    face
  Twitch with the stars that shine in thousands there.

252. The Villain

  While joy gave clouds the light of stars,
    That beamed where'er they looked;
  And calves and lambs had tottering knees,
    Excited, while they sucked;
  While every bird enjoyed his song,
  Without one thought of harm or wrong —
  I turned my head and saw the wind,
    Nor far from where I stood,
  Dragging the corn by her golden hair,
    Into a dark and lonely wood.

253. Love Speechless

  I look on Nature and my thoughts,
  Like nimble skaters, skim the land;
  But when I watch my loved one near,
  My thoughts are walkers in soft sand.

I am a man that sees a sky
Alive with stars that cannot rest;
My eyes are here, my eyes are there,
Above, and then below her breast.

Much like the summer's bee am I,
A thousand flowers before his eyes;
He, knowing each one's power to please,
No sooner settles than must rise.

I sit bewildered by those charms
That follow wave by wave all day;
When I would with one wave make free,
The others take my breath away.

254. The Dog

The dog was there, outside her door,
   She gave it food and drink,
She gave it shelter from the cold:
   It was the night young Molly robbed
An old fool of his gold.

'Molly,' I said, 'you'll go to hell –'
   And yet I half believed
That ugly, famished, tottering cur
   Would bark outside the gates of Heaven,
To open them for Her!

255. The Rat

'That woman there is almost dead,
Her feet and hands like heavy lead;
Her cat's gone out for his delight,
He will not come again this night.

'Her husband in a pothouse drinks,
Her daughter at a soldier winks;
Her son is at his sweetest game,
Teasing the cobbler old and lame.

'Now with these teeth that powder stones,
I'll pick at one of her cheek-bones:
When husband, son and daughter come,
They'll soon see who was left at home.'

256. The Cat

Within that porch, across the way,
  I see two naked eyes this night;
Two eyes that neither shut nor blink,
  Searching my face with a green light.

But cats to me are strange, so strange —
  I cannot sleep if one is near;
And though I'm sure I see those eyes,
  I'm not so sure a body's there!

257. To-day

I have no hopes, I have no fears,
Whether my dreams are gossamers
To last beyond my body's day,
Or cobwebs to be brushed away.
Give me this life from hour to hour,
From day to day, and year to year;
This cottage with one extra room
To lodge a friend if he should come;
This garden green and small, where I
Can sit and see a great big sky.
And give me one tall shady tree,
Where, looking through the boughs, I'll see
How the sharp leaves can cut the skies
Into a thousand small blue eyes.

258. How Kind is Sleep

How kind is sleep, how merciful:
    That I last night have seen
The happy birds with bosoms pressed
    Against the leaves so green.

Sweet sleep, that made my mind forget
    My love had gone away;
And nevermore I'd touch her soft
    Warm body, night or day.

So, every night deceived by sleep,
    Let me on roses lie;
And leave the thorns of Truth for day
    To pierce me till I die.

259. The Force of Love

Have I now found an angel in Unrest,
  That wakeful Love is more desired than sleep?
Though you seem calm and gentle, you shall show
  The force of this strong love in me so deep.

Yes, I will make you, though you seem so calm,
  Look from your blue eyes that divinest joy
As was in Juno's, when she made great Jove
  Forget the war and half his heaven in Troy.

And I will press your lips until they mix
  With my poor quality their richer wine:
Be my Parnassus now, and grow more green
  Each upward step towards your top divine.

260. When Leaves Begin

When leaves begin to show their heads,
Before they reach their curly youth;
And birds in streams are coming north,
With seas of music from the south ;

Then – like a snail with horns outstretched –
My senses feel the air around;
There's not a move escapes my eyes,
My ears are cocked to every sound.

Till Nature to her greenest comes,
And – with her may that blossoms white –
Bursts her full bodice, and reveals
Her fair white body in the light.

261. Passion's Hounds

With mighty leaps and bounds,
I followed Passion's hounds,
  My hot blood had its day;
Lust, Gluttony, and Drink,
I chased to Hell's black brink,
  Both night and day.

I ate like three strong men,
I drank enough for ten,
  Each hour must have its glass:
Yes, Drink and Gluttony
Have starved more brains, say I,
  Than Hunger has.

And now, when I grow old,
And my slow blood is cold,
  And feeble is my breath —
I'm followed by those hounds,
Whose mighty leaps and bounds
  Hunt me to death.

262. Love Impeached

Listen for pity — I impeach
  The tyrant Love that, after play,
Dribbles on Beauty's cheek, and still
  Refuses to be moved away.

That, not content with many a kiss
   Plays with his fingers on her lip;
And if she turns her back to him,
   Drums with his hand on either hip.

Sometimes he squeezes, then he slaps,
   I've heard he even bites her breast.
Now, how can Beauty keep her charms,
   If she gets neither sleep nor rest?

Is there no punishment, I ask –
   No small corrections, soft and mild?
For let us never once forget
   That, after all, he's but a child.

263. The Truth

Since I have seen a bird one day,
His head pecked more than half away;
That hopped about with but one eye,
Ready to fight again, and die –
Ofttimes since then their private lives
Have spoilt that joy their music gives.

So when I see this robin now,
Like a red apple on the bough,
And question why he sings so strong,
For love, or for the love of song;
Or sings, maybe, for that sweet rill
Whose silver tongue is never still –

Ah, now there comes this thought unkind,
Born of the knowledge in my mind:
He sings in triumph that last night
He killed his father in a fight;
And now he'll take his mother's blood –
The last strong rival for his food.

264. The Coming of Peace

It was the night when we expected news from France,
  To say the war was over, and the fighting done;
The tidings that would make my heart rejoice at last,
  For foe as well as friend, and make the peoples one.

And as I moved amidst that silent multitude,
  Feeling the presence of a wild excitement there,
The world appeared to me so strange and wonderful –
  I almost heard a cuckoo in Trafalgar Square!

265. April's Lambs

'Though I was born in April's prime,
  With many another lamb,
Yet, thinking now of all my years,
  What am I but a tough old ram?'

'No woman thinks of years,' said she,
  'Or any tough old rams,
When she can hear a voice that bleats
  As tenderly as any lamb's.'

266. The Coming of Spring

How I have watched thy coming, Spring,
From back in March, thy first-born day,
When smiles, all meaningless and strange,
Would twist thy face and pass away;
Such as will cross the faces of
Our babes before they grow to love,
Or wonder at the new-made light –
To this, thy great, all-smiling hour,
When thou hast soul and sight.

How I have waited for this day,
When thou, sweet Spring, art three weeks old;
And I can hear that strange, sweet voice,
To seal the wonder of thy world;
That lifts the heart of old and young
To sing an echo to that song
Which cries 'cuckoo' in every grove;
When I, who did but smile before
Must laugh outright for love.

267. A Song

My love has gone long since,
She sleeps, and yet I stay;
To think of her is my
Good night till break of day.
So, in my room, alone,
I still awake am keeping;
Thinking of my white heaven,
And all its angels sleeping.

Sleep shall not hold me yet,
  Her power I'll not obey;
I fear she has strange dreams
  To take my love away.
So, in my room, alone,
  I still awake am keeping;
Thinking of my white heaven,
  And all its angels sleeping.

268. Love's Caution

Tell them, when you are home again,
  How warm the air was now;
How silent were the birds and leaves,
  And of the moon's full glow;
    And how we saw afar
    A falling star:
It was a tear of pure delight
Ran down the face of Heaven this happy night.

Our kisses are but love in flower,
  Until that greater time
When, gathering strength, those flowers take wing,
  And Love can reach his prime.
    And now, my heart's delight,
    Good night, good night;
Give me the last sweet kiss –
But do not breathe at home one word of this!

269. Trees

They ask me where the Temple stands,
   And is the Abbey far from there;
They ask the way to old St. Paul's,
   And where they'll find Trafalgar Square.

As I pass on with my one thought
   To find a quiet place with trees,
I answer him, I answer her,
   I answer one and all of these.

When I sit under a green tree,
   Silent, and breathing all the while
As easy as a sleeping child,
   And smiling with as soft a smile –

Then, as my brains begin to work,
   This is the thought that comes to me:
Were such a peace more often mine,
   I'd live as long as this green tree.

270. What County?

What county sends me this surprise,
That had more rainbows in its skies –
More songsters in its woods and fields,
Than any other county yields?
For, judging her by her fresh look,
She never lived in grime and smoke.
So here we are, the thrush and I –
How we enjoy our ecstasy !

While one blue egg employs his tongue,
For two blue eyes I sing my song.
Yet when I think how my love's eyes
Shine with a soul so clear and wise,
Your egg, poor bird, I fear to tell,
May have no baby in its shell.
Yon cuckoo too, whose voice doth fail,
When more than one sing in one vale,
Hear how her voice becomes more sweet
Among a number, when they meet.
And yon pale star that loses light
When other stars appear in sight,
See how her light is magnified,
With other women at her side.

271. A Child's Pet

When I sailed out of Baltimore,
    With twice a thousand head of sheep,
They would not eat, they would not drink,
    But bleated o'er the deep.

Inside the pens we crawled each day,
    To sort the living from the dead;
And when we reached the Mersey's mouth,
    Had lost five hundred head.

Yet every night and day one sheep,
    That had no fear of man or sea,
Stuck through the bars its pleading face,
    And it was stroked by me.

And to the sheep-men standing near,
  'You see,' I said, 'this one tame sheep?
It seems a child has lost her pet,
  And cried herself to sleep.'

So every time we passed it by,
  Sailing to England's slaughter-house,
Eight ragged sheep-men – tramps and thieves –
  Would stroke that sheep's black nose.

272. The Flirt

A pretty game, my girl,
  To play with me so long;
Until this other lover
  Comes dancing to thy song,
And my affair is over.

But love, though well adored,
  Is not my only note:
So let thy false love-prattle
  Be in another man's throat
That weaker man's death-rattle.

Ah, such as thou, at last,
  Wilt take a false man's hand:
Think kindly then of me,
  When thou'rt forsaken, and
The shame sits on thy knee.

273. The Captive Lion

Thou that in fury with thy knotted tail
Hast made this iron floor thy beaten drum;
That now in silence walks thy little space –
Like a sea-captain – careless what may come:

What power has brought your majesty to this,
Who gave those eyes their dull and sleepy look;
Who took their lightning out, and from thy throat
The thunder when the whole wide forest shook?

It was that man who went again, alone,
Into thy forest dark – Lord, he was brave!
That man a fly has killed, whose bones are left
Unburied till an earthquake digs his grave.

274. The Clock

Every tick and every tock
That comes from my old clock,
    Keeps time to Molly's step;
And when it cries 'Cuckoo,'
Her hand should knock below.

Unless – for now I see
The clock looks down at me
    With a white and silent face –
It stops, and not one beat
Keeps time to Molly's feet.

Then, staring at that clock,
Whose every tick and tock
    Should be one step of hers.
'Why have you stopped,' I said—
'Has Molly dropped down dead?'

275. A Bird's Anger

A summer's morning that has but one voice;
    Five hundred stooks, like golden lovers, lean
Their heads together, in their quiet way,
    And but one bird sings, of a number seen.

It is the lark, that louder, louder sings,
    As though but this one thought possessed his mind:
'You silent robin, blackbird, thrush, and finch,
    I'll sing enough for all you lazy kind!'

And when I hear him at this daring task,
    'Peace, little bird,' I say, 'and take some rest;
Stop that wild, screaming fire of angry song,
    Before it makes a coffin of your nest.'

276. Bird and Brook

My song, that's bird-like in its kind,
Is in the mind,
Love – in the mind;
And in my season I am moved
No more or less from being loved;

285

No woman's love has power to bring
My song back when I cease to sing;
Nor can she, when my season's strong,
Prevent my mind from song.

But where I feel your woman's part,
Is in the heart,
Love – in the heart;
For when that bird of mine broods long,
And I'd be sad without my song,
Your love then makes my heart a brook
That dreams in many a quiet nook,
And makes a steady, murmuring sound
Of joy the whole year round.

277. One Thing Wanting

'Your life was hard with mangling clothes,
You scrubbed our floors for years;
But now, your children are so good,
That you can rest your poor old limbs,
And want for neither drink nor meat.'
'It's true,' she said, and laughed for joy;
And still her voice, with all her years,
Could make a song-bird wonder if
A rival sweetness challenged him.
But soon her face was full of trouble:
'If I could only tear,' she said,
'My sister Alice out of her grave –
Who taunted me when I was poor –
And make her understand these words:

286

"See, I have everything I want,
My children, Alice, are so good" –
If I could only once do that,
There's nothing else I want on earth.'

278. The Mint

Nature has made my mind a mint,
  My thoughts are coins, on which I live;
The dies, with which I stamp my thoughts,
  Trees, blossoms, birds, and children give.

Sometimes my die's a homeless man,
  Or babes that have no milk and perish;
Sometimes it is a lady fair,
  Whose grace and loveliness I relish.

But all my love-thoughts, until now,
  Were false to utter, and must cease;
And not another coin must pass
  Without your image on each piece.

So, you shall be my queen from now,
  Your face on every thought I utter;
And I'll be rich – although the world
  May judge my metal's worth no better.

279. Worm-Proof

'Have I not bored your teeth,' said Time,
  'Until they drop out, one by one?
I'll turn your black hairs into white,
  And pluck them when the change is done;
The clothes you've put away with care,
  My worm's already in their seams – '
'Time, hold your tongue, for man can still
  Defy you with his worm-proof dreams.'

280. Comfort

From my own kind I only learn
  How foolish comfort is;
To gather things that happy minds
  Should neither crave nor miss:
Fine brackets to adorn my walls,
  Whose tales are quickly told;
And copper candlesticks or brass,
  Which soon must leave me cold.

From my own kind I only learn
  That comfort breeds more care;
But when I watch our smaller lives,
  There's plainness everywhere:
That little bird is well content,
  When he no more can sing,
To close his eyes and tuck his head
  Beneath his own soft wing.

281. Her Mouth and Mine

As I lay dreaming, open-eyed,
With some one sitting at my side,
I saw a thing about to fly
Into my face, where it would lie;
For just above my head there stood
A smiling hawk as red as blood.
On which the bird, whose quiet nest
Has always been in my left breast,
Seeing that red hawk hovering there,
And smiling with such deadly care –
Flew fascinated to my throat,
And there it moaned a feeble note.
I saw that hawk, so red, and still,
And closed my eyes – it had its will :
For, uttering one triumphant croon,
It pounced with sudden impulse down;
And there I lay, no power to move,
To let it kiss or bite its love.
But in those birds – Ah, it was strange –
There came at last this other change:
That fascinated bird of mine
Worried the hawk and made it whine;
The hawk cried feebly – 'Oh dear, oh!
Greedy-in-love, leave go! Leave go!'

282. Let Me Confess

Let me confess, before I die,
I sing for gold enough to buy
A little house with leafy eyes
That open to the Southern skies;

Where I, in peace from human strife,
Will wish no Lazarus brought to life.
Around my garden I will see
More wild flowers than are known to me;

With those white hops, whose children are
Big, heavy casks of ale and beer;
And little apples, from whose womb
Barrels of lusty cider come.

Good food, and ale that's strong in brew,
And wine, I'll have; clear water too,
From a deep well, where it doth lie
Shining as small as my own eye.

And any friend may come to share
What comfort I am keeping there;
For though my sins are many, one
Shall not be mine, when my life's done:
A fortune saved by one that's dead,
Who saw his fellows starve for bread.

283. Love's Silent Hour

This is Love's silent hour, before the tongue
Can find expression happy in a song;
Yet your sweet, generous lips shall have their hour,
Believe me, when my song comes back to power;
So shall those eyes, so dark, so warm, and deep,
That wake for me, and for all others sleep:
Meanwhile I do no more than sit and sigh,
Watching your movements with a greedy eye.

Those birds that sing so sweet in their green bogs,
Their season over, croak like common frogs:
My thoughts, I hoped, would like those nightingales
Sing sweet for you, but still my music fails;
My music fails, and I can only kiss
Your cheek and chin, and to myself say this –
There never was a thing so fair and bright,
By sun or moon, by gas or candle-light.

284. Now That She Gives

Now that she gives my love consent,
    I hear an evil spirit near;
A mocking spirit, day and night,
    That whispers threats in either ear.

'Since you are twice her age,' it says,
    'Thick-lipped, with features large and coarse;
And she, so young and beautiful,
    Could all her life do nothing worse;

'Since she, poor girl, mistakes for love
    The feelings that possess her heart –
She must be daft, and you, strong wretch,
    Should burn in hell for such a part!'

285. You Interfering Ladies

You interfering ladies, you
    That prove your minds enjoy less rest
Than those poor mortals you advise,
    Whose habits shock your dainty taste –
Peace, let the poor be free to do
The things they like – be happy, you!

Let boys and girls kiss here and there,
 Men drink, and smoke the strongest weed;
Let beggars, who'll not wash with soap,
 Enjoy their scratching till they bleed:
Let all poor women, if they please,
Enjoy a pinch of snuff, and sneeze.

286. The Song of Life

I

A sneeze from Time gives Life its little breath;
Time yawns, and lo! he swallows Life in Death;
When we forget, and laugh without a care,
Time's Prompter, Death, reminds us what we are.

II

O thou vain fool, to waste thy breath and theirs,
Who pipes this day to make thy fellows dance;
To-morrow Death will make thy body show
How worms can dance without thy music once.

III

We are but fools, no matter what we do.
By hand or brain we work, and waste our breath;
Life's but a drunkard, in his own strange way,
Sobered at last by thy strong physic, Death.

IV

Life is a fisherman, and Time his stream,
But what he catches there is but a dream;
Our Youth and Beauty, Riches, Power and Fame,
Must all return at last from whence they came.

V

Death gives a Royal Prince the same dumb grin
As to the beggar's wayside brat of sin.
The cunning Spider soon himself must lie
Dead in that trap he sets to catch a Fly.

VI

Time grants to man no freehold property;
The power of man, however great it be,
Is only granted here for a short lease.
Voices the world has called divine must cease.

VII

Fools that we think of Fame, when there's a force
To make a coffin of this world of ours
And sweep it clean of every living thing –
What then becomes of man and all his powers?

VIII

Think of our giants now – they're auctioneers,
That shout and hammer for the people's cheers;
They blow in gales, but no good ear can find
The small clear voice that deepens Nature's wind.

IX

We call these rockets steadfast stars, and give
Them honours, wealth, and swear their works will live;
We call them giants, while the greater ones
Move like dark planets round those favoured suns.

X

This world, that licks them with its pleasant slime,
Will swallow them in but a little time;
Their Fame's like Death's, when that cold villain places
Bright looks of youth on dying old men's faces.

XI

We pass away, forgotten and neglected.
When thou, poor fool, hast lately filled thy grave,
Thy friends will bring thee cut and costly flowers,
Flowers that will leave no living seed behind,
And fade and perish in a few short hours.

XII

Perchance they'll set the soil with roots of plants
To live and bloom again there, year by year,
Moistened at times by Heaven's dew or rain –
But never once a loving human tear.

XIII

Plants that will need no help from human hands
To make thy grave look lovely, warm and sweet –
When all, except the fierce wild cat, has gone,
That lies in wait to pounce upon those birds
That beat the snails to death against thy stone.

XIV

I hear men say: 'This Davies has no depth,
He writes of birds, of staring cows and sheep,
And throws no light on deep, eternal things' –
And would they have me talking in my sleep?

XV

I say: 'Though many a man's ideas of them
Have made his name appear a shining star,
Yet Life and Death, Time and Eternity,
Are still left dark, to wonder what they are.

XVI

'And if I make men weigh this simple truth,
It is on my own mind the light is thrown;
I throw no light on that mysterious Four,
And, like the great ones, nothing I make known.'

XVII

Yet I believe that there will come at last
A mighty knowledge to our human lives:
And blessèd then will be the fools that laugh,
Without the fear Imagination gives.

XVIII

Aye, even now, when I sit here alone,
I feel the breath of that strange terror near;
But as my mind has not sufficient strength
To give it shape or form of any kind,
I turn to things I know, and banish fear.

XIX

I turn to Man, and what do I behold?
What is the meaning of this rush and tear
To ride from home by water, land, or air?
We'll want the horses soon, when our life fails,
To drag a corpse along as slow as snails.

XX

Why should this toil from early morn till night
Employ our minds and bodies, when the Earth
Can carry us for ever round the Sun
Without the help of any mortal birth?

XXI

And why should common shelter, bread and meat,
Keep all our faculties in their employ,
And leave no time for ease, while Summer's in
The greenwood, purring like a cat for joy?

XXII

For still the People are no more than slaves;
Each State a slave-ship, and no matter which
The figure-head – a President or King;
The People are no more than common grass
To make a few choice cattle fat and rich.

XXIII

They toil from morn till eve, from Youth to Age;
They go from bud to seed, but never flower.
'Ah,' says the Priest, 'we're born to suffer here
A hell on earth till God Almighty's Hour.'

XXIV

A hell on earth? . . . We'll ask the merry Moth
That, making a partner of his shadow thrown,
Dances till out of breath; we'll ask the Lark
That meets the Rain half-way and sings it down.

XXV

In studying Life we see this human world
Is in three states – of copper, silver, gold,
And those that think in silver take the joy;
Thinking in copper, gold, the poor and rich
Keep mis'ry in too little and too much.

XXVI

Though with my money I could cram a mouth
Big as an Alpine gorge with richest stuff,
Yet Nature sets her bounds; and with a lake
Of wine – to-night one bottle is enough.

XXVII

If I can pluck the rose of sunset, or
The Moon's pale lily, and distil their flower
Into one mental drop to scent my soul –
I'll envy no man his more worldly power.

XXVIII

What matters that my bed is soft and white,
If beggars sleep more sweet in hay, or there,
Lying at noon beneath those swaying boughs
Whose cooling shadows lift the heavy air.

XXIX

Not owning house or land, but in the space
Our minds inhabit, we are rich or poor:
If I had youth, who dances in his walk,
On heels as nimble as his lighter toes,
I'd set no price on any earthly store.

And wine and women, both have had their day,
When nothing else would my crazed thoughts allow;
Until my nerves shook like those withered leaves
Held by a broken cobweb to the bough.

XXXI

I touched my mistress lightly on the chin,
That girl so merciless in her strong passion:
'Since love,' she said, 'has reached that flippant mood –
With no more care than that – I'd rather you
Had struck my mouth, and dashed my lips with blood.'

XXXII

And is there naught in life but lust? thought I;
Feeble my brain was then, and small, and weak;
She held it in her power, even as a bird
With his live breakfast squirming from his beak.

XXXIII

Man finds in such a Woman's breast the tomb
Where his creative powers must soon lie dumb;
To kiss the tomb in weakness, hour by hour,
Wherein she buries half his mental power.

XXXIV

They say that under powerful drugs the tongue
Will babble wildly of some sin or wrong
That never happened – even virgins then
Tell devilish lies about themselves and men.

XXXV

Under that drug of lust my brain was mazed,
And oft I babbled in a foolish way;
And still she bounced the babies in her eyes,
For Love's mad challenge not to miss one day.

XXXVI

But that is passed, and I am ready now
To come again, sweet Nature, to your haunts;
Not come together like a snake and stone,
When neither body gives the other heat –
But full of love to last till Life has gone.

XXXVII

A little while and I will come again,
From my captivity in this strange place;
That has these secret charms to lure me on,
In every alley dark and open space;

XXXVIII

That makes me like the jealous lover who,
Eavesdropping at a keyhole, trembles more
Because the silence there is worse to him than sound,
And nothing's heard behind the fastened door.

XXXIX

To you I'll come, my old and purer friend,
With greater love in these repentant hours;
To let your Brook run singing to my lips;
And walk again your Meadows full of flowers.

XL

I'll stroke again the foreheads of your Cows,
And clothe my fingers in your Horses' manes;
I'll hear that music, when a pony trots
Along your hard, white country roads and lanes.

XLI

Kissed with his warm eyelashes touching mine,
I'll lie beneath the Sun, on golden sheaves;
Or see him from the shade, when in his strength
He makes frail cobwebs of the solid leaves.

XLII

I'll see again the green leaves suddenly
Turned into flowers by resting butterflies;
While all around are small, brown, working bees,
And hairy black-and-ambers, twice their size.

XLIII

And there'll be ponds that lily-leaves still keep –
Though rough winds blow there – lying fast asleep.
And pools that measure a cloud from earth to sky,
To sink it down as deep as it is high.

XLIV

And many a charming truth will I discover;
How birds, after a wetting in the rain,
Can make their notes come twice as sweet; and then
How sparrows hop with both their legs together,
While pigeons stride leg after leg, like men.

XLV

Nature for me, in every mood she has;
And frosty mornings, clear and cold, that blind
The cattle in a mist of their own breath –
Shall never come and find my heart unkind.

XLVI

And I'll forget these deep and troubled thoughts;
How, like a saucy puppy, Life doth stand
Barking upon this world of crumbling sand;
Half in defiance there, and half in fear –
For still the waves of Time are drawing near.

XLVII

Would birds, if they had thoughts of their short days,
Stand on the boughs and carol such sweet lays?
Is it not better then that we should join
The birds in song than sit in grief and pine?

XLVIII

Come, let us laugh – though there's no wit to hear;
Come, let us sing – though there's no listener near;
Come, let us dance – though none admire our grace,
And be the happier for a private place.

XLIX

A quiet life with Nature is my choice
And, opening there my Book of Memory,
The record of my wild young roving blood –
I'll sail the seas again, and reach strange ports,
And light a fire in many a silent wood.

L

Under white blossoms spread all over him,
Have I not seen the Ocean laugh and roll;
And watched a boundless prairie, when it lay
So full of flowers it could employ the whole
World's little ones to pick them in a day?

LI

I'll sail the great Atlantic, whose strong waves
Could lift the ship *Tritonia* up so high
That to my wondering mind it ofttimes seemed
About to take the air above, and fly!

LII

Up North I'll go, where steel, more cold than death,
Can burn the skin off any naked hands –
Down to those woods where I'll at midnight read
By one fat glow-worm's light in Southern lands.

LIII

I'll see again, in dreams, the full-rigged Ship
Wearing the Moon as a silver ring at night
On her main finger; while the water shines,
Fretted with island-shadows in the light,

LIV

With all the wealth of Heaven: those perfect stars
That draw near earth in numbers to amaze;
The bubble-light of others deep impooled,
The shadowy lustre of those lesser rays.

I'll see again, in my long winter dreams,
That iceberg in the North, whose glorious beams
Fluttered in their cold prison, while the Sun
Went up and down with our good ship, like one.

I'll dream of Colorado's rushing stream;
And how I heard him slap his thighs of stone
So loud that Heaven had never power to make
His cañon hear more thunder than his own.

There will I live with Nature, there I'll die;
And if there's any Power in Heaven above,
A God of vengeance, mercy, and sweet love –
If such a judge there be, I can but trust
In Him for what is only fair and just.

I'll place my hope in some few simple deeds
That sacrificed a part of my own needs
All for the love of poor Humanity –
Without a single thought, O Lord, of Thee.

287. I Could not Love Him More

I could not love him more –
Though he were richer than
A summer's night
That bubbles over with
A flood of starry light.

I would not love him less –
Though he were poorer than
A winter's morn
That struggles wildly with
A sun that's never born.

288. See how the Glow-worm's Light

See how the glow-worm's light is found
To shine upon a nameless mound:
So, though my lover's life is false,
In being true to none,
And, like that worm's, his beauty shines
Upon a past unknown;
Yet still I ask no more than this –
The knowledge that is in a kiss.

289. A Chant

With all our mirth, I doubt if we shall be
Like Martha here, in her serenity,
When we're her age; who goes from bed to bed
To wash the faces of the newly dead;
To close their staring eyes and comb their hair,
To cross their hands and change the linen there;
Who helps the midwives to give strength and breath
To babes, by almost beating them to death
With a wet towel; and half drowns them too,
Until their tender flesh is black and blue.
Not all the revels, Martha, we have been to
Can give us, when we're old, a peace like yours –
Due to the corpses you have gone and seen to.

290. Beggar's Song

Good people keep their holy day,
  They rest from labour on a Sunday;
But we keep holy every day,
  And rest from Monday until Monday.

And yet the noblest work on earth
  Is done when beggars do their part:
They work, dear ladies, on the soft
  And tender feelings in your heart.

291. On What Sweet Banks

On what sweet banks were thy pure fancies fed,
  What world of smiling light has been thy home;
In what fair land of rainbows wert thou bred,
  From what green land of cuckoos art thou come?

By all that shining wonder in thine eyes,
  Baffled and vexed I stand before thy smile;
Thy thoughts, like angels, guard thee from surprise,
  We see them not, yet feel them all the while.

That smile which, like the sun on every thing,
  Now falls on me with no increased delight,
Must either go behind a cloud and bring
  Death to my hopes or give my love more light.

292. Drinking Song

Ah, Life, we are no sooner dressed
Than we must strip:
Come, Bacchus, then, you wondrous boy,
You god of laughter, peace and rest,
With friendship smiling on your lip –
There's nothing in this world can move
Us like good wine and love.

293. Around that Waist

Around that waist, scarce bigger than my neck,
    Where my two arms can make a double band,
That's how I'd like to hold her in a knot,
    Clasping my elbow fast with either hand.

To feel her soft round body slip and turn,
    And still to feel no bones; that clings to me,
Till she becomes at last the trembling flower
    Kissed without mercy by a powerful bee.

294. Her Body's a Fine House

Her body's a fine house,
    Three stories I have reckoned;
Her garter marks the first,
    A belt of silk the second;
Her necklace marks the third,
    And know – before I stop –
The garden of that house
    Is planted on the top.

295. Oh for a Glass of Wine!

Oh for a glass of wine!
A glass of ruby wine, that gives the eyes
A light more wonderful than Love supplies.

Oh for a glass of ale!
A glass of sparkling ale, where bubbles play
At starry heavens, and show a Milky Way.

296. The Woods and Banks

The woods and banks of England now,
   Late coppered with dead leaves and old,
Have made the early violets grow,
   And bulge with knots of primrose gold.
Hear how the blackbird flutes away,
   Whose music scorns to sleep at night:
Hear how the cuckoo shouts all day
   For echoes – to the world's delight:
Hallo, you imp of wonder, you –
Where are you now, cuckoo? Cuckoo!

297. Without Contentment, what is Life?

Without contentment, what is life?
   Contented minds, like bees, can suck
Sweet honey out of soot, and sleep,
   Like butterflies, on stone or rock.

Contented minds are not in towns,
  Where stars are far away and cold,
That tremble till they almost fall,
  When they draw near to Nature's world.

Such quiet nights we'll have again,
  And walk, when early morning comes,
Those dewy cemeteries, the fields –
  When they are white with mushroom tombs.

298. When Autumn's Fruit

When Autumn's fruit is packed and stored,
And barns are full of corn and grain;
When leaves come tumbling down to earth,
Shot down by wind or drops of rain:
Then up the road we'll whistling go,
And, with a heart that's merry,
We'll rob the squirrel of a nut,
Or chaffinch of a berry.

When Winter's bare and cold for all,
Save lovers with their spawny eyes,
And, like a horse that fleas annoy,
We stamp, to make our spirits rise:
Then out of doors we'll whistling go,
And, with a heart that's merry,
We'll feed – while richer squirrels sleep
The birds that have no berry.

299. Now that the Tears

Now that the tears of love have reached
Their flood-time in my throat,
What thoughts I launch for your sweet sake,
What dreams I set afloat;
How when I've caught you fast asleep,
I'll sit awake and trace
The curved and round perfections in
Your head, your neck and face.

If there is such a passion now,
With so much strength to move,
What shall we do if you inflame
With jealousy that love:
That jealousy, whose eyes can see
More than the deaf and dumb,
And hears far more than one that's blind —
What then shall we become!

300. The World May Charge

The world may charge a man with sin,
    That to no woman can be proved —
Until she finds a part that shows
    She is by him no longer loved.

When they walk out, and trust in him
    Is shining in her happy face,
Who'll dare to show them with cold looks
    They think one thought of his disgrace?

301. Where She is Now

Where she is now, I cannot say –
   The world has many a place of light;
Perhaps the sun's eyelashes dance
   On hers, to give them both delight.

Or does she sit in some green shade,
   And then the air that lies above
Can with a hundred pale blue eyes
   Look through the leaves and find my love.

Perhaps she dreams of life with me,
   Her cheek upon her finger-tips;
O that I could leap forward now,
   Behind her back and, with my lips,

Break through those curls above her nape,
   That hover close and lightly there;
To prove if they are substance, or
   But shadows of her lovely hair.

302. Men that have Strength

Men that have strength to rule their sex
   Leave women still unmoved;
Men that by women are preferred –
   By that strange sex adored and loved –
Will rise by neither deed nor word.

When women's dainty heroes are
    Conferring with strong men,
They sit in fear, as dumb as graves;
    So, ladies, your sweet darlings, then –
What are they but our strong men's slaves?

303. Night is the only Time I Live

Night is the only time I live,
    Wherein I find delight;
For then I dream my lover's near,
    To make a day of night.

But when I wake from those sweet dreams,
    And find that he's away,
My night again begins its course,
    With every break of day.

304. When Diamonds, Nibbling in my Ears

When diamonds, nibbling in my ears,
Are sparkling there in wild delight,
They'll dance as free of my close flesh
As any stars that shine at night.
What joy to see those diamonds burn
Their own clear space to dance and turn!

311

305. With thy Strong Tide of Beauty

With thy strong tide of beauty I must go,
Where my love leads I follow in her tow;
And all my hope is that I sing for her
Fresh songs whose breath is April's all the year.

There, with the flowers and butterflies, and bees
That grumble more the more their blossoms please -
We'll live secure from this vain world's pretence,
Till we acquire a second innocence.

We'll shun all human scandal, though our words
May oft discuss the private life of birds;
And prying into every move and sound,
Surprise a bee before his blossom's found.

306. Who Bears in Mind

Who bears in mind misfortunes gone,
   Must live in fear of more;
The happy man, whose heart is light,
   Gives no such shadow power;
He bears in mind no haunting past
   To start his week on Monday;
No graves are written on his mind,
   To visit on a Sunday;
He lives his life by days, not years,
   Each day's a life complete;
Which every morning finds renewed,
   With temper calm and sweet.

307. The Hour of Magic

This is the hour of magic, when the Moon
  With her bright wand has charmed the tallest tree
To stand stone-still with all his million leaves!
  I feel around me things I cannot see;
I hold my breath, as Nature holds her own.
  And do the mice and birds, the horse and cow,
Sleepless in this deep silence, so intense,
  Believe a miracle has happened now,
And wait to hear a sound they'll recognize,
To prove they still have life with earthly ties?

308. The Beautiful

Three things there are more beautiful
  Than any man could wish to see:
The first, it is a full-rigged ship
  Sailing with all her sails set free;
The second, when the wind and sun
  Are playing in a field of corn;
The third, a woman, young and fair,
  Showing her child before it is born.

309. Impudence

One morning, when the world was grey and cold,
  And every face looked dull and full of care,
There passed me, puffing clouds of silver breath,
  A lovely maiden, with a jaunty air.

The red carnations flamed in both her cheeks,
   Her teeth were white and shown; while either eye
Shone like a little pool on Christchurch Hill
   When it has stolen more than half the sky.

And when I saw such beauty, young and fresh,
   So proud, although the day was grey and cold,
'Who ever saw,' I laughed, and stared amazed,
   'Such impudence before in this old world!'

310. Wasted Hours

How many buds in this warm light
Have burst out laughing into leaves!
   And shall a day like this be gone
Before I seek the wood that holds
   The richest music known?

Too many times have nightingales
Wasted their passion on my sleep,
   And brought repentence soon;
But this one night I'll seek the woods,
   The Nightingale and Moon.

311. Two Women

The Mother

The midwife nearly drowned my son,
   And beat him hard, before he'd give
That cry a mother longs to hear
   To prove her precious babe will live.

I wish that she had drowned him quite,
   Or beat your precious babe to death;
Since he has grown so fierce and strong
   He'll beat me out of my last breath.

Your precious babe is now a man,
   But, mother, he's not worth the skin —
As husband, father, or a son —
   That he was made for living in.

312. Pastures

That grass is tender, soft and sweet,
   And well you young lambs know't:
I know a pasture twice as sweet,
   Although I may not show't;
Where my five fingers go each night
   To nibble, like you sheep,
All over my love's breast, and there
   Lie down to sleep.

313. Her Merriment

When I had met my love the twentieth time,
   She put me to confession day and night:
Did I like woman far above all things,
   Or did the songs I make give more delight?

'Listen, you sweeter flower than ever smiled
   In April's sunny face,' I said at last —
'The voices and the legs of birds and women
   Have always pleased my ears and eyes the most.'

And saying this, I watched my love with care,
   Not knowing would my words offend or please:
But laughing gaily, her delighted breasts
   Sent ripples down her body to her knees.

314. Joy

Poor souls, who think that joy is bought
      With pelf;
The bait that captures joy is joy
      Itself.
My joy, it came mysteriously
      At birth;
I give it to, not take it from
      The earth.
Have pity on my enemy:
      Again,
And yet again, my triumph gives
      Him pain.
Come, Death, give me life's perfect end;
      Take me
In my sleep, Oh Death, and do not
      Wake me.

315. Lamorna Cove

I see at last our great Lamorna Cove,
Which, danced on by ten thousand silver feet,
Has all those waves that run like little lambs,
To draw the milk from many a rocky teat,
Spilt in white gallons all along the shore.
Who ever saw more beauty under the sun?
I look and look, and say, 'No wonder here's
A light I never saw on earth before –
Two heavens are shining here instead of one.'
And, like the wild gulls flashing in my sight,
Each furious thought that's driving through my brain
Screams in its fresh young wonder and delight.

316. Wild Oats

How slowly moves the snail, that builds
A silver street so fine and long:
I move as slowly, but I leave
Behind me not one breath of song.
Dumb as a moulting bird am I,
I go to bed when children do,
My ale but two half-pints a day,
And to one woman I am true.
Oh! what a life, how flat and stale –
How dull, monotonous and slow!
Can I sing songs in times so dead –
Are there no more wild oats to sow?

317. The Grief of Others

Once more I see the happy young
  Broken by grief and pain;
That tears have made like earth's red worms
  Turned white by days of rain.
Once more I see the new-made wife
  From her dead husband torn;
When down she sits and weeps, and laughs,
  And rocks her babe unborn.
And when I see a hearse that takes
  A coffin through the town,
Or pass the quiet house of death,
  That has its blinds drawn down –
Such pity moves me for the dear
  Ones left to mourn behind,
That I am glad my loves are dreams
  Made purely of the mind:
That take expression for their grave,
  When they have served their hour;
And I create a younger brood
  To charm me with new power.

318. The Portrait

She sends her portrait, as a swallow,
To show that her sweet spring will follow;
Until she comes herself, to share
With me a pillow and her hair.
To this fine portrait of my Dear,
With nothing but dead matter near,
I whisper words of love, and kiss
The cardboard dewy with my bliss.

This is her hair, which I will bind
Around my knuckles, when inclined
To bandage them in skeins of gold.
These are her lips, in paper mould,
Which when I touch appear to move,
As conscious of my burning love.
These are her eyes, now hard and set,
And opened wide, which Love will shut.
Lord, is my kiss too poor and weak
To make this portrait move and speak,
And close these eyes in fear of this
Strong love of mine, half bite, half kiss?
This kiss that would in fierce delight
Burn on her soft white flesh, and bite
Like a black fly when, stiff and old,
He's blind, and dying of the cold!
Now, when I rest awhile from kissing,
My room looks lonely with her missing.
Now empty seems that chair, where she
Could sit this night and smile to see
Her own light fingers work with grace
Straight cotton into cobweb lace;
Or when they rub that small gold band
That makes her mine, on her left hand.
O that my love were sitting there,
Before me, in that empty chair;
Rocking the love-light, where it lies
Cradled for joy in her two eyes.
Till in the flesh she comes to kiss,
Be happy, man, that she sends this –
Her own dear portrait, as a swallow,
To show that her sweet spring will follow.

319. A Thought

When I look into a glass,
   Myself's my only care;
But I look into a pool
   For all the wonders there.

When I look into a glass,
   I see a fool:
But I see a wise man
   When I look into a pool.

320. Our Sussex Downs

My youth is gone – my youth that laughed and yawned
In one sweet breath, and will not come again;
And crumbs of wonder are my scanty fare,
Snatched from the beauty on a hill or plain.
So, as I look, I wonder if the land
Has *breathed* those shadows in the waters blue!
From all first sounds I half expect to hear,
Not only echoes, but *their* echoes too.
But when I see – the first time in my life –
Our Sussex Downs, so mighty, strong and bare
That many a wood of fifteen hundred trees
Seems but a handful scattered lightly there –
'What a great hour,' think I, 'half-way 'twixt Death
And Youth that laughs and yawns in one short breath.'

321. Telling Fortunes

'You'll have a son,' the old man said –
  'And then a daughter fair to meet
As any summer nights that dance
  Upon a thousand silver feet.'
'You dear old man, now can you tell
If my fair daughter'll marry well?'
The old man winked his eye and said,
  'Well, knowing men for what they are,
She'll break their hearts, because she'll not
  Be half as good as she is fair.'
The new-made wife was full of pain,
And raised her head and hoped again.
'And will my son be fine and smart
And win a noble lady's heart?'
The old man winked his other eye –
'Well, knowing women as we do,
  The kind of man they most prefer,
He'll break their hearts, because he'll be
  A fool, a coxcomb, and a cur.'

322. The Collar

Who taught fair Cleopatra how to bring
Mark Antony to her knees – the touch of love,
As soft as velvet, that could stroke the wing
Of a butterfly and take no powder off;
The gentle purr that made eternal Rome,
With all its marble, melt in that sweet sound,
And vanish like the mist, when it has come
Into a man's full height above the ground?

When I see how a cat has, even now,
With its own body curled and crouching low,
Made a large, heavy collar, soft and warm,
For that girl's neck, I think, with no alarm,
If, young one, that's your friend – as it was Hers –
I'll watch you round the corner of my fears.

323. To a Fool

If, when thy body's end has come,
Thy mind must find another home,
  Make no mistake with man again;
Come into flesh the thing thou art
In all except thy body's part –
  Come as a silly ass, and plain.

Such were my thoughts, their honest parts,
But oh, what liars are kind hearts!
  What smooth false words such hearts demand
'Thy dreams,' said I, 'give more surprise
Than when I chased bright butterflies,
  And missed them with my snapping hand.'

324. Strength

What lies I read, that men of strength
Have keen and penetrating looks
That, flashing here and flashing there,
Command success – what foolish books!
For when we go to life we find
The men and dogs that fight till death

Are sleepy-eyed, and look so calm
We wonder if they live by breath!
Love, too, must hold her saucy tongue,
And turn on us two sleepy eyes,
To prove she is no painted doll,
And full, like books, of pretty lies.

325. To Bacchus

I'm none of those – Oh Bacchus, blush!
    That eat sour pickles with their beer,
To keep their brains and bellies cold;
    Ashamed to let one laughing tear
Escape their hold.

For only just to smell your hops
    Can make me fat and laugh all day,
With appetite for bread and meat:
    I'll not despise bruised apples, they
Make cider sweet.

'Tis true I only eat to live,
    But how I live to drink is clear;
A little isle of meat and bread,
    In one vast sea of foaming beer,
And I'm well fed.

326. A Woman's History

When Mary Price was five years old,
   And had a bird that died,
She laid its body under flowers;
   And called her friends to pray to God,
And sing sad hymns for hours.

When she, before her fifteenth year,
   Was ruined by a man,
The neighbours sought him out, and said –
   'You'll come along and marry her,
Or hang till you are dead.'

When they had found the child he wronged,
   And playing with her doll,
'I'll come along with you,' said she –
   'But I'll not marry anyone
Unless my doll's with me.'

With no more love's heat in her than
   The wax upon her arm;
With no more love-light in her eyes
   Than in the glass eyes of her doll –
Nor wonder, nor surprise.

When Mary Price was thirty-five,
   And he was lying dead,
She wept as though her heart would break:
   But neighbours winked to see her tears
Fall on a lover's neck.

Now, Mary Price is seventy-five,
     And skinning eels alive:
She, active, strong, and full of breath,
     Has caught the cat that stole an eel,
And beaten it to death.

327.   The Trance

The Moon is beautiful this night:
She is so clear and bright,
That should she smile
On any sleeping face awhile,
The eyes must then their slumber break,
And open, wide awake;
And should she pass a sleeping bird,
Where no leaves touch or meet,
He'll wake and, in his softest voice,
Cry Sweet! Sweet! Sweet!
The Moon is beautiful, but who is this
That hides his face from hers;
That, when she makes eyes through the leaves,
Is full of trembling fears?
The night breeds many a thing that's strange:
The wretched owl that in distress
Hoots every star that comes to help
The evening in her loveliness;
The half-blind bats that here and there
Are floundering in the twilight air;
The rat, that shows his long white teeth
Of hard, unbreakable bone –
That take him where his notions go,
Through wood and lead, cement and stone;

And cats, that have the power,
About the midnight hour,
To hide their bodies' size
Behind two small green eyes.
The night has these – but who is this
That like a shadow glides
Across the shadows of the trees,
And his own visage hides?
He hides his face – we wonder what
That face would look like in the sun:
Perhaps an ugly bloated thing
That has more heavy chins than one;
Or is it sharp and white and thin,
With a long nose that tries to hook
Almost as sharp a chin –
And with a cold, hard, cruel look?
We cannot say, but this is sure –
If we this night saw *it*,
We'd rush to strike that monster down,
To drown him in our common spit.

*   *   *   *   *

This morning, when the blackbird near
Was frightened from his thirteenth song,
There was a lady buried here –
A lady, beautiful and young.
And all the rings she wore in life,
As one betrothed and as a wife,
Were left upon her fingers still,
According to her living will.
But there was one who thought and thought,
Until one thought possessed his head;
And now he goes, though full of fear
Of that clear moon, to rob the dead.

326

I will not say
Whose beauty had less fault:
That lady, where she lay,
Or that fair moon outside,
That kissed the mouth of her black vault.
Oh God, it was a lovely sight:
She was so beautiful in death,
That, till her own looks pitied her,
No mortal could, with living breath.
But what cared he for her fair face
When, by his lamp, in that dark place,
He saw the jewels there,
Shaking with life, and greedy, where
They nibbled at the small, gold bands
On her cold, lifeless hands:
But though he turns those rings around,
They make no downward move, when pulled,
To come from her white hand to his —
He'll cut her fingers off for gold.
But ah, no sooner had he cut
One finger with his knife,
Than her white flesh, so firm and smooth,
Rippled with sudden life!
Now if a cobweb touched his face,
This moment, in that haunted place,
He would have fallen to the ground,
Caught in a net of steel, and bound;
A little leaf, dropped on his head,
Would be a bolt to strike him dead:
But when he heard the lady sigh,
And saw her body rising there,
A second fear released the first,
From stupor into active fear;
And when outside that vault again.

With space to use his trembling knees,
He ran and ran – nor thought of light,
Or shadows under trees.
The first thoughts of that lady
Were delicate and pure:
She looked to see if her fair body
Was covered well and sure;
Her second thoughts were home and love –
And quickly did that lady move
Home to her husband, where that man,
In misery full and deep,
Kneels at an empty chair and sobs;
To her two little ones that sleep –
They are so small in size
That their sweet tender mouths are still
No bigger than their wondering eyes.
What joy, and what astonishment
For him, who suffers for her sake!
But the little ones will certainly
Expect their mother when they wake.

328. The Poet's Horse

Come, show the world your mettle now,
Come, come, my horse of wind and fire –
   Your Master rides no more alone;
   And say, when her young beauty's shown,
Her weight with mine increased your power.

Come from that silver manger, where
You eat the golden corn and hay,
  To give her mount, who is my Bride;
  Whose beauty makes her fit to ride
Bareback through Heaven, and twice a day!

329. The Rainbow

Rainbows are lovely things:
  The bird, that shakes a cold, wet wing,
Chatters with ecstasy,
  But has no breath to sing:
No wonder, when the air
Has a double-rainbow there!

Look, there's a rainbow now!
  See how that lovely rainbow throws
Her jewelled arm around
  This world, when the rain goes!
And how I wish the rain
Would come again, and again!

330. Love, Like a Drop of Dew

When I pass down the street and see
  The people smiling so,
It's clear enough that my true love
  Was there awhile ago.

Her lips that, following her two eyes,
  Go smiling here and there,
Seem newly kissed – but 'tis my faith
  That none but I would dare.

Love, like a drop of dew that joins
  Two blades of grass together,
Has made her mine, as I am hers,
  For ever and for ever.

331. The Nature Lover

The years passed by, and my pure love
For Nature did no longer grow:
'I'll get that love back soon,' thought I –
'By living with more men than now.'
But I made enemies; so I
Return to Nature, where my pain
Shall be forgotten, and my love
For humankind come back again.
When through the woods and fields I go,
No thought is mine of human care;
Under a rainbow's jewelled arch,
No foe can find a lodgment there;
And when our fearless nightingales
Sing in a summer's thunderstorm,
Like choir boys when an organ's played –
Where are such tongues as whisper harm?
So, with this changed and sweeter mind,
Nature for me has saved mankind.

332. One Token

The power was given at birth to me
To stare at a rainbow, bird or tree,
　　Longer than any man alive;
And from these trances, when they're gone,
My songs of joy come, one by one.

But what I want I cannot have:
One token from beyond the grave,
　　That hour I neither dream nor sleep,
To prove death but a veil to hide
Another life on the other side.

333.　Rogues

The nearer unto Nature's heart I moved,
In those sweet days of old, the more I loved:
The nearer to the heart of man I move,
As days and weeks go by, the less I love;
Where can I find a true and honest mind?
Men rob me, and my Love is still unkind.

You cruel rogues, that come this day to borrow
A sum that's promised but not paid to-morrow;
That take like wasps the fruit that's on its way
Towards my mouth, and never fear my nay –
Go to that girl and state your happy case,
That you can see more kindness in my face.

Tell her that though I kiss so wild and oft
Her flesh that's like a baby's, white and soft,
Yet kind consideration, at the back,
Can fear a kiss will bruise and turn it black:
Go to her, rogues, and show her all the signs
Where in my face a foolish angel shines.

334. Leaves

Peace to these little broken leaves,
    That strew our common ground;
That chase their tails, like silly dogs,
    As they go round and round.
For though in winter boughs are bare,
    Let us not once forget
Their summer glory, when these leaves
    Caught the great Sun in their strong net;
And made him, in the lower air,
    Tremble – no bigger than a star!

335. At Night

One night I heard a small, weak voice,
    Born into a silent, sleeping world:
Was it a new-born baby, or
    A new-born lamb, a minute old?

But when I saw the sky was one
    Big loaded orchard of bright lights,
I almost cried like that young child,
    For Earth, and all her little mites.

The silence of those mighty heavens,
  That infant's cry, so weak in power,
Made me half wish that Day had brought
  Her sparrow with his common flower.

336. The Pond

So innocent, so quiet – yet
  That glitter in the water's eye
Has some strange meaning there, I fear;
  Did waves run wild and butt this bank
With their curled horns, when it happened here?

Beneath these heart-shaped lily-leaves,
  In water, lies a broken heart:
And one white lily in this place –
  In this deep, silent, leaf-bound pond –
Is that dead woman's upturned face.

337. See Where Young Love

See where Young Love sits all alone,
  And sucks his thumb, and broods:
And all because you women have
  These ever-changing moods.

See how he sits in this cold air,
  That has the breath of tears:
Waiting until your mood has changed,
  And one round drop appears.

Till one round trembling tear-drop leaps
  From the corner of your eyes –
To show your mood has changed again,
  And tears have made you wise.

338. A Miracle

Let women long for dainty things,
  Expecting twins – content am I:
I want no more, no more than the sea
  Wants water, that was never dry.
The ale was strong, and I had three,
  Three glasses only, on my soul!
I *could* have walked home straight, but still
  Preferred a proud, Atlantic roll.

'Those stars in Heaven are frisking lambs,
  Not flocks of steady sheep,' I think;
'Poets who call them flocks of sheep,
  Are fools, or either lie or drink.'
As I said this, the earth broke up,
  And danced in parts, like living things;
Till, falling on their backs, I twirled
  Around and around, in countless rings.

The worm may turn, it matters not,
  It helps the bird, and nothing more:
I turned and turned, but still those parts
  Danced faster than they did before.
Till, rolled and rocked to sleep at last,
  I lost, it seems, my senses nine:
The sun stood still, in Joshua's day,
  But how the earth has danced, in mine!

339. The Rivals

Pleasure is not the one I love:
  Her laughter in the market-place
Makes every fool her echo there;
  And from her finger-tips she throws
Wild kisses in the open air.

Give me that little miser, Joy,
  Who hoards at home her quiet charms;
And offers with her two soft lips
  A warmer kiss than any thrown
By Pleasure, from her finger-tips.

340. Earth Love

I love the earth through my two eyes,
  Like any butterfly or bee;
The hidden roots escape my thoughts,
  I love but what I see.

A tree has lovely limbs, I know,
  Both large and strong, down under earth;
But all my thoughts are in the boughs,
  That give the green leaves birth.

My friend, his thought goes deeper down,
  Beneath the roots, while mine's above:
He's thinking of a quiet place
  To sleep with his dead Love.

335

341. Love's Payment

All fish and fowl, all fruit, and all you drink,
   Lie at the bottom of my purse, and I
Demand at will two kisses for my one;
   This is my certain charge – I swear it by
Our honest cows, that turn those meadows white
With mushrooms, where they passed a summer's night

Whether it is the seal or silver fox,
   The sable, silk, or plain white calico –
Two kisses for my one I charge at will,
   Since by my power these changes come and go:
I swear by sheep, that let the brambles pull,
In payment for their leaves, some soft white wool.

342. In Spring-Time

There's many a pool that holds a cloud
   Deep down for miles, to float along;
There's many a hedge that's white with may,
   To bring the backward birds to song;
There's many a country lane that smells
   Of beanfields, through the night and day:
Then why should I be here this hour,
   In Spring-time, when the month is May?

There's nothing else but stone I see
   With but this ribbon of a sky;
And not a garden big enough
   To share it with a butterfly.

Why do I walk these dull dark streets,
  In gloom and silence, all day long –
In Spring-time, when the blackbird's day
  Is four and twenty hours of song?

343. My Garden

The lilac in my garden comes to bloom,
  The apple, plum and cherry wait their hour,
The honeysuckle climbs from pole to pole –
  And the rockery has a stone that's now a flower,
Jewelled by moss in every tiny hole!

Close to my lilac there's a small bird's nest
  Of quiet, young, half-sleeping birds: but when
I look, each little rascal – five I've reckoned –
  Opens a mouth so large and greedy then,
He swallows his own face in half a second!

344. The Schemes of Love

Sleeping in some green bower, and wrapped
In wool for twenty breathless years –
Was that the way your beauty kept?
You're but a dribbling baby yet,
My cuckoo-flower with the soft moist mouth –
Your kisses always leave me wet.
If Love had time I would not rest
Until I reached your heart at last,
And kissed a tunnel through your breast!
But Life's too short for Love's long dreams –

337

How many ages would we need
To reach the end of one of his schemes?
Disturbed in life, from morn till night,
We pass away like butterflies,
That snatch their kisses in their flight.

345. The Meadow

Leafy with little clouds, the sky
   Is shining clear and bright.
How the grass shines – it stains the air
   Green over its own height!
And I could almost kneel for joy,
   To see this lovely meadow now:
Go on my knees for half a day,
   To kiss a handful here and there,
While babbling nonsense on the way.

346. Cant

What cant, oh, what hypocrisy
   Is centred in this life of man!
Self-preservation is his God,
And has been, since his life began.
He sits to breakfast with no care
   Of others that have none;
He keeps more idle rooms than two,
   While *families* live in one;
He saves his gold, and yet he sees
   Others without a penny;
He hoards his clothes, and knows full well
   Of children without any.

He makes his own sweet life secure,
    And then – to crown all this –
Insults a God by thinking he'll
    Get everlasting bliss!

347. The Trick

No answer, yet I called her name,
I shook her, but no motion came,
    She showed no signs of having breath;
When, in my fear, the light was sought,
The hussy laughed: 'Is this,' I thought –
    'Some strange convulsion after death?'

I could have murdered her that hour,
To think that she had used such power
    In making me betray a love
Secret and vast, and still unknown;
A love half-dreamt, till life is done,
    And only Death himself can prove.

348. Breath

How those wet tombstones in the sun
    Are breathing silently together!
Their breath is seen, as though they lived,
    Like sheep, when out in frosty weather.
The dead beneath, that once could breathe,
    Are nothing now but breathless bones;
And is this breath the same as theirs,
    Now coming from their own tombstones?

So, when the end has come at last,
   And we're consigned to cold damp earth,
Our tombstones in the sun will show,
   By their vain breath, what ours was worth.

349. The Cave

Once, in that cave, I heard my breath:
I heard my breath, as cowards do,
And guilty men; or misers, when
They sort their old coins from the new.
Tread softly there: in there a sigh
Has left a heavy groan behind;
Each whisper turns to thunder, and
A whistle to a gale of wind;
Hold tight your breath, nor cry for help
Where, though you perish, none may come:
And softly creep, before you're crazed,
Back to the open light and home.

350. The World Approves

The shade and colour of her eyes can wait,
It is the light of love that matters there;
But the spider's threads that catch the morning's pearls,
All for the Sun, could make no finer hair.

Our milk-fed kitten has no warmer skin,
My neighbour's pigeon has no softer voice;
Our black-mouthed puppy has no whiter teeth –
And the world approves of Dinah and my choice.

340

351. Down Underground

What work is going on down underground,
Without a sound – without the faintest sound!
The worms have found the place where Beauty lies,
And, entering into her two sparkling eyes,
Have dug their diamonds up; her soft breasts that
Had roses without thorns, are now laid flat;
They find a nest more comfortable there,
Than any bird could make, in her long hair;
Where they can teach their young, from thread to
    thread,
To leap on her white body, from her head.
This work is going on down underground,
Without a sound – without the faintest sound.

352. The Fear

Oft have I thought the Muse was dead,
    Nor dreamed she ever needed sleep;
And as a mother, when she sees
    Her child in slumber deep,
Wakes it, to see one sign of breath –
So did I think of my love's death.

Sleep, sleep, my love, and wake again,
    And sing the sweeter for your rest;
I am too wise a parent now
    To think each sleep the last –
That you are dead for ever, love,
Each time you sleep and do not move.

353. The Fates

When I was lying sick in bed
The Fates said, 'Come, we'll have some sport
   Your mother's life,' they said, 'is done:
You have no strength in hand or foot,
   And she is calling for her son.'

A second blow struck down my love,
   And she was taken from my side –
   The one who watched me night and day;
And strangers came and offered help,
   But all their love was talk of pay.

And then the Fates struck out again:
They filled these strangers with distrust,
   That I had done my love some wrong:
'Ah, cruel Fates,' thought I, 'you lose,
   For now you make my spirit strong.'

354. The Two Stars

Day has her star, as well as Night,
   One star is black, the other white.
I saw a white star burn and pant
   And swirl with such a wildness, once –
That I stood still, and almost stared
   Myself into a trance!
The star of Day, both seen and heard
Is but a little, English bird;
The Lark, whose wings beat time to his
   Wild rapture, sings, high overhead;
When silence comes, we almost fear
   That Earth receives its dead.

355. The Rabbit

Not even when the early birds
Danced on my roof with showery feet
Such music as will come from rain –
Not even then could I forget
The rabbit in his hours of pain;
Where, lying in an iron trap,
He cries all through the deafened night –
Until his smiling murderer comes,
To kill him in the morning light.

356. To a Lady Friend

Since you have turned unkind,
  Then let the truth be known:
We poets give our praise
  To any weed or stone,
Or sulking bird that in
  The cold, sharp wind is dumb;
To this, or that, or you –
  Whatever's first to come.

You came my way the first,
  When the life-force in my blood –
Coming from none knows where –
  Had reached its highest flood;
A time when any thing,
  No matter old or new,
Could bring my song to birth –
  Sticks, bones or rags, or you!

343

357. The Two Heavens

When, with my window opened wide at night,
To look at yonder stars with their round light,
In motion shining beautiful and clear –
As I look up, there comes this sudden fear:
That, down on earth, too dark for me to see,
Some homeless wretch looks up in misery;
And, like a man that's guilty of a sin,
I close my blinds, and draw my body in.
Still thinking of that Heaven, I dare not take
Another look, because of that man's sake;
Who in the darkness, with his mournful eyes
Has made *my* lighted home his paradise.

358. The Doll

Dinah is young, and I am old;
She takes two cushions to attack
Me, and her kisses close my eyes;
She combs my hair, that still is black.
Ah, my poor child, you do not know
The state of your live doll;
When you are gone out shopping, he
Sits thinking of it all.
The cushion-fights will soon be done,
He'll need a pillow for his head;
And fingers, not your kisses, love,
Must close his eyes, when he lies dead.
You'll not sit laughing on his knee
To comb his hair when white as snow,
Or when a few thin hairs remain
Of all its tangled blackness now.

Blinded by his young spirit, you
Can see no signs that he must die:
Your doll, my child, will make of you
A serious woman, by and by.

359. The Snowflake

When we are young and wake from sleep,
　What pillow-fights we share with Life!
We laugh and punch, and never dream
　How Death can end that joyful strife.

We'll not let Time destroy that dream,
　But in old age our spirit brave
Shall, like a snowflake in its fall,
　Dance while it hovers o'er the grave.

Contented men are still my theme,
　Who – though too poor for ivory keys –
Still whistle with their naked lips
　Their happy tunes of careless ease.

360. Secrets

Had I a secret plan by which,
　In pressing a small button, I
Could wreck this world entire – would not
　That button, with a snake's bright eye,
Flutter my bird-like finger down,
　Till I, bewitched and uncontrolled,
Must press with sudden impulse, and –
　Good-bye, my pretty world!

If Dinah knew how great my love is,
  My worship of her small white face,
Which deserts of grim silence hide,
  And many a waste of commonplace –
Would she not serve me some mad trick,
  To test my passion's utmost power,
And break that silent world of love
  In one weak foolish hour?

361. Our Longer Life

Some little creatures have so short a life
  That they are orphans born – but why should we
Be prouder of a life that gives more time
  To think of death through all eternity?

Time bears us off, as lightly as the wind
  Lifts up the smoke and carries it away;
And all we know is that a longer life
  Gives but more time to think of our decay.

We live till Beauty fails, and Passion dies,
  And Sleep's our one desire in every breath,
And in that strong desire our old love, Life,
  Gives place to that new love whose name is Death.

362. When Love is Young

I, who had eyes to wander here and there,
  No longer have my vision unconfined:
Love brings the first grave thoughts of majesty
  Into the free republic of my mind.

The time is grave with doubting of my power
  To serve her well, that she may always smile:
Love-at-first-sight is oft, as hundreds know,
  Made Love-lies-bleeding, in too short a while.

Some day I'll take love easy, as a child
  Will drink his mother's milk while half-asleep:
But when Love's young he's troubled – like Old Age –
  With breath that's short, that still no time can keep.

363. Dust

If Life is dust, is not dust Life?
We're walking on the backs of living things!
On things that live we sleep.
I kick a stone that – were its life released –
Could in its fury leap
Into my face and be a frantic beast.
What things lie sleeping all around,
That may awake at last
And, joining in our mortal strife,
Defend their rights as living dust!

364. Pity

Though you are gone and I am left alone,
With but this shadow by my body thrown,
And nothing more;
Though you are gone, and I am feeling poor,
Yet still the root is fed
Of my self-love, and but the leaves are dead.

347

But if, when I am old, and in the street
With a new love that's young, we three should meet;
And she should say,
'Who's that old hag that stares so hard this way?' –
What answer should she meet?
May I drop dead in pity at your feet!

365. The Joy of Life

How sweet is Life, how beautiful,
    When lying curled in innocent sleep!
Without one thought that, soon or late,
    Death will unbend that graceful curve
And stretch him out, all stiff and straight.

Go, happy Life, and say to Death –
    'I gave this man sufficient joy
To last him for a thousand years.'
    Then ask him why my time's as short
As one whose breath is full of tears.

366. Violet and Oak

Down through the trees is my green walk:
It is so narrow there and dark
That all the end, that's seen afar,
Is a dot of daylight, like a star.
When I had walked half-way or more,
I saw a pretty, small, blue flower;
And, looking closer, I espied
A small green stranger at her side.

If that flower's sweetheart lives to die
A natural death, thought I –
What will have happened by then
To a world of ever restless men?
'My little new-born oak,' I said,
'If my soul lives when I am dead,
I'll have an hour or more with you
Five hundred years from now!
When your straight back's so strong that though
Your leaves were lead on every bough,
It would not break – I'll think of you
When, weak and small, your sweetheart was
A little violet in the grass.'

367. Evil

How often in my dreams have I beheld
   An enemy with a grinning, loathsome face;
And then, before the dream is over, lo!
   A smiling friend has taken that enemy's place.

So, when unkindness comes my way, I think
   Of an enemy first; but in the end
It follows, two to one, the secret blow
   Is struck by one who calls himself my friend!

Call me a Nature poet, nothing more,
   Who writes of simple things, not human evil;
And hear my grief when I confess that friends
   Have tried their best to make a cunning devil!

368. A is for Artist

See what a light is in those painted clouds!
Surely the man's immortal, who has wrought
This lovely picture with his hand and brain!
But at this thought
The glorious Sun in Heaven
Burst through a window-pane, and caught
The fringes of those clouds with such a light
That I fell back amazed –
To see that man
Made so much less immortal in my sight!

369. B is for Beauty

My girl has reached that lovely state
    That's half a bud and half a flower;
But I am near my berry time,
    Outnumbering her by many an hour.
Yet Love – who sometimes raises kings
    To the level of our common race –
Can see no difference in our state,
    In look, in word or grace.

The Moon to her has life and power –
    It is the Earth's white ghost to me ;
Which tells the Earth of its decay,
    And mine, which Love's too blind to see.
Love her, my heart, that she may give
    My ghost this praise she gives the Moon:
Let not her shudder when she sees
    It thin away so soon.

370. C is for Child

See how her arms now rise and fall,
    See how, like wings, they beat the air:
An arm to balance either foot,
    She moves, half-fluttering, here and there.

And still those motions will suggest
    A different life that's left behind
In early days, remote and strange;
    Felt in that little unformed mind
For one short season, after birth –
Before her feet are claimed by Earth

371. D is for Dog

My dog went mad and bit my hand,
    I was bitten to the bone:
My wife went walking out with him,
    And then came back alone.

I smoked my pipe, I nursed my wound,
    I saw them both depart:
But when my wife came back alone,
    I was bitten to the heart.

372. E is for Eyes

I need no glass to help my eyes,
    My naked sight shows no decline;
A rich blind man would give his all
    For one of these two jewels of mine.

But I'd give any poor blind man
  One of these precious jewels free –
Could he restore the inward sight
  That Time is taking away from me.

373. F is for Fiddles

What an enchanted world is this,
  What music I have heard: And when
I hear these Master fiddlers play,
  I ask – 'Are these not marvellous men?'
So, since such men command the sweetest sounds,
  I'll have no fear to leave my solitude
Of woods and fields,
  And join the human multitude;
To hear a Master's hand express
The very soul and tenderness
  Heard when a pigeon's cooing there;
To hear him make the robin sob again,
  In Autumn, when the trees go bare;
Till – touching one lamb-bleating string –
We leap the Winter into Spring.

374. G is for Garden

I'll have the primrose grow in grass,
Held up in hands of soft, green moss.
If in twelve months no green moss grows
On that dark stone, then out it goes.
Above my window-top there'll be
A creeper that grows wild and free;

Until so many leaves have grown,
They'll make a curtain half-way down.
In that round corner place shall grow
A holly tree, for Winter's snow;
There shall the Robin Redbreast sing,
Till snow – that feathers everything
That has no life-blood pulsing through –
Would feather his warm feathers too!
This lime, now old, I'll slowly kill
With creeper-sucker leaves; until
The leaves that grow around its bole,
Makes it a child all beautiful –
When with her naked knee that's brown,
She stands with half her stocking down.
A lovelier death no man shall see –
Than seen in my half-strangled tree.

375. H is for Hedge

I climb a tree to bring them down –
 The yellow eyes of my black kitten ;
The laurel hedge that's left behind –
 Whose shoulders measure three feet wide –
Is swaying lightly in the wind.

But when I looked from my high place,
 With my black kitten safely tucked
From danger, under my left arm –
 I saw that laurel's thick, broad back
Was wriggling like the thinnest worm.

376. I is for Implements

What lovely dark blue flames, O Spade,
    Shine in thy steel so bright:
See how the shadows smoke and play;
    How thou hast laboured, year by year,
To reach this silver day.

But thou, poor shining Sword, must wait
    Till sloth and idleness
Can tell the world that splendid story:
    Nothing but rust, a bloodless rust,
Shall cover *thee* with glory.

377. J is for Jealousy

I praised the daisies on my lawn,
And then my lady mowed them down.
My garden stones, improved by moss,
She moved – and that was Beauty's loss.
When I adored the sunlight, she
Kept a bright fire indoors for me.
She saw I loved the birds, and that
Made her one day bring home a cat.
She plucks my flowers to deck each room,
And make me follow where they bloom.
Because my friends were kind and many,
She said – 'What need has Love of any?'
What is my gain, and what my loss?
Fire without sun, stones bare of moss,
Daisies beheaded, one by one;
The birds cat-hunted, friends all gone –

These are my losses: yet, I swear,
A love less jealous in its care
Would not be worth the changing skin
That she and I are living in.

378. K is for Kings

Love's touch is soft, and Death
  Is gentle, when he takes
A sleeping child's light breath,
  Before it wakes;
But neither Death nor Love
Moves softer than I move.
Great is my ecstacy,
Till generous I
For common pence have sold
The world my purest gold.
No man that's blind
  Has ears more quick to hear;
No man that's deaf and dumb
  Has eyes more sharp and clear.
No wonder then that kings,
Envying the man who sings,
Aspire to wear his crown,
And scorn their own;
No wonder kings aspire
  For crowns not made of gold,
Which – though Time's born a thief –
  Escape his hold.
Two kings have won –
David and Solomon.

379. L is for Light

What lovely meadows have I seen in the Sun,
  With their large families of little flowers
Smiling beneath the quiet, peaceful skies!
  Let no man trespass on these happy hours,
And think acquaintance waits in my two eyes.

This glorious light that makes the butterfly
  Go staggering like a drunkard through the air,
Till he lies dazed and panting on a stone –
  This light I feel is both my light and fire,
And Love may bleed to death, till it has gone.

380. M is for Mother

It was a long, long time ago,
Since I was at my mother's knee –
Trying in vain on my tipped toe
To stand as tall as she could sit.
'Your cousin,' said my mother to me,
'Was the loveliest girl in Pontypool,
Or through the Rhondda Valley; still
The girls would look at her sweet face,
As though there were no boys; for she
Had heaps of hair which, when combed down,
Could be a coat, or half a gown.
Until one day when full of joy,
To hear my baby coo so well,
She tossed that hair, and its full weight
Breaking her slender neck – she fell.
Your cousin died – to end our story
Killed by a thing that was her glory.'

381. N is for Nature

Day after day I find some new delight:
  It was the grass that pressed upon my cheeks,
That had a touch as soft as Death's, when he
  Comes to a sleeping child that never wakes.

And now the wind and rain: it was the rain
  That made the wind reveal his breath at last;
But 'twas the wind that, travelling high and far,
  Furrowed the Heavens with clouds from East to
    West.

And when the night has come, perhaps the Moon,
  With her round face all shining clear and bright,
Will ride the dark, humped clouds with camels' backs –
  And end my day with that last new delight.

382. O is for Open

Are those small silver tumps a town,
  And are those dewdrops windows there;
Is that dark patch a hill or cloud,
  And which is Earth, and which is air?
Lord, when I see a world so vast,
  This large, bewildering stretch of land;
The far-off fields, the clumps of woods,
  The hills as thin as clouds beyond –
When I see this, I shrink in fear,
  That if I once but close my eye,
The ends will sink, and leave me dazed
  Before a monstrous, empty sky!

357

383. P is for Pool

I know a deep and lonely pool – that's where
  The great Kingfisher makes his sudden splash!
He has so many jewels in his plumes
  That all we see is one blue lightning flash.

But whether that fine bird comes there or no,
  There I'll be found before the coming night –
Beside that dark, deep pool, on whose calm breast
  Sleep a young family of pools of light.

And near my pool an ancient abbey stands,
  Where I, when lying in the longest grass,
Can see the moonlight, tener, soft and fair,
  Clasped to the rugged breast of that black nurse.

384. Q is for Question

The man who tells me he has seen a ghost,
  He either lies, was drunk or full of fears;
But if by chance a ghost should come my way,
  This is my question, ready for his ears –
'What lies beyond this life I lead to-day?'

One night I dreamt I met a spirit man,
  But when I told that ghost what I would know,
He laughed 'Ha, ha! I knew what you would say;
  And that's the question I am asking now –
"What lies beyond this life I lead to-day!" '

385. R is for Remembrance

I have no memory of his face,
  A bearded man or smooth and bare;
I never heard my mother call
  My father either dark or fair.

All I remember is a coat
  Of velvet, buttoned on his breast;
Where I, when tired of fingering it,
  Would lay my childish head and rest.

His voice was low and seldom heard,
  His body small – I've heard it said ;
But his hoarse cough made children think
  Of monsters growling to be fed.

If any children took that road,
  And heard my father coughing near,
They whispered, 'Hist! Away, away –
  There's some big giant lives in there!'

386. S is for Swimmer

When I had crossed the hill at last,
  And reached the water's brink,
'For once, in all my life,' thought I –
  'I'll swim in water fit to drink.

'In this calm lake, so clear and pure,
  Which has no weeds or thorns,
I'll send a thousand small blue waves
  To butt the rocks with milk-white horns.

'I'll laugh and splash till, out of breath,
    My life is almost done;
And all that's left is one wild hand
    Above me, clutching at the Sun!'

387. T is for Time

You false church clock, whose long-drawn chimes
    Tell me Life moves like some slow snail –
The watch beneath my pillow beats
    So fast my breath doth almost fail.
Your solemn chime, that says I walk
    Sedately to my grave – doth lie;
I gallop faster to my doom
    Than any mortal bird can fly –
I gallop like a startled horse,
    That leaping flames and whirlwinds chase –
Until his eyes have left his head,
    And stretch beyond his frantic face.

388. U is for Union

If Time and Nature serve us both alike,
    I shall be dead for years, when you are dying;
Remember then how much I loved the birds:
    That should you hear a gentle bird-voice crying
'Sweet! Sweet!' You'll know at once whose lover waits.
    I shall be there in all good time to show
The way that leads to a new life and home –
    Ere Death can freeze one finger-tip or toe.

But we'll have years together yet, I trust,
　　In this green world: how many sparrows came
To breakfast here this morning, with the frost
　　As plump as snow on window-sill and frame?

389. V is for Venus

Is that star dumb, or am I deaf?
　　Hour after hour I listen here
To catch the lovely music played
　　By Venus down the evening air.

Before the other stars come out,
　　Before the Moon is in her place –
I sit and watch those fingers move,
　　And mark the twitching of her face.

Hour after hour I strain my ears
　　For lovely notes that will not come:
Is it my mortal flesh that's deaf,
　　Or that long-fingered star that's dumb?

390. W is for Will

If I should die, this house is yours,
　　A little money too:
It's but a poor reward I make,
　　For all this care from you.

And though you take a second mate,
　　And think that man the best,
I would not change – if dead men could –
　　One word of this bequest.

Would that I could bequeath to you
  My joy in Earth and sky –
Worth more than gold or precious stones,
  To be remembered by.

391. X is for Expecting

Come, come, my Love, the morning waits,
What magic now shall greet our sight!
  What butterflies
  Before our eyes
Shall vanish in the open light!

Come, while the Sun has power to strike
Our household fires all dead and cold!
  How softly now
  The wind can blow –
When carrying off a field of gold!

Come, when behind some leafy hedge
We'll see a snow-white, new-born lamb
  No man has set
  His eyes on yet –
Where it lies sleeping near its dam.

Come, come, my Love, the morning waits,
The Sun is high, the dew has gone!
  The air's as bright
  As though the light
Of twelve May mornings came in one.

392. Y is for Youth

Would I had met you in my days of strength,
  Before my tide of life had turned, my Love;
These lightning streaks, that come in fitful starts,
  Are not the great forked lightnings you deserve;
Too many silver moons has my life worn
Into an old thin rim, since I was born.

What you deserve are those enchanted notes
  We sing in dreams at night; so pure and sweet
That kings and queens sit down with bended heads,
  And listen with their crowns laid at their feet:
Those songs that pass, without a voice on Earth,
And perish in the brain that gives them birth.

393. Z is for Zany

Why does a woman change her moods?
  That man may have no thought but hers,
When man has silent, unknown dreams,
  Oh, how it troubles her with fears:
Her words, what jealous fear they prove –
'A penny for your thoughts, my love.'

When I would think, she laughs and talks,
  That I shall know a woman's there;
She stops my hand, when it would write:
  I took her for my staff, but swear –
By every devil and every god –
This woman's love is now my rod!

394. The Rock

Love kissed me in a strange, untruthful hour,
   All for a smiling lip and shining eye;
Not knowing that my thoughts were far from her,
   Set on a wonder in the years gone by.
It was the vision of a mighty rock
   That faced the East, across Long Island Sound;
From which a hundred tongues of water burst,
   And sang me into slumber on the ground.
And how I, waking in the night-time, saw
   A large, white butterfly of moonlight clinging
To that rock's forehead, while each silver tongue
   Shook faster than a lamb's tail, in its singing.

395. The Poet

When I went down past Charing Cross,
   A plain and simple man was I;
I might have been no more than air,
   Unseen by any mortal eye.

But, Lord in Heaven, had I the power
   To show my inward spirit there,
Then what a pack of human hounds
   Had hunted me, to strip me bare.

A human pack, ten thousand strong,
   All in full cry to bring me down;
All greedy for my magic robe,
   All crazy for my burning crown.

364

396. A Lonely Coast

A lonely coast, where sea-gulls scream for wrecks
  That never come; its desolate sides
Last visited, a hundred years ago,
  By one drowned man who wandered with the tides:
There I went mad, and with those birds I screamed,
  Till, waking, found 'twas only what I dreamed.

397. The Perfect Life

Who knows the perfect life on earth?
  It lies beyond this mortal breath;
It is to give the same kind thoughts
  To Life as we bequeath to Death.

It is to show a steadfast love;
  As faithful to our friends that live
As our dead friends are to ourselves –
  Sealed up from gossip, in the grave.

But who can lead this saintly life,
  When friends are false and men unkind;
And every man will cheat a man
  Whose trust, like faith in God, is blind?

Hang this pale fool, Philosophy!
  Kind hearts obey themselves, no other:
Why like a saint can I take pain
  And not inflict it on another?

398. The Two Loves

I have two loves, and one is dark,
    The other fair as may be seen;
My dark love is Old London Town,
    My fair love is the Country green.

My fair love has a sweeter breath,
    A clearer face by day; and nights
So wild with stars that dazzled I
    See multitudes of *other* lights.

My dark love has her domes, as round
    As mushrooms in my fair love's meadows:
While both my loves have houses old,
    Whose windows look cross-eyed at shadows.

399. No-man's Wood

Shall I have jealous thoughts to nurse,
When I behold a rich man's house?
Not though his windows, thick as stars,
    Number the days in every year;
I, with one window for each month,
    Am rich in four or five to spare.

But when I count his shrubberies,
His fountains there, and clumps of trees,
Over the palings of his park
    I leap with my primeval blood;
Down wild ravines to Ocean's rocks,
    Clean through the heart of No-man's Wood.

400. Come Away, Death

Come away, Death, make no mistake,
　There's no one in that house to die;
She's young and strong, though suffering pain,
　And waits to hear her first-born's cry.

'Nay,' answered Death. 'there's no mistake,
　I've been to this same house before;
Though no one saw a corpse come out,
　Or any mourner at the door.

'I've been to this same house before,
　I know it well from any other:
And now I come again, to see
　A dead-born child destroy its mother.'

401. One Night, when I was Sleeping

One night, when I was sleeping all alone,
Close to a forest, far from any town,
Up with a cry I started – what was that
Which shook me here, as though I were a rat?
I met a black man in the morning light,
Who said – and fear had made him ashen white –
'Where were you when this earth of ours
Shook terribly in the early hours?'
And shall the Himalayas and the Alps
Wriggle like worms, when the Earth gulps
Half the Pacific in one breath?
Think of the death

Of countless people –
When the bells in each surviving steeple
Toll for the dead in every shaken land,
Without a touch from any mortal hand;
Until this Earth lies down again to rest,
And sleeps without a conscience in her breast.
Is not the fear of this sufficient then
That War must cease and Friendship come to men?

402. The Life of Man

All from his cradle to his grave,
Poor devil, man's a frightened fool;
His Mother talks of imps and ghosts,
His Master threatens him at school.
When half a man and half a boy,
The Law complains of his high blood;
And then the Parson threatens him
With hell, unless baptized for good.
Soon after, when a married man,
He fears the humours of his Spouse;
And, when a father, fears to spend
One shilling that his Babes might lose.
Then comes Old Age, Lumbago, Gout,
Rheumatic Pains that ache and sting:
All from his cradle to his grave,
Poor devil, man's a frightened thing.

403. Traffic

This life in London – what a waste
  Of time and comfort, in this place;
With all its noise, and nothing seen
  But what is stone or human face.
Twigs thin and bare, like sparrows' legs.
  Yet back to Nature I must go –
To see the thin, mosquito flakes
  Grow into moths of plumper snow.

What is this life, if, like bad clocks,
  We keep no time and are but going;
What is my breath worth when I hear
  A hundred horns and whistles blowing;
The rushing cars that crunch their way,
  Still followed by the heavy carts;
Till I, with all my senses stunned,
  Am deafened to my very thoughts?

404. The Bust

When I went wandering far from home,
I left a woman in my room
To clean my hearth and floor, and dust
My shelves and pictures, books and bust.

When I came back a welcome glow
Burned in her eyes – her voice was low;
And everything was in its place,
As clean and bright as her own face.

369

But when I looked more closely there,
The dust was on my dark, bronze hair;
The nose and eyebrows too were white –
And yet the lips were clean and bright.

The years have gone, and so has she,
But still the truth remains with me –
How that hard mouth was once kept clean
By living lips that kissed unseen.

405. How Sordid is this Crowded Life

How sordid is this crowded life, its spite
And envy, the unkindness brought to light:
It makes me think of those great modest hearts
That spend their quiet lives in lonely parts,
In deserts, hills and woods; and pass away
Judged by a few, or none, from day to day.
And O that I were free enough to dwell
In their great spaces for a while; until
The dream-like life of such a solitude
Has forced my tongue to cry 'Hallo!' aloud –
To make an echo from the silence give
My voice back with the knowledge that I live.

406. The Treasured Three

Here with my treasured Three I sit,
    Here in my little house of joy,
Sharing one fire, and on one mat:
    My wife and my dog, Beauty Boy,
And my black Venus of a cat.

But while they sleep I sit and think;
    Will Death take my black Venus first;
Shall I be first, or Beauty Boy,
    Or Dinah, whom I love the most –
To leave this little house of joy?

407. The Song of Love

I

The oak bears little acorns, yet
    Is big in branch and root:
My love is like the smaller tree,
    That bears a larger fruit.

II

In Spring, when it is leafing time,
    We know what plants will live;
But love need never wait for Spring,
    To show its power to thrive.

III

Trouble may come, yet love will stay:
    No heavy rain can beat
The lightning down and out – and birds
    Wet through sing twice as sweet.

IV

Love is a staff, and Love's a rod,
    A wise man and a fool;
I thought that I was wise, until
    Love sent me back to school.

Scorn not because my body lives
  In such a little place;
Think how my mind, on that account,
  Inhabits greater space.

My smallest blossom sometimes is
  The Moon or setting Sun;
Seas are my pearls, and forests vast
  Have no more trees than one!

The finest scarf or collar made,
  To keep a woman warm,
By night or day, on sea or land,
  Is still a lover's arm.

Last night I dreamt that Dinah's ghost
  Was standing near my bed:
What brings you here this hour of the night,
  Picking your cheek? I said.

She picked her cheek with her right hand,
  Then held her arm out firm:
She made my hand a present then
  Of a tiny little worm.

X

Lie here, I said, my poor dead love,
  I'll not live many hours;
And take my word that I'll return
  A worm of mine for yours.

XI

I thought when I was thirty years,
  My marrying time had come;
But in that year the girl I love
  Was in her mother's womb.

XII

But when she brought her twenty years
  To my two score and ten,
I heard a cuckoo in a place
  It never charmed till then.

XIII

Time, my love said, is sprinkling his
  White jewels in my hair;
To join like dewdrops soon, and make
  One big white diamond there!

XIV

So let her still praise Age and Time,
  The more our years are told,
And say a garden's beauty's grown
  The more as it grows old.

Six months in friendship, side by side,
  Like blades of grass we grew;
Love pinned us then together with
  One diamond of his dew.

Since then our love has vaster grown,
  Far up the branches reach;
Our smallest twigs as big as trunks
  Of full-grown oak or beech.

And though my years outnumber hers
  By thirty years all told,
My healthy fear of Death remains
  To prove I am not old.

Who can deserve a dog's pure love,
  Which any villain can have?
One of the richest things on earth
  Goes cheap to any knave.

My dog and I are waiting now,
  His love is safe at least;
But never think my love can be shamed
  By the love of my beast.

XX

Let's marry soon, and live no more
   Like disappointed flowers
Whose heads are wet, but not their feet –
   When mocked by passing showers.

XXI

Where shall we live, in some green vale,
   Or on a hill that's high?
Sometimes a hill and wood are one,
   With tree-tops in the sky.

XXII

And should we live in London town
   Shall we by chance not meet
Two horses with a load of hay,
   Sweetening a crowded street?

XXIII

A sight as fair as when the Sun
   Is burning on a pool,
And, standing on their heads in water,
   The ducks keep calm and cool.

XXIV

When I was rich without a care,
   And lived with wandering men –
My belly spread across my back
   Was all my bed-clothes then.

375

XXV

But when I say a house is mine,
  The tax-collectors come
To show a man is poor indeed,
  Who keeps a little home.

XXVI

I'll go into the country now
  And find a little house;
And though its eyes are small, they shall
  Have heavy, leafy brows.

XXVII

A house with curtains made of leaves,
  Hanging from every stone;
I'll pass before the windows oft,
  And it shall not be known

XXVIII

I'll have a garden full of flowers,
  With many a corner-place;
Where love can learn from spiders' webs
  To make her mats of lace.

XXIX

When I am at one end of the garden
  And she at the other end,
I'll see the Sun's bright face and hers
  Into each other blend.

XXX

Until her face alone is seen,
    And nothing she has on;
I'll see her shining face, with no
    More body than the Sun.

XXXI

We'll sit in our garden, with a joy
    That's great enough to give
The Sun our pity with his poor
    Few million years to live.

XXXII

We'll keep a pool where under leaves
    The fish swim out and in;
Sometimes we'll see a breast of gold,
    Sometimes a silver fin.

XXXIII

And though I scorn a painted skin,
    Think not my tongue could scold her,
Should such fair things as butterflies
    Encourage her to powder.

XXXIV

And if, when I've been out with some
    Bass-singing, belted bee,
I take a drink or two myself –
    Will she not pardon me?

377

XXXV

One time I thought it was my brain
    That made the songs I sing;
But now I know it is a heart
    That loveth every thing.

XXXVI

And while his heart's blood feeds his brain,
    To keep it warm and young,
A man can live a hundred years,
    And day break into song.

XXXVII

How sad it is when Age has lost
    Imagination's power,
And with a feeble, active tongue
    Can jest of his last hour.

XXXVIII

But when I hear no birds in song,
    And beauty there is none,
That is the hour when Death can strike –
    With all my wonder gone.

XXXIX

The hour I hear a nightingale,
    Or see a dragonfly,
Shall not be my last hour on earth –
    For then I cannot die.

XL

My love grows large when I behold
  A blossom sucked by a bee ;
Or leaves with sails of butterflies,
  Floating like ships at sea.

XLI

So will my love increase when I
  Can cast some kindly light
Of human thought on matter dead,
  That's lovely to my sight.

XLII

Our life is dust, and dust is life:
  When I am heavy and sigh,
A paper rag that rides the wind
  Is greater far than I.

XLIII

I pass through life a laughing man,
  Untouched by any sin:
Death makes us all, both king and fool,
  Lie down at last to grin.

XLIV

And who can tell, when stripped by Death,
  A monarch from his clown;
Who knows which head has worn the bells,
  And which has worn the crown?

379

XLV

Day after day, and night by night,
    The silly game is fought:
Life makes a question mark, and Death
    Answers it with a nought.

XLVI

No matter what we say or do,
    Or what it's all about,
There's that lean fellow, Death, behind,
    Waiting to blot it out.

XLVII

Is Death a mask that Life puts on
    To curb our foolish laughter;
And shall our spirits, living still,
    Enjoy the jest hereafter?

XLVIII

Is Death's dark tunnel endless night
    Where, entering, none can choose;
Or is a greater light to come
    Beyond the light we lose?

XLIX

Answer, you poets, one and all,
    Answer us from the Height;
Speak from your Many-jewelled Mountain
    Are we wrong or right?

L

But the more I question things unknown
  The more my mind is lost;
My voice is Echo's echo, and
  My life a Shadow's ghost.

LI

For while I speak the thunder growls;
  My dog, without a whine,
Barks fiercely back, and proves his voice
  To be as vain as mine.

LII

When as a little boy I saw
  The water break and stir,
I wondered what mysterious life
  Had brought those bubbles there.

LIII

Now as a man full-grown and strong,
  And known to many men,
I watch those bubbles still, and know
  No more than I did then.

LIV

Is there a God, I ask, and smoke –
  But fear, with reverence,
To foul the Face of a God with smoke
  And a mortal's arrogance.

381

LV

My pipe goes out, I sit in thought,
    A humble man and sad:
And then a voice within me says –
    You have done well, my lad.

LVI

The great broad rivers, miles in width,
    Are for the world to roam;
But little streams, for paddling feet,
    Whisper of Heaven and home.

LVII

Could we survive the breathless leap
    That brought her door to mine,
I would not care if a whirlwind made
    Our houses toe one line.

LVIII

I would not care if an earthquake came
    And opened its mouth wide,
If when it closed and shrunk the earth,
    It brought her to my side.

LIX

When deer and tigers flee from fire,
    Which is the master then?
Love shares the power with Fear to bring
    Equality to men.

LX

The king who would not rather see
　His queen without a crown,
Is but a king, and less a man
　Than any lover in town.

LXI

Who is this creature that has come
　Between her life and mine?
I saw the look she gave my love,
　And took it for a sign.

LXII

I saw the hard and cruel look,
　To wither, dry and wilt:
Where were her adder-bracelets then,
　And deadly scorpion-belt?

LXIII

We'll not make Jealousy our foe,
　A hound to track us down;
That sleepless hound, with bloodshot eyes,
　Shall be to us unknown.

LXIV

Give Jealousy his shadows, let
　Him still gnaw lifeless stones,
And in his wild delirium think
　He works on meaty bones.

383

LXV

All other women that I know,
    I'll look on them as men;
She'll look on other men as women –
    There'll be no trouble then.

LXVI

My rival has a pleasant wife,
    But who has heard her name?
Let him praise his, as I'll praise mine,
    And leave the rest to Fame.

LXVII

See how my horse can fret and stamp
    To pass a bird in flight:
My rival's horse is stamping too –
    To shake off fleas that bite.

LXVIII

A donkey's gallop, rare and short,
    Gives joy to all that see't:
My rival's horse gives joy to none –
    Except its own vain poet.

LXIX

Would that some power would turn all things
    To mirrors that reflect him;
To haunt him with his own vain face,
    Till later days neglect him.

LXX

If our contented hearts are blind
　　To what the world calls great,
How can that world, whose pride is wealth,
　　Look down on our low state?

LXXI

The thing we call a truth to-day
　　Is but to-morrow's lie;
We change our minds, our bodies change,
　　Until we come to die.

LXXII

To-day I swear that music's best,
　　To-morrow swear by books;
If there's one truth that stays unchanged,
　　It's Love, and how she looks.

LXXIII

The story of my love shall be,
　　When I am one with Her,
Far richer than a Blackbird's yarn
　　In merry April's ear.

LXXIV

I praise the Blackbird's golden bill
　　Because of his golden song:
Were Love less kind than she is fair,
　　The devil could take my song.

385

LXXV

When she, poor bird, is croaking hoarse
    After her glorious June,
The Nightingale shall wonder much
    To hear my love in tune.

LXXVI

Skylarks sing well for meadows green,
    But for ploughed land sing sweeter:
When I was single I sang well,
    But married men sing better.

LXXVII

When rats bite rats and snakes bite snakes,
    They seldom die from harm:
Could Dinah live if one of these
    Should bite her leg or arm?

LXXVIII

We'll live beyond our fellow's reach,
    From gossip, slander, strife,
And leave those human rats and snakes
    To their own poisoned life.

LXXIX

So when my foe, who knows far less
    Than He who knows all life,
Has taken a mistress from my side,
    God gives me a good wife.

LXXX

A fool without experience, poor,
  Began one day to think
How rich he'd be with scores of friends –
  And wrote that down in ink.

LXXXI

A rich man said, with scores of friends,
  Who wisely understood,
'How poor am I with these false friends!'
  And wrote that down in blood.

LXXXII

I met a lonely man who had
  No friend, no child, no wife:
O what a wretched thing, said I,
  Is this poor mortal's life!

LXXXIII

But when I met a poorer man,
  With neither friend nor foe,
This man is doubly damned, said I –
  With twice the other's woe.

LXXXIV

But Love has saved me from that state,
  I shall not live alone,
A weak, unloved, unhated thing,
  Unnoticed and unknown.

LXXXV

Though we are two are we not one?
  Aye, even as that Pair
Of scissors, which we hold in turns,
  To cut each other's hair.

LXXXVI

One – like our Pair of household tongs,
  There with his crookèd thighs,
His long thin legs, his little head
  With neither mouth nor eyes.

LXXXVII

My love is fair, but fairer still
  With eyes a little wild,
When she forgets how fair she is,
  And wonders like a child.

LXXXVIII

Let not her face be doted on
  Too much by stranger men,
For when her back is turned their eyes
  Dart on her ankles then.

LXXXIX

When flies are old and going blind,
  They bite all things they touch:
But never think that Age or Time
  Will trouble Love so much.

XC

And when a Spider damns the dew
  For pearls on every string,
My Love will clap her hands, and say –
  'Look at this lovely thing!'

XCI

I've seen six bees together kiss
  A Sunflower's golden face;
But still she turns towards the Sun,
  And follows face to face.

XCII

So, thinking of my greater love,
  I live on her good looks;
And give my second thoughts, not first,
  To music, verse, or books.

XCIII

The kiss of Love is half a bite,
  And worth a thousand others;
Girls who have no desire for that
  Should never leave their mothers.

XCIV

Should she complain no kiss of mine
  Has left one little bite,
I'll let her take a needle and thread
  And sew my mouth up tight.

XCV

If cheek or chin of hers can say
    It never felt one nip,
I'll let her take a packet of pins
    And pin me lip to lip.

XCVI

In Winter, when the evergreens
    Have seen their plumpness go;
When all the little holly leaves
    Wear padded gloves of snow –

XCVII

We'll pay the birds for their past songs,
    In bread that's white and new:
Jack Frost, the finest artist known,
    Shall be the kindest, too.

XCVIII

Her birthday comes, and I will buy
    A pair of buckled shoes;
With two silk stockings cradled there,
    Between the heels and toes.

XCIX

Her right leg's stocking shall contain
    A comb to dress her hair;
In her left stocking she shall find
    A silver thimble there.

See how my hands stretch out to take
  The hand of Her I love:
Did Noah make more haste when he
  Reached out to take God's Dove?

408. The Time of Dreams

What sweet, what happy days had I,
When dreams made Time Eternity!
Before I knew this body's breath
Could not take life in without death.
As fresh as any field of grass
This breath of life was, then; it was
An orchard with more fruit than leaf,
And every owl enjoyed his grief.
No Winter's morn, when I went forth,
Could force on me a sunless North;
When I would watch the bees for hours
Clinging to their love-bitten flowers;
And, dreaming to the songs of birds,
Would still delay my deeds and words;
And every common day could place
A shining Sunday in my face.
O for my greater days to come,
When I shall travel far from home!
On seas that have no shade in sight,
Into the woods that have no light;
Over the mountains' heads so tall,
Cut by the clouds to pieces small;
Across wide plains that give my eye
No house or tree to measure them by.

And all the wonders I shall see
In some old city new to me;
Haunting the ships and docks, and then
To hear the strange, sea-faring men
That with their broken English prove
More lands than one to roam and love.
What sweet, what happy days had I –
When dreams made Time Eternity!

409. Frost

What swords and spears, what daggers bright
He arms the morning with! How light
His powder is, that's fit to lie
On the wings of a butterfly!
What milk-white clothing he has made
For every little twig and blade!
What curious silver work is shown
On wood and iron, glass and stone!
'If you, my slim Jack Frost, can trace
This work so fine, so full of grace,
Tell me,' I said, 'before I go –
Where is your plump young sister, Snow?'

410. Mad

When she was but a little child,
    And only two feet high,
She clapped her hands and cried, 'Shoo, Shoo!'
    To make the small birds fly;
Till with her mouth as sweet as a bee's,
Her laughter shook the old folks' knees.

But no one laughs when this small child,
    Grown to a woman soon,
Claps her two hands and tries to shoo
    Away the stars and moon;
As though one star should leave its place,
Even for her afflicted face.

411. One by One

Few are my friends,
    But kind and true;
One by one,
    I lose my few.

Again a friend
    Must leave this world;
One by one,
    His limbs go cold.

Before the Sun
    Has left yon wall,
One by one
    The blinds will fall.

My visits change
    From house to tomb:
One by one
    My friends leave home.

412. Hill and Vale

Day by day the man in the vale
    Enjoyed his neighbour's hill above;
Day by day the man on the hill
    Looked down his neighbour's vale with love.

If either one would see how fair
    Was his own home, at any hour,
He, walking up the hill or down,
    Enjoyed it from his neighbour's door.

So, down the vale and up the hill,
    These neighbours travelled, to and fro;
One man to see his own green hill,
    And one to see his vale below.

413. The White Horse

What do I stare at – not the colt
    That frisks in yon green field; so strong
That he can leap about and run,
    Yet is too weak to stand up straight
When his mother licks him with her tongue.

No, no, my eyes go far beyond,
    Across that field to yon far hill,
Where one white horse stands there alone;
    And nothing else is white to see,
Outside a house all dark and still.

394

'Death, are you in that house?' think I –
  'Is that horse there on your account?
Can I expect a shadow soon,
  Seen in that horse's ghostly ribs –
When you come up behind, to mount?'

414. The Mask

When I complained of April's day,
  Her silent birds, her absent Sun;
And how her mist but added tears
  Unto the dew's, that had not gone –

Young April heard and, suddenly,
  Came leaping from her strange disguise;
Off came her dark-November mask,
  And showed the world her laughing eyes.

415. Giants

I take no pride in body's growth
Nor in my strength of mind,
Nor should my life exceed in both.
For only he whose heart is kind
And gentle enough to laugh and play
At snowballs in a fairy's game –
Deserves a giant's name.

416. Advice

Now, you two eyes, that have all night been sleeping,
Come into the meadows, where the lambs are leaping;
See how they start at every swallow's shadow
That darts across their faces and their meadow.
See how the blades spring upright, when the Sun
Takes off the weight of raindrops, one by one.
See how a shower, that freshened leaves of grass,
Can make that bird's voice fresher than it was.
See how the squirrels lash the quiet trees
Into a tempest, where there is no breeze!
Now, you two eyes, that have all night been sleeping,
Come into the meadows, where the lambs are leaping.

417. The Spoiler

When I put out my thoughts to grass
    Among the horses, sheep and cows,
And let them run with squirrels, when
    They raise a storm in leafy boughs;
When I had dreams of pools and lakes,
    The Earth's bright eyes that never close –
There came a man to fill my mind
    With all about our dry old laws.

To spoil my dreams of little buds
    That smile in March's troubled face;
Of woodnuts, mostly born in twins,
    Among the leaves that interlace;
Of babies wearing on each wrist
    Bracelets of fat; and toddlers small,
That work their arms, like wings, to fly –
    The moment they begin to fall !

396

418. Storms

She fears not me —
  Neither my thunder,
Nor my lightning, startles her
  To make surrender.

But when my friend
  In Heaven makes thunder,
Her spirit breaks, and turns
  To fear and wonder.

Lightning and thunder,
  Give her no rest:
Bring her head back again,
  Back to my breast.

419. Property

A dog has bones to spare and hide,
  Squirrels have nuts in plenty:
Though I own houses, Lord, and work,
  Yet still my purse is empty.

A poet with five houses, Lord,
  Though but a common sinner,
Should at the least expect in rent
  A shilling for his dinner.

But though my houses, Lord, are hens
  That lay no eggs for me,
Thou knowest well they never fail
  To lay for my Trustee.

Lord, since Thy bounty is for all,
  Shall my Trustee, John White,
Be eaten alive by fleas before
  A worm can get one bite!

420. Sun, Tree and Crow

There, on a branch, he stands alone,
And, dangling from his knotted claws,
  His prize – a little, trembling eye!
Shall we exult at last,
To see this power – that once was Earth's –
  No longer held by any sky?

The power that once was Heaven's is changed,
It comes to Earth, it comes to Earth –
  What mercy shall we show!
Our leaves, our common leaves, have caught
The Sun's great eye, all shrunk and small –
  And gives it to that old, black crow!

421. Shooting-Stars

A little porch with roof and sides
  Cobwebbed by overhanging leaves,
Led into that old woman's house;
  The lattice windows almost blind
From heavy, leafy brows.

'Each time we see a shooting-star,
    A child is born on earth,' she said;
'Six stars were mine, six children born,
    But all my little chicks are dead.'

Eyes budded like a cat's by day,
    They only showed sufficient light
To keep her little house all clean –
    And flowered full large at night.

For well it pleased that poor old soul
    To see the stars give children birth,
Sitting, inside her porch, alone;
    Counting those babes, if any came,
And thinking of her own.

422. A Dull Spirit

I see the houses, but I swear
    They're all alike this day;
I see no difference in the birds,
    In sparrow, thrush or jay.
Cows, horses, sheep, and cats or dogs
    Are all the same in look;
I see no change in bark or leaf,
    From sycamore to oak.
The chaffinch, with his laughing song,
    Is but a bird to me;
The cherry, in her summer snow,
    Is nothing but a tree.

My wonder's gone, and my sick muse
    Burns dead, without a flame;
And that's why different birds and trees,
    And houses, look the same.

423. The Dragonfly

Now, when my roses are half buds, half flowers,
    And loveliest, the king of flies has come –
It was a fleeting visit, all too brief;
    In three short minutes he had seen them all,
And rested, too, upon an apple leaf.

There, his round shoulders humped with emeralds,
    A gorgeous opal crown set on his head,
And all those shining honours to his breast –
    'My garden is a lovely place,' thought I,
'But is it worthy of so fine a guest?'

He rested there, upon that apple leaf –
    'See, see,' I cried amazed, 'his opal crown,
And all those emeralds clustered round his head!'
    'His breast, my dear, how lovely was his breast' –
The voice of my Belovèd quickly said.

'See, see his gorgeous crown, that shines
    With all those jewels bulging round its rim' –
I cried aloud at night, in broken rest.
    Back came the answer quickly, in my dream –
'His breast, my dear, how lovely was his breast!'

424. Light and Darkness

The world is sleeping, and the earth is dark,
  The lamps are out, the window lights are gone:
Was that a bird that twittered in its sleep,
  Or was it but a fancy, here alone?

Who said the earth is dark – the Moon has come
  To silver many a tump and hollow place;
Dark Earth and Moonlight – and I see a child
  Stroke with her tender hand a blinded face.

425. The Evening Star

See how her body pants and glows,
  See how she shakes her silver wings!
Ten thousand stars, and more, are mute,
  And she, and she alone, that sings.

Ten thousand stars, and more, are mute,
  All listening in the quiet sky,
While that bright star sings wildly there
  And happy they hear more than I.

Bring me my strange invention now,
  That I may sit at home in ease
And have fresh music brought by air
  From towns beyond the curly seas.

In vain, in vain; the power to hear
  The music of those heavenly spheres
Is but a wild, fantastic dream –
  But who can read the unborn years?

426. Old or Young

I questioned Poetry, 'Say,' I said –
   'What am I, old or young?'
'Young as the heart remains,' she smiled –
   'While laughter comes, and song.'

  Say, am I old or am I young?'
   I asked Philosophy.
'The way that women look at you
   Should answer that' – growled he.

So, when I claim, by my high blood,
   A life still young and jolly,
Women, with their indifferent looks
   Reprove me for my folly.

427. An Epitaph

Beneath this stone lies one good man; and when
We say his kindly thought towards all men
Was as generous to the living as to the dead –
What more for any mortal could be said?
His only enemies were those he tried
To help, and failed; who blamed him, in their pride,
Forgetting that his power was not as great
As his intention – and their own weak state.
And if he met with men too slow to move
Into the fullness of his own clear love,
He looked for the fault in his own self, and not
Blamed other men – like our more common lot.

His boundless trust and innocence of evil
Tempted the base and mean, and helped the devil.
Since such a man, without suspicion, kind,
Was duped by many a false, ungrateful mind,
He's gone to Heaven – because he lived so well
That many a wretch through him has gone to hell.

428. Sport

Hunters, hunters,
Follow the Chase.
I saw the Fox's eyes,
Not in his face
But on it, big with fright –
Haste, hunters, haste!

Say, hunters, say,
Is it a noble sport?
As rats that bite
Babies in cradles, so,
Such rats and men
Take their delight.

429. Winter Fire

How bleak and cold the air is now –
The Sun has never left his bed:
He has a thick grey blanket pulled
All over his shoulders and head.

Big birds that only have one cry,
  And little birds with perfect songs,
Are silent all, and work their wings
  Much faster than they work their tongues.

I'll turn that black-faced nigger, Coal,
Into an Indian painted red;
And let him dance and fire wild shots
  Into the chimney overhead.

430. To a Contemporary

By my fast horse that knows no rest
And, like its rider, never tires;
By my strong concentration, which
Shall take me where my heart desires;
By my great power to stand transfixed
At beauty, when my mind commands it;
By my strong faith that I'll not fail
At morning, noon or night to find it;
By my desire for longer life,
My ecstacy in mortal breath;
By all my healthy hate and fear
In thinking of the hour of death;
By all this joy, by this content,
By all my faith in what I plan;
By all these all-sufficing friends –
How can I envy any man?
True to a heart that joy makes kind,
And praising things of little worth;
Still giving praise where none is due –
No greater liar walks the earth.

431. Peace and Goodwill

On Christmas day I sit and think,
Thoughts white as snow, and black as ink.
My nearest kinsman, turned a knave,
Robbed me of all that I could save.
When he was gone, and I was poor,
His sister yelped me from her door.

The Robin sings his Christmas song,
And no bird has a sweeter tongue.
God bless them all — my wife so true,
And pretty Robin Redbreast too.
God bless my kinsman, far away,
And give his sister joy this day.

432. Friends Unborn

With this one friend — I ask no more —
    To love me till I die,
I sing my songs that, after death,
    My friends may multiply.
To make this world, when I am gone,
    Think all the more of me —
Each time a rainbow's in the sky,
    Or bird is on a tree.
That God may say, when I am judged —
    'This sinner did his duty:
Who made men worship Me the more,
    By his great love of beauty.'

433. The Richest Stones

My wandering days have run their course,
   And Age is in my flesh and bones:
Of all the temples, domes, and towers,
   Where have I found the richest stones?

The little house where I was born,
   And where my early childhood lies,
Was built with solid blocks of gold,
   And all its walls had diamond-eyes!

434. This Bantam Star

Is this the Blackbird's richest song –
   Is this his greatest hour?
And still the Bee stands on his head
   To suck his sweetest flower;
While I, a poet with my pen,
Make music only known to men.

How merrily this bantam world
   Can clap his wings and crow!
Is there a merrier world than this?
   'No,' says the Blackbird – 'No!
No other worlds, though bigger far,
Can match this little bantam star!'

435. If Love Survives

If nothing takes away our power
    To think of what is past –
What matters where our spirits go,
    What life we lead at last?

Whether we burn in summer's heat
    Or freeze in winter's cold,
Whether we float on silver waves,
    Or ride on beams of gold:

No matter where or what we are,
    To work, my love, or play;
In Heaven or Earth, our cry shall be –
    'How old is Love to-day?'

436. Hand or Mouth

This, then, is Pleasure's bower,
    Where every thing can please;
Her cushions are of silk,
    She plays on ivory keys.
She gives her hand to kiss,
    Before I leave her bower:
'I thank you, pretty one,
    For this light hour.'

Out in the garden now
    Young Joy sits all alone;
The cushion she sits on
    Is nothing but a stone;

Her naked lips are all
   The music she can play;
She gives her mouth to kiss –
   Sweet Joy, I stay!

437. Ambition

I had Ambition, by which sin
   The angels fell;
I climbed and, step by step, O Lord,
   Ascended into Hell.

Returning now to peace and quiet,
   And made more wise,
Let my descent and fall, O Lord,
   Be into Paradise.

438. For Sale

Four hundred years this little house has stood
Through wind and fire, through earthquake
      and through flood;
Still its old beams, though bulged and warped,
      are strong,
In spite of gaping wounds both deep and long.
The doors are low and give such narrow space
We must walk humbly in this little place.

The windows here, no longer square or straight,
Are able now, from their fant·stic state,
To squint down their own walls, and see the
    flowers
That get more drippings from the eaves than
    showers.
Six hundred pounds for all this precious stone!
These little, quaint old windows squinting
    down;
This orchard, with its apples' last appeal
To dumpling or sweet cider; this deep well,
Whose little eye has sparkled from its birth –
Four hundred years in sixty feet of earth!

439. Birthdays

My friend has a birthday;
And what can I say
To young Betty Blake
With her wonderful cake
And seven pink candles there –
One candle for every year?
'How many candles shall I see
On yours?' asked Betty Blake of me.
'Sixty!' I cried, excited by it –
Steady, old heart! Lie quiet!

440. Uncertainty

Shall I confess my love?
  No, no – it will not do;
Not while Uncertainty
  Can keep a woman true.

She shall not know that I,
    Being absolutely won,
Release her thousand charms
    For something new in man.
So let the game go on,
    Which Love calls 'Yes or No,'
Till Death says, 'Come with me –
    Come to a quiet show.'
Where she, or I, alone,
    Inside the cold, black vault,
Train worms to skip a hair,
    And make a somersault.

441. Charity

Things that are dear to me at home
    Need all my help, and more;
And many a kindly thought I kill,
    For the stranger at my door;
Yet every generous impulse slain,
    Is a ghost that haunts me still.

It's better that a woman had
    A love-child at her breast,
Than live a heartless, selfish maid;
    It's better that a man should trust
A worthless knave, than never have
    His love or innocence betrayed.

442. A Dream of Winter

These flowers survive their lover bees,
    Whose deep bass voices filled the air;
The cuckoo and the nightingale
    Have come and gone, we know not where.

Now, in this green and silent world,
    In Autumn, full of smiling light,
I hear a bird that, suddenly,
    Startles my hearing and my sight.

It is the Robin, singing of
    A silver world of snow and frost;
Where all is cold and white – except
    The fire that's on his own warm breast.

443. A Child's Fancy

His chin went up and down, and chewed at nothing,
His back was bent – the man was old and tired;
Toothless and frail, he hobbled on his way,
Admiring nothing, and by none admired;
Unless it was that child, with eager eyes,
Who stared amazed to see so strange a man,
And hobbled home himself, with shoulders raised
Trying to make his chin go up and down;
Unless it was that much affected child,
With rounded shoulders, like the old man seen –
Who asked his mother why he was not made
The wonderful strange sight he might have been.

444. Wild Blossoms

No lilies all for milk,
　Nor roses rich in blood,
Can settle my best thoughts
　To browse in solitude.
But where the daisy grows,
　Primrose and violet,
In their first happy state,
　No mortal hand has set:
Where these wild blossoms grow
　All in the grass and moss –
I'll raise my hand, O Lord,
　With a sign of the Cross.

445. A Silver Wonder

Shall I this night, amazed and full of wonder,
　Forget the Heavens and worship this new toy;
Shall I betray the stars and fall before
　A strange new Image, with a greater joy?
Caught in the searchlights' fingers, gleaming bright,
　A silver wonder, with a strange device,
Has made the stars, the great eternal stars,
　Peep out of their dark holes like timid mice!

446. Peace and Rest

Under this tree, where light and shade
  Speckle the grass like a Thrush's breast,
Here, in this green and quiet place,
  I give myself to peace and rest.

The peace of my contented mind,
  That is to me a wealth untold —
When the Moon has no more silver left,
  And the Sun's at the end of his gold.

447. Moss and Feather

Pools but reflect his shape and form,
  And nothing of his lovely hues;
Could he but see his jewels' light,
  Would this Kingfisher choose
To live alone with Weeping Willows,
Diving, and making toys of billows?

Her shadow shows this Stone her frame,
  But not her plumpness, round and simple;
Could she but see what moss she has,
  To jewel every dimple —
Could this rich Stone but see her face,
Would she lie idle in one place?

Were I a great Magician now,
  I'd bring this Bird and Stone together,
Lord, what a glorious pair they'd make,
  To dance, in moss and feather —
Nine times in sunshine, keeping step,
And twenty when the Moon is up!

448. Pot and Kettle

'Away!' I cried, to a spiteful Wasp,
　　Who challenged me to fight;
'Would you, a paltry dram of flesh,
　　Attack a hundredweight?
Go, little upstart, try your mettle
On some old spider, bug or beetle.'

'Your pardon, Sir,' the Wasp replied:
　　'If man attacks a God in Heaven,
Why can't a Wasp attack a man –
　　Which is the most uneven?
This wise discourse, on power and mettle,
Should please your Masters – Pot and Kettle.'

449. Eyes and Ears

Would that the Powers that made my eyes so keen,
　　To stare at things intently, near or far;
That I discover twins at last, in what
　　I thought at first was but a single star –
Would that those Powers had made my ears the same,
　　To tell the Oak and Maple in the dark,
To recognize their songs in wind or rain,
　　Before I knew their names by leaf or bark.

450. The Blest

The Vision came, all grey and cold,
  And cast his shadow on my bed —
But I could live a thousand years,
  And never wish that I were dead.
'You do not know,' said Death, to me,
  'How many men have called me "Blest";
The millions that have squeezed my hand
  In gratitude for peace and rest;
When they are old, and no one wants them,
  They lie their heads upon my breast.'
And he looked so gentle and kind,
  And his voice came so soft to my ear,
That I gave him a cherry to eat,
  And the dew on its skin was a tear.

451. The Idiot

The hand that rocked his cradle once
  Lies buried with his father's rings;
Yet in his cradle still lives he —
  He rocks it by himself, and sings.

He knows no heaviness at heart,
  He cannot feel his body's old;
The cradle that his mother rocked
  Is still his joy, and all his world.

All by himself he rocks and sings —
  Until he makes old Death at last
Measure him in his cradle for
  A coffin to contain his dust.

452. Letters

If these six letters came from birds,
  What gossip we would hear!
The Thrush would tell me how he sang
  For twenty hours in twenty-four.
The Starling, too, would thank me for
  A ribbon found down here;
To give his home a lovely line,
  As well as comfort there.
And hear what Robin Redbreast says,
  I read his letter now:
'My happiest hours are when my legs
  Are more than half-way up in snow.'
Hear what the poor Hedge Sparrow writes,
  To ease her troubled breast;
She says a Cuckoo lately dumped
  An extra youngster in her nest.
The Cuckoo, that forgiven bird,
  Writes from his Mediterranean place –
'I hope to be in England soon,
  The tenth of April, by God's grace.'
And, Lord, to read the Nightingale –
  'My voice,' she says, 'to my own wonder,
Rose into Heaven, all clear and strong,
  To lead a chorus full of thunder!'

453. Day or Night

Again I wake and cry for light!
  My golden day has gone,
And, looking through my window now,
  I see the stars and moon.

Which shall I sacrifice to sleep,
  With both beyond my praise?
So lovely are these silvery nights,
  So bright these golden days!

454. Hunting Joy

How sad a face this Knowledge wears!
  How strange is Truth, which none can doubt!
How easy is an Eden made,
  How hard to keep the Serpent out!
How easy to create a Joy,
  How hard to hold it safe and fast;
Since half the world would hunt it down,
  As Fame, or Love, can prove at last.
I'll make my Joy a secret thing,
  My face shall wear a mask of care;
And those who hunt a Joy to death,
  Shall never know what sport is there!

455. A Young Thrush

What power of will – to follow now,
  In this cold hour of fear,
His studies in dead sticks and stones,
  With all this danger near!
So here we stand with breathless looks,
  As figures made of stone;
Till knowing that the poor thing's heart
  Beats faster than my own,
I, creeping backward, silently,
  Am happy to be gone.

456. Born of Tears

A thing that's rich in tears is sweet –
No sounds in all the world are sweeter.
A robin redbreast in the fall,
    The nightingale in June;
The bleating of young lambs in March,
    And the violin in tune:
These are the sounds that haunt my ears,
And all of them are born of tears.

A thing that's rich in tears is fair –
No sights in all the world are fairer.
How lovely is a summer's eve
    That's full of heavenly light;
When tears of joy, called shooting stars,
    Run down the face of night.
While every rainbow that appears
Could say – 'My mother's name is Tears.

457. Heaven and Earth

It may be true the stars are worlds,
    And twenty times the earth in size;
But all I know, or care to know,
    Is in the limit of my eyes.
Which proves that any star can see
    Her face in one small drop of dew;
And that the Moon, the lovely Moon,
    With half her heaven of stars in view,
Can see their beauty, all in full,
    Down in one little wayside pool.

458. In Winter

The cold, ice-sucking Wind has gone,
　　The air breathes quietly;
The Rain has come, as warm as spray
　　That sprinkles ships at sea.

And I remember how I woke,
　　Before my time to rise,
And heard a Robin and a Thrush
　　Cheering the winter skies.

Now when my Summer fails to shine,
　　And skies are cold and grey –
I'll let my Memory warm her hands
　　At this fine winter's day.

459. My Life's Example

Stand with eyes fixed, the Cuckoo calls –
　　Let all the world go blind!
Should any search be made at all,
　　Let it be for the Wind!

At Birdland Corner, where I live,
　　And daffodils appear –
The hero of my life and dreams
　　Cries 'Cuckoo' every year.

He is my life's example, and
  His spirit fills my place;
That I, like him, would be a voice,
  And never show my face.

And let my notes be cries of joy,
  Too simple to despise;
That children from their cradles love,
  And hearts grown old and wise.

460. When and Where

What man was in the Moon last night?
  Her silver ore lies scattered here!
What time I go, or where I work,
  Not even Love knows when or where.
Who hears a voice inside the Wind's,
  Has heard a poet chant his verse;
For any jewels in his song,
  Look to a Rainbow for their source.
The gold-dust on my leaves of song
  Proves where my morning's work was done;
For I'm the man – that spot and speck –
  That worked in gold, inside the Sun!

461. Silver Hours

Come, lovely Morning, rich in frost
   On iron, wood and glass;
Show all your pains to silver-gild
   Each little blade of grass.

Come, rich and lovely Winter's Eve,
   That seldom handles gold;
And spread your silver sunsets out,
   In glittering fold on fold.

Come, after sunset; come, Oh come –
   You clear and frosty Night:
Dig up your fields of diamonds, till
   The heavens all dance in light!

462. Here Am I

The World has shared my joy and pain,
   And I have had my day;
My little life is almost done,
   And I must haste away:
So, quietly, before I leave –
I'll do no more than sit and breathe.

How many friends – and two are dogs –
   Beguile me to the end:
That by their love that cannot change,
   Make Death a greater friend.
When Death cries 'Next!' and I must die,
Soft be my answer – 'Here am I.'

463. Flowers

What favourite flowers are mine, I cannot say –
My fancy changes with the summer's day.
Sometimes I think, agreeing with the Bees,
That my best flowers are those tall apple trees,
Who give a Bee his cyder while in bloom,
And keep me waiting till their apples come.
Sometimes I think the Columbine has won,
Who hangs her head and never looks the Sun
Straight in the face. And now the Golden Rod
Beckons me over with a graceful nod;
Shaped like a sheaf of corn, her ruddy skin
Drinks the Sun dry, and leaves his splendour thin.
Sometimes I think the Rose must have her place –
And then the Lily shakes her golden dice
Deep in a silver cup, to win or lose.
So I go on, from Columbine to Rose,
From Marigold to Flock, from Flock to Thrift –
Till nothing but my garden stones are left.
But when I see the dimples in her face,
All filled with tender moss in every place –
Ah, then I think, when all is said and done,
My favourite flower must be a Mossy Stone!

464. Mangers

Who knows the name and country now,
    Of that rich man who lived of old;
Whose horses fed at silver mangers,
    And drank of wine from troughs of gold?

He who was in a manger born,
    By gold and silver undefiled –
Is known as Christ to every man,
    And Jesus to a little child.

465. Ships and Stars

As soon as I began to name a star,
Or judge a ship by rigging, mast or spar,
I, seeing more with eyes than with my mind,
Had fears that I would soon go beauty blind.
But now, not caring if the ship that's seen
Is schooner-rigged, a barque or brigantine,
I look beyond my eyes to where she rides
Under a rainbow, beautiful; or glides
Before the wind, on one side of her belly.
And as young lambs or sheep all white and woolly,
I see the stars in one flock nibbling go
Across the Heavens, whose names I will not know.

466. Starlings

This time of year, when but the Robin sings,
    Shall I reproach those Starlings, chuckling near?
What Spring-like green is in their feverish haste
    To pock the face of my half-ripened pear!

When I remember my own wilful blood,
    The waste, the wildness of my early years –
Shall I not chuckle with those birds, when they
    With wicked music waste my sweetest pears?

467. Poison

When this strange world speaks ill of me,
  With tongues of poison, and unkind –
What can I do but seek the poor,
  And leave my silver mark behind?

When I, a silent stranger, make
  Them wonder if Christ comes again –
Have I not found a shilling cure,
  When suffering from a poisoned brain?

One silver shilling, white and clean,
  Left with a poor man, old or blind –
And here I stand, all poison-proof,
  Till every tongue grows sweet and kind.

468. A Prayer

Lord, hear my morning's prayer!
  Increase, O Lord, my power,
That as I feed Your birds
  From such a slender store,
Turn all these crumbs to pounds,
To feed a thousand men –
As easy as I feed
  A sparrow, tit, or wren.
But God, being jealous still,
  Can only smile and say –
'Serve me as you do now;
  Feed My small birds and pray.

One dog to share one bone,
    One woman to one hearth;
One man to share one house –
    One Christ to share My Earth!"

469. Old Friends

Forgive me, World, if I outlive my welcome;
    Still look on me with gracious thoughts and kind;
Remembering all the love of my old friends
    That lie at rest, and never change their mind.

Forgive me, World, if I an old and think
    A silver love deserves return in gold:
An old dog friend – whose kennel was my shadow –
    Has left it empty, and I feel the cold.

470. Wonderful Places

I am haunted by wonderful places –
And not by human faces;
My only ghosts, by day or night,
Are Nature's own, of sound or sight.
I see again the hollow, deep and round,
Filled with a murmuring sound;
Where Summer sent her flowers, with bees
And humming-birds to play with these.
Again, and still again, I dream
How Colorado's stream
Squeezed his huge body through
A narrow gorge, and never knew
That Heaven's thunder
Was but a whisper to his own down under.

Again I see the mighty leap
Made by the wild Pacific deep
At Rarotonga, off a coral bed –
With his own mist to hide his face and head.
I am haunted by wonderful places –
And not by human faces.

471. What Light?

I know my Body well,
    I know both foot and hand;
How far I swim in water,
    How fast I walk on land.
I know what drink, I know what food
Can do my Body harm or good.

My Body is but clay:
    An earthquake sucks it down
While still a Rainbow shines
    And smiles as it looks on.
Yet ere that Body's gone to Earth –
What light shall smile my Spirit forth?

472. Old Autumn

Is this old Autumn standing here,
    Where wind-blown fruits decay;
Dressed up in limp, bedraggled flowers
    That Summer cast away?

Within whose mist no dewdrops shine,
  And grass, once green, goes yellow;
For whom no bird will sing or chirp,
  On either Ash or Willow?

If this is his poor, pelted face,
  With dead leaves soaked in rain,
Come, Winter, with your kindly frost
  That's almost cruelly sane;

Take him, with his unwanted life,
  To his last sleep and end –
Like the cat that cannot find a home,
  And the dog that has no friend.

473. Trails

He leaves his silver trail behind,
  But has no silver on his way;
His path is rough, and sometimes dark,
  And troubles come by night and day:
Slowly he moves – this humble snail –
And never sees his silver trail.

So, men who give us golden lines
  Have written them in blood and sweat,
Time never turns a thought to gold,
  Unless a tear has made it wet:
They suffer – like these humble snails –
And never see their golden trails.

474. The Poor

Give them your silver, let the poor
   Put on a braver show;
Let not their cold and sullen looks
   Depress the world with woe.

But to the poor who laugh and sing
   Nor look depressed nor cold –
What can we give to these sweet souls,
   Worth twice their weight in gold?

475. No Careless Mind

A granted joy can make a careless mind,
   To take or leave at any hour I choose;
Yet every wind that blows has its own song,
   And sings a music that I dare not lose;
While every tree that grows in field or wood
Has qualities that change, like flesh and blood.

The Sun comes out and like a dog am I,
   That starts a scent that's new to him and strange,
And where it burns I follow till it dies;
   The stars at night, whose beauty knows no change,
Still lead my hopes to see, at any hour,
A seed of light throw up a magic flower!

476. A Fleeting Wonder

See where he rides, all hot and fast —
  High on his horse that kicks
Lightning and thunder out of wind,
  While fools applaud his tricks.

A year or two, and there he lies,
  A bleeding thing, and thrown;
Down in the dust he dribbles blood,
  Forgotten and unknown.

Whoa! Steady now, my little horse,
  A gentle canter past:
Though faintly cheered, there's nothing gained
  By riding wild and fast.

477. Kiss and Blow

He takes that woman with his kiss,
  Yet strikes her man a heavy blow:
  Would she have gone off smiling so
For any other Power that's known —
  If she had seen the cruel blow
That struck her man and lover down?
  A blow and a kiss, in a single breath —
  How kind and cruel, how clever is Death!

478. The Visitor

Her beauty is a wasted thing,
  She's neither sweet nor kind;
And flowers that have no other eyes
  Than raindrops soon go blind.

She is a park that has no deer
    To give it life or grace;
Until I think the wilderness
    A more enchanted place.

Her Ten Commandments are her own,
    She knows no other Creed;
The only babies in her eyes
    Are selfish thoughts and greed.

Her beauty is a wasted thing,
    Is Nature's loss and pain;
When will the little, plain, brown bird
    Come back and sing again?

479. The Chase

The Moon his mare, all silver-bright,
    And he all gold, to match her –
When will that stallion, called the Sun,
    Come near enough to catch her?
With time to spare, and love to waste,
    What years and years of fire and haste!

When his bright eye grows cold and dim,
    His nostrils blow less fire –
Will he, the shadow of himself,
    Pursue her with the old desire?
When Earth has not one living eye –
    What ghostly horse shall course the sky?

480. Age and Youth

The music's dull – I trust my Ears;
  The day is cold – I blame no Blood;
The air is mist – I trust my Eyes;
  My breath is stale – my Teeth hold good;
My bed is hard – I blame no Bones;
  My drink is Sour – I trust my Tongue.
Ears, Blood and Eyes; Teeth, Tongue and Bones –
      Tell me what's wrong,
      And speak the truth.
'It's strange, Old man, but no complaint
      Has come from Youth.'

481. The Prayer of Daft Harry

Lord, since this world is filled with fire.
  Inside this rounded mould –
Let's turn it inside out, O Lord,
  While hands and feet are cold.

Let's split the world in half, O Lord,
  As open as my palm,
Until the snow has melted down,
  And hands and feet are warm.

Let's turn the world all inside out,
  And glorify Our Name;
Until Our fire makes Jesus laugh,
  While I blow up the flame.

Let's do it now, this minute, Lord,
    And make a glorious blaze:
Till Jesus laughs and claps his hands,
    While Mary sings Our praise!

482. A Sweeter Life

No bitter tongue, no grief for what is gone,
    Shall enter here, where Love with me is staying;
Only from books we'll know what Sorrow means,
    And keep sad thoughts for when there's Music
        playing.
Give me a simple, sweet, dove-tempered spirit,
    That thinks unpleasing Truth must be a lie;
To lose all memory of unfriendly men,
    Where all unkindness has gone home to die.
From what, think you, comes this exalted state,
    That makes life now so rich in joy, and full;
What woman taught me that it needs four hands
    To hold her skein and wind a ball of wool?

483. Epitaph on John Keats

Some poets die consumed by love
    Of their own dreams – here lies John Keats:
Who died because he had no power
    To stop his craving after sweets.

484. Epitaph on a Child

They killed her lamb, and no one wept,
   Save this small child, to find it gone;
O Lamb of God, and Lover of lambs –
   This was the Little One.

485. Come, Melancholy

Come, Melancholy, come, Delight:
   Let's croak of misery, like a frog.
Let us pretend the window's shut
   For the cat, and a door for the dog.
Let us pretend that every door's
   Made fast, to all except the Bee –
Who finds a keyhole every time,
   And passes in without a key.
Let us pretend that Life's a babe
   All wrapt in clay, with pins of ice,
Without a nurse to tuck it in,
   Or sooth it with a softer voice.
And when we have imagined these,
   Refusing peace, and scorning mirth –
We'll light our pipes and blow a smoke
   That casts a halo on our birth!

486. Jewels

Twice in one hour I've seen this lovely Night,
   Flustered at having all those jewels there –
Spilling her stars, that fall from Heaven to Earth,
   As though she carried more than she could bear.

While I, a struggling dreamer, all day long,
  That tries to polish one poor little rhyme –
Though breathed on hard, and rubbed with ecstasy,
  Still call on Night to see my wasted time.

487.   The Legacy

She died when I was wild and young,
  And I myself am old by now;
And still her small, few shillings come,
  Like shoots from a severed bough.
Though they have dwindled, year by year,
  Can I despise these tiny gains –
Worth little more than children's weeds
  Picked in the woods and kissed in lanes?
Not while I think her spirit lives
  And, close beside me, understands
The grateful love – so long delayed –
  In the kiss on her ghostly hands.

488.   Clocks

Still comes no answer to my greatest question –
Am I two clocks, or am I only one?
I know my Body is wound up to go
A certain number of days, and all is done.
But is my mind another clock, wound up
To add its chimes to those immortal spheres;
One clock for Earth, to run its numbered days,
The other for my more-than-mortal years?
That is my question; this, my only finding –
One clock or two, there'll be no further winding.

489. A Child's Mint

When young, I kissed a miser man,
  A brand new penny for my pain;
In case he asked for a ha-penny back,
  I kissed him once and then again.

With kisses here, and kisses there,
  I kissed for all that I could get;
I had a mint so rich and full
  That kisses paid my every debt.

My kisses now are wind, not breath,
  In refuse-heaps they lie unsold;
All debts and favours, all demands,
  Cry out for silver, and for gold.

490. The World Dictates

The World dictates my life from day to day,
  It holds my purse, and cuts my pleasures down,
If I would ride, it tells me I must walk,
  It counts my concerts when I live in Town.
Yet when I see yon lovely hill this morning,
  All white and sepia with its trees and snow –
Who'll think I'd be a wiser, better man
  To sit in cushions at a gilded show?
So let the World dictate my daily life,
  Let beauty last till Summer brings me more –
Where lovers, paired together, laugh and play,
  As they go wobbling sideways past my door.

491. The Enemy

Though I am all for warmth and light,
For my full share of Earth's delight,
  How often must I stand perplexed!
Knowing that Death has little care
Who answers to his call, or where –
  When his cold voice comes crying, 'Next!'

If Joy should falter any day,
Have no unkindly thoughts, and say –
  'How hard and strained is this man's note!'
But rather think Death sometimes comes
For early practise here, and hums
  His hard, dry rattle in my throat.

492. The Lady of Light

Though I must sleep, and give my body rest,
  Still must I love this Moon with all my heart;
Like silly lovers, walking to and fro,
  We see each other home, and cannot part.

And when at last the final moment comes,
  When I have said 'Good Night,' from under cover –
I still have hopes to see her pass my window,
  As she goes home alone, without her lover.

Night after night we play this lover's game,
  We come and go, from place to place we roam:
Yet no fair Lady, half so sweet, should be
  The last at night to see her lover home.

493. Playmates

That is your little playmate, Jane,
   His coffin, with its flowers;
You will not play with him again,
   For hours, my child – and hours!

With head bowed down to hide her grief,
   She faltered, with a sigh:
'To have such lovely flowers as his –
   Would any child not die!'

494. Sick Minds

When I am sick and dark depression
   Lies all around with chilly breath –
What herbs or drugs shall I prescribe,
   To save me from the hands of Death;
What remedy can I then find
To bring relief to my sick mind?

The teachings of my Master, Christ,
   Are all the herbs or drugs I need;
To help one poorer than myself,
   That is a remedy indeed:
To give a joy where there is none,
Is magic that restores my own.

495. Bird and Cloud

Lord, if that Cloud still grows and swells,
  To reach the Sun at last –
What a fine nipple she will have
  On the top of her white breast!
And does this Blackbird, singing here,
  Up on my Sycamore bough,
Make that his richest Summer's yarn,
  To last the season through;
Or is he blind, to Cloud and Sun,
  And sings but from content –
Because his body feels no pain,
  And his mind has no complaint?

496. Ourselves

We live to read each other's soul –
  We dare not read our own for shame!
But since I dare to know myself,
  Where I condemn I share the blame.

I know my very seeds of thought,
  Before they flower, or leaves are shown:
I see your fault with lazy eyes,
  To cast their lightning on my own!

497. The Mourner

When all your bitter grief is gone,
With anger and rebellion done,
Think then, with your more even breath –
How lovely was the face of Death!
Say you remember her sweet face,
    The light, the loveliness;
The smile that passed beyond this world,
    To rest no more on us:
That, knowing now how Death is loved –
You follow her, and stand reproved.

498. Loyalty

Kings, who would have good subjects, must
    Be loyal subjects in themselves:
We poets – like women with their hair –
    Who sing before a looking-glass,
Can count our loyal subjects, there!

You, who have found young Cupid's thumb
    So soft and white, from constant sucking –
Sit down and think how sweet it was:
    Until your poet, grown sincere,
Can sing without his robe or glass.

499.　No Place or Time

This curly childhood of the year,
　　These days of dancing blood –
Is Spring the proper time for breath
　　To be resigned for good?

When Summer's face is bright and clear,
　　And all the trees are green –
Shall I believe the time has come
　　To creep away unseen?

When Autumn shuffles leaves of gold,
　　And deals them in one heap –
Must I agree that that's the hour
　　For everlasting sleep?

And when the world is white with snow,
　　With Winter in his prime –
I'll still maintain that Death's a fool,
　　That knows no place or time.

500.　Dreamers

There was a poet once who died,
His casement opened wide;
With his two hands he clasped his book,
And died with his last look
Fixed on the brightest star –
How great some poets are!
I too have my ambitious end,
With one green leaf in either hand –
And save the small breast-feather
Of a little bird for the other!

501. Wild Creatures

They say wild creatures hide themselves,
   And seek a quiet place to die:
Would that my end were such as theirs,
   So strange, so wild a thing am I.

Let no man sneer at me, and say –
   'We know this poet hides with care;
Inside the Abbey's sacred walls
   He hides himself – if anywhere.'

I, who have lived for Nature's love,
   Think nothing of your sculptured stones –
Who sees a dingle lined with moss,
   And one small row of clean, white bones?

502. Aye

How many years since I, a wandering man,
   Sat at a forest fire, for warmth and light!
With but one mate, a bird unseen, and strange
   That kept on crying, all the livelong night –
'Aye! . . . Aye! . . . Aye!'

Though times are changed, and different fires are mine,
   Yet if that strange, wild bird could but restore
The youth I lost when in his forest glade –
   Would I not come again in rags, and poor?
'Aye . . . Aye . . . Aye.'

503. Magpies

I have an orchard near my house,
    Where poppies spread and corn has grown;
It is a holy place for weeds,
    Where seeds stay on and flower, till blown.
Into this orchard, wild and quiet,
    The Magpie comes, the Owl and Rook:
To see one Magpie is not well,
    But seeing two brings all good luck.
If Magpies think the same, and say,
    'Two humans bring good luck, not one' –
How they must cheer us, Love, together,
    And tremble when I come alone!

504. A Dog's Grave

My dog lies dead and buried here,
    My little Pet for five sweet years.
As I stand here, beside her grave,
    With eyes gone dim, and blind with tears –
I see it rising up and down,
As though she lay in a sleeping-gown.

Forgive me, Pet, that half these tears,
    Which make my eyes go dim and blind,
Should come from thoughts of love betrayed,
    When I had trust in my own kind:
And Christ forgive this living breath
That links such lives with my dog's death!

442

505. Dogs

When I was once a wandering man,
   And walked at midnight, all alone –
A friendly dog, that offered love,
   Was threatened with a stone.

'Go, go,' I said, 'and find a man
   Who has a home to call his own;
Who, with a luckier hand than mine,
   Can find his dog a bone.'

But times are changed, and this pet dog
   Knows nothing of a life that's gone –
Of how a dog that offered love
   Was threatened with a stone.

506. On Finding a Dead Bird Under My Window

Here you lie, with feathers cold and wet –
To dig a grave for you will cause no sweat!
I never felt your body warm with blood,
And now I hold you longer than I should.
What does it matter, if we live or die –
You with a cherry-tempted heart, or I?
The sun in Heaven has his own heat and glow,
And, when all flesh is gone, the grass will grow.
Yet still I hope that you have left a son
Or daughter here, to do what you have done –
To tap my window sharply, without warning,
And be the first to wish a friend 'Good Morning'.

507. Crumbs and Guineas

How many plates of crumbs, my little friend,
    Have I now scattered twice and thrice a day?
Have I not crushed a ton or more of bread,
    In payment for your pretty songs and play?

'When you have said what you have done for us,'
    A saucy Sparrow answered, speaking bold –
'Then tell the World what we have done for you,
    Whose well-invested bread has brought you gold:
Give us our daily bread – not worth a penny –
    And make a song of it, to charge a guinea!'

508. Voices of Scorn

When I had thought my end was near,
    And I must soon prepare to die –
'Be quick! Be quick!' the Mavis called,
    And 'Haw, Haw, Haw!' the Rooks did cry.

What bird, with even greater scorn,
    Has come so quickly following after?
Is this the Chaffinch – how his voice
    Reproves me with its wholesome laughter!

444

509. One Poet Visits Another

His car was worth a thousand pounds and more,
A tall and glossy black silk hat he wore;
His clothes were pressed, like pretty leaves, when they
Are found in Bibles closed for many a day;
Until the birds I love dropped something that –
　　As white as milk, but thick as any cream –
Went pit, pit, pat! Right on his lovely hat!

*　　　　*　　　　*

Lead this unhappy poet to his car –
　　Where is his longing now, where his desire?
When left alone, I'll ride him to his grave,
　　On my own little horse of wind and fire.

510. My Rockery

Here in my garden I have lovely stones,
　　All old and grey and some with knobs of pearl;
Stones with their silver sides, and amber backs,
　　With mossy dimples and with horns that curl.

Would that this rockery were my grave indeed,
　　The monument where lie my buried bones:
Though people – coming here to think of me –
　　Might well forget, and stay to worship stones!

511. To Play Alone

A Tom Tit clinging upside down,
    Needs nothing more to raise his wonder;
A lonely Trout will play until
    His own deep whirlpool sucks him under.

So when my money all is spent,
    And all my merry friends are gone –
What little Tom Tit, Trout, or Child,
    Will teach me how to play alone?

512. Flying Blossoms

These Butterflies, in twos and threes,
    That flit about in wind and sun –
See how they add their flowers to flowers,
    And blossom where a plant has none!

Bring me my hat of yellow straw,
    To greet them on this summer's morn –
That they may think they see in me
    Another crop of golden corn!

513. A Bright Day

My windows now are giant drops of dew,
    The common stones are dancing in my eyes;
The light is winged, and panting, and the world
    Is fluttering with a little fall or rise.

See, while they shoot the sun with singing Larks,
  How those broad meadows sparkle and rejoice!
Where can the Cuckoo hide in all this light,
  And still remain unseen, and but a voice?

Shall I be mean, when all this light is mine?
  Is anything unworthy of its place?
Call for the rat, and let him share my joy,
  And sit beside me here, to wash his face.

514. Breast to Breast

What strange commotion, Love,
  Is seen on yonder bough?
'It's only a bird,' said she –
  'Or little winds that blow.'
Only a bird, my Love?
  Who sees the best –
When bird and leaf together
  Are fluttering breast to breast!

515. The Cuckoo

When I was sitting near a stream,
  And watched the waves that came in turns
To butt the rocks that kept them in,
  Breaking their milk-white horns –
'Twas then a Cuckoo, full of joy,
  No man had seen in any place,
Perched on a tree before my eyes,
  And shouted in my face!

447

516. Owls

What music, Lord, these birds must feel,
   That makes no pleasant tune:
They fail by throat, yet in their hearts
   How they enjoy the Moon!

When I sit thinking of my money,
   Or lie in bed and snore –
'Te-who! Te-who!' they cry in wonder,
   For the beauty at my door.

517. Old and Crazy

Though rising early with the Lark –
How can she sing, whose mind is dark?
She burns her lamp by night and day,
To keep the evil spirits away;
With windows opened wide at night,
She puts the lurking devils to flight.

How many nights have heard her wrath,
That cursed all things in Heaven and Earth!
Till, tired of all her terrible speech,
Only the Owl was left to screech.
When children wake and, trembling, cry –
Who blames the poor old Owl? Not I.

518. Little Flower

Little Flower, I hold you here,
   Between my finger-tips;
Can I do more for your sweet smell
   Than kiss you with my lips?
               Little Flower,
I am an old man –
   But a child could do no more.

519. Drink

Say that the House that makes our Laws
   Is but an Infants' School;
Say that the World is old and doomed,
   Where every man's a fool;
Say that the worms make skipping-ropes
   Of Beauty's hair at last;
That Love must die, as Age comes cold –
   To prove it was but Lust:
Say what you like, and I'll be calm,
   No matter what I think;
But if you value blood and bones –
   No disrespect to Drink!

520. Eyes

The owl has come
   Right into my house;
He comes down the chimney,
   To look for a mouse –
And he sits on the rim of my old black table.

Lord, since I see
  Those wonderful eyes,
As big as a man's
  Or a maiden's in size –
Have I not proved his wisdom is no fable?

521. On a Cold Day

My sacrament of wine and broken bread
  Is now prepared, and ready to be done;
The Tit shall hold a crust with both his feet,
  While, crumb by crumb, he picks it like a bone.
The Thrush, ashamed of his thin ribs, has blown
  His feathers out, to make himself look fat;
The Robin, with his back humped twice as high,
  For pity's sake – has crossed my threshold mat.
The Sparrow's here, the Finch and Jenny Wren,
  The wine is poured, the crumbs are white and small·
And when each little mouth has broken bread –
  Shall I not drink and bless them one and all?

522. The Dead

Not till my Spirit's naked and ashamed,
  And free of mortal flesh, would I desire
To sit in close communion with the dead.
  I would not hear a friend exclaim in ire –
'When I was poor and kept your borrowed money
You sulked and let our blood go cold and thin.'

I would not sit and hear a woman say –
'What do you want with me, poor child of sin;
Where did you hide your face for ten long years –
The face I missed beside my dying bed?'
Not till my Spirit's naked and ashamed,
And free of flesh, would I approach the dead.

523. The River Severn

This is the morning bright and clear,
To stand on top of Christchurch Hill;
We'll see the Severn, looking down,
In all his silver beauty, Love –
Where he lies basking in the sun.

My lovely Severn shines as bright
As any moon on trucks of coal,
Or sun above our greenest meadow;
Till I again defy the world
To search his face and find a shadow.

524. The Bee Lover

He comes with a song,
With his strong healthy blood,
To find a young Blossom
All fresh the bud.
With his body like amber,
And his kisses to come –
Is she deaf to his voice,
This Blossom so dumb?

451

He comes with a song,
  This gallant young lover,
And he fusses about
  Till his passion is over:
Till he lies like a baby –
  With love in a mist –
To dribble and sleep
  On the face he has kissed.

525. A Lovely Day

A cloudless path from East to West,
  Undimmed, and shining still –
The Sun has died as he was born,
  And only changed his hill.

What words can praise him for this day,
  To show my joy and pride –
But that I'd give my life for it,
  And die, as he has died.

526. Bells

The Worlds march on and circle in their place,
Thousands of Worlds march on through Time and
    Space;
Each World a bell that, with its different toll,
The Master strikes to One Harmonious Whole.
His ears are keen, and He can always tell
If any World rings false, and name the bell.

And even I, with all these birds in song,
And grass all round me growing green and long;
Yes, even I – though shadows mark the Moon –
Could name the guilty World that's out of tune.

527. Beggar's Luck

Where did you sleep in the Country, Lad?
   'It was a field of hay.'
Did you sleep soundly there, and well?
   'Till after break of day.'

Where did you sleep in the City, Lad –
   Where did you rest your bones?
'They gave me neither straw nor feather,
   And drove me away with stones.'

528. The Vagabond

Tormented day and night by fleas,
   With but your shadow for a friend –
Have you no wish that such a life
   Were coming to a quiet end?

*

'Had I no life there'd be no shadow,
   And worms would pick my bones,' he said;
'And shall I make that damned mistake,
   And wish that I were cold and dead?
My fleas but bite, and keep me warm,
   And worms would do me little good;
My shadow follows – though I swear
   And eat up all the bloody food!'

453

529. Sound and Light

When I stand here alone at night,
　And see but nothing hear –
The silence of so many stars
　Is almost pain to bear.

Yet if I heard one creak in Heaven,
　One little break or move –
What would become of Faith and Hope,
　And of the Gods we love?

If but one star cried out at night,
　To burst like any pod –
Where shall we find, in all the Heavens,
　A chapel for our God?

530. The Man of Moods

Sometimes I blow and praise a bubble,
　And then I stab, to break its light;
This morning I despised a lamb,
　And now a rat would please my sight.
Lately I called my birth divine,
　And kings came second; now, my Soul
Takes penance in the cold, dark earth,
　In a cell with the snail and a mole.
To-day I love; to-morrow rue't:
Your prophet, sage and friend – the Poet.

531. Logic

My years to come are numbered on two hands,
  Ten fingers do the trick, and that is all;
Yet when this Cuckoo's dead, and comes no more,
  Shall I not live to hear his grandchild call?

So when I give a year-old dog my heart,
  With three-score years and more, and he so young –
Judged by our life we live on equal terms,
  Because his life is short, while mine is long.

To end this logic with that bird again,
  Be it enough to say I hope one thing –
That I'll be here when this contemporary's dead,
  Ten Aprils hence, to hear his grandchild sing.

532. Compensation

When these sweet spirits, my most faithful friends,
  No longer fill my reservoirs of song,
And pass me by as one whose work is finished,
  To help new poets who are young and strong –
Then, like a man that's blind, whose ears acquire
  A double strength, to follow every sound,
So shall I triumph in another's voice,
  And hear more clear, since my own tongue is bound.
Who are these spirits, that have not yet failed
  To fill my reservoirs of light and song?
Helped by their love, all scratches, cuts and wounds
  Close up like water, when the times go wrong.

533. Bewitched

Give me a night in June that's clear and quiet,
  That I may stare at Heaven until I see
Her face all twitching to her farthest star –
  Conscious of one true man's idolatry.

I stare at dewdrops till they close their eyes,
  I stare at grass till all the world is green;
I stare at rainbows all their precious life,
  Till nothing's left to prove what I have seen.

I stare at Robin Redbreast on his bough,
  Till he comes down with many a pretty dance:
I stare at my own Self, and walk the earth
  With half my spirit in a wonder-trance.

534. Seed and Flower

The seed-time of this lovely life,
  So long, so long ago;
Before it grew and came to flower –
  No man shall ever know.

How long it lay within this Earth,
  We shall not understand;
We can but guess from whence it came,
  And Bless the Vanished Hand.

We'll never know the seed, my Love,
  But here's a life in flower –
To kiss and smell, and call it sweet
  A thousand years and more!

535. The Little Devil

The Sun has his spots, the Moon has her shadows,
  The Sea has his wrinkles, the Land has her warts;
Sweet Faith has her doubts, and lovers their quarrels,
  And nothing is perfect in all its parts.

How lovely is a garden when neglected!
  What could be uglier than a perfect face!
Shall I then call my Love a perfect angel
  Sent down from Heaven to take a mortal's place?

How could she wear and last this common life,
  Unless her charms had some alloy of evil?
An Angel, no; but by Love's two extremes,
  Of ice and fire — *'Come here, you little devil!'*

536. When We Forget

When we forget that Nature gives
  No other home to lovers than
The haunted house of Death —
  Let us then call our love immortal,
Nor think we waste our breath.

But Love, still looking for a place
  To lean her head against, and sing,
Should never have her childish brain
  Vexed by a thought so cold and grave,
To turn her joy to pain.

537. Love and Money

I count my pounds as three times two,
    And five times one, my shillings;
Six pounds, five shillings for my Love,
    To buy a coat with frillings.

But as she takes the light and air,
    So will she take my money;
And all the thanks I'll get will be
    A quiet — 'Kiss me, Honey'.

And so I will, at such a rate
    That, long before it's over —
A deer pursued by fire and wind
    Shall fly to safer cover!

538. Where We Agree

Give her her ribbon, belt or scarf —
    To match my rainbow in the sky;
Let her prefer her looking-glass,
    When dewdrops meet me, eye to eye.
Give her her pretty flowers or stars,
    Embossed in silk and figured lace;
While I prefer their living forms,
    Set in a green or azure place.
Give her her choice, and give me mine,
    Remembering still Love's greater worth —
That she and I prefer each other
    To any thing in Heaven or Earth.

539. Brother Gods

If woman's a delightful creature,
    A dog can be another;
But, Lord, who ever saw such fools,
    When they are out together!

Cupid and Bacchus are the same,
    Delightful in their way;
But when these youngsters share one life —
    The very devil's to pay!

As fast as Cupid builds his dreams,
    Young Bacchus knocks them down;
He leaves poor Cupid limp with tears,
    And struts about the town.

So let us all be warned in time,
    When brother fights with brother;
Let's make our choice of one, and then —
    The devil take the other.

540. Spirits and Bodies

Two spirits in two bodies, Love,
 We live together here, and thrive;
If one of these two bodies die,
 How much of us will then survive?
If either you or I die first,
 What comfort has the passing bell?
Two spirits in one body, Love,
 Can hold together fairly well.
So when there's but one body left,
 And that dies too, let it be known
That two fond spirits leave together,
 As neither one could go alone.

541. Regret

How strange that Love should be like this,
 So miserly and mean;
To wrap such radiant corn in leaves
 Where little can be seen.

When sweet affection wastes its time
 On gravestones white and cold —
Shall we not pity their remorse,
 Whose love was never told?

542. To-morrow

What can I find in my wild orchard,
   To please your pretty eyes to-morrow;
A kitten mewing, short and sweet,
   Like the chirp of a sleeping sparrow?
A bee as big as a little bird;
   Flowers red or white, pink, blue or yellow?
Or a bird as small as the bumble bee —
   To please your pretty eyes to-morrow?

543. To-night

What can I find in the city shops,
   To please your pretty eyes to-night;
A lovely gown that's made of silk,
   Soft to the hand, and gossamer-light?
A little book with silver clasps,
   With golden words on all its pages?
Two bowls of glass, wherein the lights
   Flit here and there, like birds in cages?
A dog to wind up like a clock,
   That's made to growl, and then to yap?
Or Cupid as a fountain, made
   To piddle in his mother's lap?

544. Married Couples

When Love is strong in married couples,
   They grow in looks like one another;
Till strangers think they see a son,
   And then a daughter, of one mother.

Come, Time, and make us look like twins,
  My wife, my sister, I her brother;
That this amazing proof may show
  How she and I have loved each other!

545. The Laws of Beauty

The laws of Beauty and its patterns
  Must all conform to blood and race;
A nose that's tilted, round and small,
  Is not for any Jewish face.
To say that she is tall and plump
  Would be a blemish in Japan;
A foot coercion makes no smaller
  Would never please a Chinaman.
To say her skin's as white as foam,
  With sea-blue eyes, so soft and mellow,
Would please no race whose beauties must,
  Like all their gods, be brown or yellow.
But let these laws be what they will,
  And differ with our blood and race;
Come, fair or dark; come, white or brown —
  Where shall I find a sweeter face?

546. This Green Orchard

The healthiest place for Love is here,
  And not in any room;
Out in this old, green orchard, with
  The apple trees in bloom.

For here we see no idle hooks,
  No empty shelf or box,
To set Love's thoughts on sable scarves,
  Or stoles of silver fox.

The first sweet lovers known to life,
  Had nothing more than this:
Shall we, far richer, when compared,
  Be poorer in our bliss?

547. Love Lights His Fire

Love lights his fire to burn my Past —
  There goes the house where I was born!
And even Friendship — Love declares —
  Must feed his precious flames and burn.

I stuffed my life with odds and ends,
  But how much joy can Knowledge give?
The World my guide, I lived to learn —
  From Love, alone, I learn to live.

548. Past and Present

I who have seen a tiny cloud,
  No bigger than my Lady's puff,
Powder the Heavens with miles of soot,
  And make the seas all wild and rough;

I who have seen that speck at last
  Sink half a fleet and drown its men,
With waves, like eagles, swooping down
  To carry off both sheep and pen;

I who have felt and seen all this,
  And trained my thoughts to quiet scorn —
Am still the man to dress Love's finger,
  Scratched by a little pin or thorn.

549. Love Ten Years Old

Our love this day is ten years old.
  What thoughts are in my sweetheart's mind?
'A kinder, sweeter tempered man,'
  Says she, 'no woman could ever find.'

What says the World, that knows me less,
  And judged me of another kind —
That robs a poor man of his dog,
  And knows the man is old and blind!

550. True or Fickle

Who would not be a poet, when
  The girl he loves is sweet and kind,
And fancies burn and tickle;
  When both his Love and Muse are true,
And neither one is fickle?

And if there is but one that's true,
  To smile or prattle, kiss or sing,
He will not scorn the other;
  But take a joy that's half complete,
As poet, or as lover.

464

But when the both of them are false,
  His sweetheart turned contrary,
And Thought still sulks from Word —
  Who'll praise him for his peevish chirps?
Who wants that moulting bird?

551.   Alone

When we're together, how the moments fly!
  We toss them up like jewels in the sun;
We catch them lightly as a falling leaf,
  To find a light that's new in every one;
Life then to us is all a game of play
With leaves and jewels, and too short a day.

But when alone with Time, and you away,
  I hear those heavy, deadly strokes of his
At Life's foundations, aiming at our years,
  That fall in thuds from blows that never miss;
What are our moments then, so weak and small —
When years of life are heard to crash and fall!

552.   The Shadow

She flies from my shadow,
  To her lover, the Sun;
Yet for her rare beauty,
  I still follow on.

Her wings tipped with silver,
  Jet-black, and of gold,
She flies to her lover,
  From a shadow that's cold.

Stay, Butterfly, stay,
　My Love's full of laughter:
Why fly from a shadow?
　She still follows after!

553.　Love's Rivals

What glorious sunsets have their birth
　In Cities fouled by smoke!
This tree — whose roots are in a drain —
　Becomes the greenest Oak!
No hand's more gentle than a thief's,
　Greed has the brightest eyes;
And by their straight, clear, honest looks,
　Great villains live on lies!
Yet Love, whose source is sweet and pure,
　Still makes no question why
A thief should have more gentle hands,
　Or Greed a brighter eye.

554.　A Foolish Tongue

Her face is full of silent Pain —
　Forgive my foolish tongue;
I with my one desire in life,
　To praise our love in song.

If I should do this thing again,
　Lord, let Thy vengeance come;
Take back Thy precious gift of song,
　And strike me cold and dumb!

466

If I again forget her love,
    And utter words of blame,
Let my own mother from her grave
    Rise up, and cry — 'For shame!'

555. Faults

The healthiest trees bear fruits that fail,
    By worm or frost they drop decayed;
The very Heavens have weakling stars
    That fall from their high state, and fade.
But as a thousand silver stars
    Stand firm and fast for one that's lost;
And many a strong and golden pear
    Survives the worm, the wind, and frost:
So must I think, when Love's at fault,
    Of charms secure and manifold —
As stars whose silver numbers last,
    And pears that reach the age of gold.

556. Competitors

I had a friend to smoke and drink,
    We dined at clubs and saw the Play;
Till Love came, like the smallest wind,
    And looked him quietly away.

So Friendship goes, and Love remains,
    And who can question which is best —
A Friendship reared on the bottle, or
    A Love that's reared at the breast?

557. Fortunes

'This house is worth a thousand pounds,
You'll not be very poor;
My pictures and my books,' said I —
'May fetch a thousand more.'
But I, who thought to see her smile,
With nothing strange or wild,
Turned round to find her limp and cold,
And crying like a child.
It seems that I, a living man,
Though life was but a linger —
Was worth a thousand cold, dead hands
With a fortune for each finger.

558. Great Lovers

Why did we think no power in Heaven
    Would ever chill or blind that loving eye?
Sweet Earth, so young and green, so beautiful,
    Your lover is but mortal, and must die.

Burning himself to nothing, day by day,
    Your lover, that great Sun, is slowly dying;
And where you smile, a Queen of beauty now,
    There'll be a poor, unhappy lady, crying.

559.   Let Love Live On

Love is the precious jewel in our Life,
   The sweetest thing this Earth has ever known,
Found in a labourer's cottage, on a stool,
   Then in a palace, sitting on a throne.
She lets no Knowledge cloud our mortal hours,
   Or cast its shadows on her glorious eyes;
All hope of Life immortal after Death
   Springs out of Love's abiding qualities.
Love judges neither blood, nor pomp, nor state,
   She questions for its *heart* each living thing:
What kind of woman is our English queen,
   What kind of man her husband and our king.

560.   The Ghost

Seek not to know Love's full extent,
   For Death, not Life, must measure Love;
Not till one lover's dead and gone,
   Is Love made strong enough to prove.
What woman, with a ghostly lover,
   Can hold a mirror to her hair?
A man can tell his love with tears,
   When but a woman's ghost is there.
Our greatest meeting is to come,
   When either you or I are lost:
When one, being left alone in tears,
   Confesses to the other's ghost.

561. Pecking

One kiss to open up the day,
    One kiss at night to close it fast;
Sometimes a kiss or two between,
    To help the first and last.
But when I woke this morning early,
    I caught her pecking at my face;
Greedy for grain, she pecked and pecked
    All over the golden place.
And artful I, still feigning sleep,
    Lay quiet, while that little chick
Enjoyed the grain Love scattered there —
    And still went on to peck.

562. Words and Kisses

She pecks the earth for every second,
    Young Jenny Wren, while on the run:
'Come, Love, and watch this little darling;
    Come, see this pretty little one.'

'Why waste such precious words on birds?'
    Said jealous Love, not liking this.
'They are but words, my Love,' said I —
    'To make birds jealous when we kiss!'

563. Good and Evil

A wealth of stars in Winter time
  Brings frost severe and cold;
And Winter's coppers are no more
  Than Autumn's wasted gold:
While Love herself, this very morning,
Scorned me without one word of warning.

Had I not seen a Bumble-bee
  Stand on his head in clover;
Parting the folds with hairy legs,
  For comfort under cover;
Had I not seen this Bee and wondered —
Could I have left Love's scorn unpondered?

564. The Peacemaker

When she threatened to leave me,
  And I, full of evil,
Cried 'Hoi, tiddlee, hoi,
  Here's work for the devil! — '

With a sharp, single cry,
  With a quick, sudden burst,
Up sat our little blind dog,
  And begged to be nursed.

565. The Supper

Since music is Love's milk and keeps him strong,
Give him his supper, let the feast last long;
Let it begin like thunder, with a power
That in mid-June our nightingales adore.

Then let it come to whispers, low and deep,
As a dreaming Bee that buzzes in his sleep;
While Love's small head, that on your shoulder lies,
Has fixed on me his large, unwavering eyes.

566. Marvellous Ears

That speckled Thrush, that stands so still,
   Is listening for the worms to stir;
He hears a worm — what marvellous ears!
   That he can live by ear alone,
And save his eyes to guard his fears.

So when I have a secret care,
   And think my voice is well controlled,
Love, like the Thrush that hears a worm,
   Detects it with her marvellous ear —
No matter what her eyes affirm.

567. Beauty and Song

The Peacock, that fine-feathered bird,
  Has but a screeching voice;
The Robin, with a lovely breast,
  Sings once, and quarrels twice.

I married you for youth and beauty,
  The first to please my mind;
And found Love's strength was in her voice —
  To keep it sweet and kind.

568. Three Score and Ten

Ten Junes to hear the Nightingale,
  Ten Aprils for the Cuckoo's coming;
And only ten more Februarys, Love,
  To celebrate our wedding.
Come, happier thoughts, and cry 'Good Morrow'!
  Though we but kiss three times a day,
Three hundred days and sixty five,
  In every year, must come our way!
Think how these kisses too will make
  One thousand and ninety-five a year!
And all the thousands that must follow
  In ten years' reckoning up, my Dear!

569. Let Us Lie Close

Let us lie close, as lovers should,
    That, if I wake when barn-cocks crow —
I'll feel your body at my side,
    And hear your breathing come and go.

When dreams, one night, had moved our bodies,
    I, waking, listened for your breath;
I feared to reach and touch your face,
    That it was icy-cold in death.

Let us lie close, as lovers should,
    And count our breaths, as some count sheep;
Until we say 'Good night', at last,
    And with one kiss prepare for sleep.

570. Light and Darkness (ii)

Though I sit brooding here, with my eyes closed,
Yet have I seen the light go suddenly;
Though I had shut them fast, to see no light,
A sudden wave of darkness, without warning,
Broke on their trembling lids, and forced my sight.

So when my Love has gone out quietly,
And left me here alone, all lost in dreams,
I see the shadow of her absence fall
Across my vision, that had been too blind
To see her body in the light at all.

571. Stings

Though bees have stings, I doubt if any bee
  Has ever stung a flower in all his life:
Neither, my love, can I think ill of you,
  Though half the world and I may be at strife.

Can I forget your coming, like the Moon
  When, robed in light, alone, without a star,
She visits ruins; and the peace you brought,
  When I with all the world was still at war.

572. Last Thoughts

If my last thoughts contain no wish
  To feed the wild birds here;
If I forget to pity you,
  And show no mark of care;
If I forget your kindness, love,
  And hasten to my grave:
Then, false to all that made life sweet,
  What good shall I deserve?
Then, though I see Heaven close at hand,
  And hear the music too,
May twenty devils seize my soul —
  Until I think of you!

573. A Lullaby of Rest

Workhouse and Bedlam, Refuge, Den,
   For Passions deaf and blind —
How many strange and peevish things
   Have harboured in my mind!

Ambition, Pride and Greed, with all
   The Body's Appetites,
Knocked at my door for lodgings, and
   Disturbed my days and nights.

Till, treading softly, like a bird,
   When young ones fill her nest —
Love sits beside me here, and sings
   A lullaby of rest.

574. Beauty and Brain

When I was old, and she was young,
   With all the beauty hers —
I wooed her with a silver tongue,
   With music for her ears;
And shall I now complain to find
That Beauty has so small a mind?

If this young Chit had had more sense
   Would she have married me?
That she gave me the preference,
   Proved what a fool was she:
Then let me die if I complain
That Beauty has too small a brain.

476

575. The Tyrants

Love came about the Cuckoo's time,
    Two months ago, or more;
In April I was rich in joy,
    But June has left me poor.

Love cried for money all day long,
    For more than I possessed;
The Cuckoo, making echoes fast,
    Destroyed my quiet rest.

Now, in July, in this dead calm,
    When both are gone away —
I sit alone, a peevish man,
    And miss them every day.

576. Three Loves

My silver love is shared by all,
    With every flower and bird;
With every man that greets me well,
    A friendly nod or word.
My golden love is kept for two,
    That share my fire and mat;
A little dog with simple ways,
    And my self-conscious cat.
My diamond love, more precious far,
    Is shared by only one;
And where She is that love prevails,
    On mat or grass, or stone.

477

577. His Throne

When Love has lost his bite and sting,
  And all his fire has gone —
What other god shall take his place,
  And fill his golden throne?

Where Love has sat, there let him lie,
  Whether he lives or dies;
Still on that throne, where none succeeds,
  Embalmed in memories.

578. Flirting

Should her flirting prove a danger,
What's the proper thing to change her;
Shall I, marching up and down,
Stamp and tremble, sulk and frown?
Since no woman will obey,
Bid her go, and then she'll stay.
When a woman's lost to reason,
That's the stuff to stop her treason.

Sing a song of 'Flirt, my Pretty,
Flirt and flit, I need no pity;
Though you mend my shirt, or never —
Why should I be pledged to either!'
Sing a song of 'Heigh, Heigh Ho,
What care I what Women do!'
When a woman's lost to reason,
That's the stuff to stop her treason.

579. The Jealous Lover

Who is this man that, brain on fire,
  Can reason without rule;
The fastest thinker known to life,
  And yet the greatest fool?
This man is blind, and yet can see
  Beyond our common eyes,
This man is deaf, yet hears plain words
  When others hear but sighs.
Thinking that silence proves our guilt,
  And speech is all a lie,
He cries aloud, 'My name is Truth —
  Who calls me Jealousy?'

580. Love Me No More

Since Love cries out for money, still,
  Where little is, or none —
Love me no more till I am dead,
  And every penny gone.

Is there one tender thought to come,
  When I have nothing more —
To show the World that Love, though small,
  Can be secure and pure?

Love me no more till I am dead,
  And dangers all removed;
When, though my worms can spin no silk,
  I lie unblamed, and loved.

581. The Faithful One

The bird that fills my ears with song,
  The Sun that warms me with his fire;
The dog that licks my face and hands,
  And She whose beauty I desire —
Each of these think that he or she
Creates in me the joy they see.

But when my dog's gone off with a bitch,
  And there's no Sun, nor bird in song;
When Love's false eyes seek other men,
  And leave me but her lying tongue;
Still will my Joy — though forced to roam —
Remember me and come back home.

582. Eardrops

This bag of cherries for my Love:
  She takes one lovely Pair,
And makes an eardrop of each one,
  To fit in either ear.
Until I swear it seems to me,
  To see those Cherry stones,
They almost match in loveliness
  The flesh that's on her bones.
They match her eyes in light and size,
  With such a glowing stain —
That every precious pearl is hurled
  Back to its sea again!

583. The Players

To-day I acted Christ,
   While Joy played Lazarus;
I buried her in ferns
   And heaps of gathered grass.
And when I cried 'Come forth!'
   Up from the grave she rose
And, with a peal of bells,
   Threw off her burial clothes.

When Sleep this night has come,
   With feathers for our grass,
Shall we reverse our parts
   Of Christ and Lazarus?
When I — a buried man —
   Hear 'Lazarus, come forth!'
I'll rise and, with both hands,
   Ring every bell on earth!

584. The Birth of Song

I am as certain of my song,
   When first it warms my brain,
As woman of her unborn child,
   Or wind that carries rain.
The child and rain are born at last,
   Though now concealed from sight —
So let my song, unshaped and crude,
   Come perfect to the light.

585. Man

Come, let us measure
  The greatness of Man;
The marvellous things on earth
  Conceived and done.

He who would measure
  How little is Man,
Must cry himself to sleep,
  Like some lost Little One.

586. This is a Joy

This is a joy no laughter shakes,
  Nor shall my body rock;
It hears the Cuckoo's voice in Spring,
  And sends no echoes back.
When Music plays, it claps no hands,
  To twirl on nimble toes;
It sits as quiet as a bird,
  With all its young up close.
It is a joy that reconciles
  The smallest with the greatest;
From what I was, and am, until
  Life's sweetest breath comes, latest.

587. All's Well

The cat has her milk,
    The dog has his bone;
The man has his ale,
    And his week's work is done,
He sits at a fire,
    And he sees his young wife
Give suck to her babe —
    All's well with his life.

588. A New World

A new World calls, in voices loud and strange,
    But what they mean or say no man can prove;
Like cats at night, we do not know their game,
Whether they scream for murder or for love.

They come along with many a blinded rush,
    And have no sense in sight, or force of will;
Like drunken men, impelled to walk or run,
    Because they have no power to stand up still.

Beauty and Music lie beyond their thoughts,
    And what they say or mean, no man can know;
They give us warts in place of Beauty's moles—
    And Music that was once an Irish row.

589.   Street Criers

(Written for Music)

When Poll stays here, her Jack goes there,
　　To earn their provender;
Her cries are all in Bethnal Green —
　　'Sweet Lavender! Sweet Lavender!
Who'll buy Sweet Lavender?'

And oft she wonders if her Jack
　　Enjoys a man's success;
Who cries on top of Stamford Hill —
　　'Young Watercress! Young Watercress!
Who'll buy Young Watercress?'

590.   Scandal

This is God's poorest lambing-time,
　　Our life is one of evil;
Who'll bring me news that's kind and sweet,
　　Where Mercy shames the devil?
We leap like fleas before we look,
　　On any sin or lie;
Unless I hear more kindness soon,
　　I'll laugh until I die.
I'll put this injured Bee to rest,
　　Safe on a mossy stone —
Till Scandal, blackening all that's white,
　　Has said 'Good-bye', and gone.

591. Love in Trouble

The World is poor, and Love is lonely,
  He sits alone, and has no toy;
He sits beside a dying fire,
  And sucks his thumb for all his joy.

What thoughts have we for song or beauty,
  In this old World, so sad and poor?
We count and fear to spend our pence,
  And think no more of bird or flower.

The World is poor, and Love is lonely,
  His dying fire no longer heats:
He dreams of sugar, cakes and toys,
  And sucks his thumb for all his sweets.

592. Tell Me, World, and Tell Me, Nature

No spoilt, no pampered child am I,
  Neither by Nature nor the World;
Enough to keep my Body in breath
  Is all I get in silver and gold.
How many pools have been my haunts,
  Which but a Moorhen stirred,
To see my great Kingfisher twice —
  That wild and lovely, life-sought Bird!
And many a Rainbow too has come
  All silently in Heaven, and gone,
Between last Blackberry-time and this —
  While I saw only one!
Then tell me, World, and tell me, Nature —
  Am I a spoilt and pampered creature?

593. The Conquerors

Who are these men with quiet smiles —
　How came these two together?
I'd walk ten miles to meet with one
　Or ten to miss the other.

The one man smiles because the World
　Is conquered by his love;
The other smiles because the World
　Must fear his every move.

594. Catching the Devil

Not while her charms are still in flower,
　We'll trust no woman then;
Not till her beauty's gone for good,
　Can she be safe with men.
I thought I loved an angel once,
　Without one breath of evil —
Till, smiling in my cunning trap,
　I saw the very devil!
I set my trap in my friend's face,
　With his weak face my glass;
Till, with his looks reflecting hers —
　O Lord, how false she was!

595. Named

As I marched out one day in Spring,
  Proud of my life and power —
I saw an infant, all alone,
  Kissing a small, red flower.
He looked at me with solemn eyes,
  As only children can,
And — in a voice that might be God's —
  He called distinctly — 'Man!'
Though I had been the Pope of Rome,
  Our English King or Heir,
A child has called in God's own way,
  And I have answered — 'Here!'

596. The Witness

The witness to my document
  Was called a woman of shame;
She takes my pen, and lifts her clothes,
  To kneel, and write her name.

With head bowed down, on bended knees,
  She kneels before my chair;
And, writing slowly, rises up —
  As a little child from prayer.

597. The Age of Gold

A silver shilling for his white-haired Granny,
That child is richer far with but a penny;
Compared with Youth, that has but little more,
Old men with gold must still be counted poor.
When you have spent your three score years and ten,
And tell how you have prospered in the end —
Think then of others in their golden Youth,
That still have all their precious years to spend.
When you are old, and live for Memory's sake,
What are you but all tail, and nothing more?
Think of your Youth, with all its lovely dreams,
When you, all eyes, were richer far, though poor.

598. The Mongrel

Your Laurel Hedge, with its broad leaves,
    Keeps fresh and green from year to year;
While that poor Wayside, Mongrel hedge,
    In Winter time goes thin and bare.
But when October's in his prime,
    How beautiful that Mongrel grows —
Where Blackberry, Thorn and other leaves
    Can make a hundred shining hues!
In singles, twins, and triplets too,
    In bunch and cluster, high and low,
I see his fruits in heavy folds,
    Or fluttering lightly to and fro.
The Apple with her beauty-moles,
    The beady Currant, glassy-eyed;
The golden Corn, all naked there,
    Without a leaf on either side.

The nippled Pear and misty Plum,
  The yellow Quince and Cherry red;
The crimson Strawberry, full of dimples,
  Now lying so low in her bed.
Let no man touch this Mongrel now,
  Nor dare to pick his fruit, for fear
That Wizard turns his gorgeous feast
  To shrivelled leaves, all limp and sere.

599.   The Lily of Our Valley

(Written for Music)

Once on a time, in Pontypool,
There lived a maid, all beautiful;
And every time she went abroad,
The people cried, with one accord —
'Here comes our Sweetest, lovely Sally!
Sally, the Lily of our Valley!'

As sweet as any nut put by,
Selected by a Squirrel's eye;
As pure as any drop of dew
A bird drinks, after looking through —
No wonder every voice cried 'Sally!
Sally, the Lily of our Valley!'

600. Combing

All for the sake of lovely dreams,
   I search the World, and everywhere;
I comb the hours for golden thoughts,
   As a mermaid combs her hair.
And as she sometimes combs out gold,
   That shines like shreds of silk;
That makes the sand she sings on rich,
   As cream enriches milk;
And sometimes combs out mud or weeds,
   All gathered from her miles afloat —
So I, who find a dream at times,
   Am sometimes left without a thought.

601. Song of the Miners

When starving cattle see
   Their blades of grass
Locked up in ice that cuts
   Their mouths, like glass —
What can they do but lie in heaps and die?

And shall our people starve,
   Like these wild herds?
We, with our power to think,
   Our gift of words —
Shall we lie down like these dumb brutes and die?

602. Father and Son

'While we enjoy this meat, my Son,
   This tongue so savoury,
Bear this in mind — it was a tongue
   That never told a lie!'

'Now, Father, tell me this at once,
   Explain the reason why:
Is it no sin to kill and eat
   A tongue that told no lie?'

603. Good Friends

I brought two friends to share my fire,
   To crack a joke or two;
I kissed one friend, and smacked my lips,
   And sighed, as lovers do.
And never think, when I had slept
   And, waking, found them gone —
That I abused my absent friends,
   To find myself alone.
Now, shall I call my friends by name,
   That shared this fire of mine?
Well, one was called 'Young Walnuts', and
   The other was 'Old Wine'.

604   To W.S.—On his Wonderful Toys

Lend me your precious toys,
  But for one day and night;
I'll take them under my orchard boughs,
  And nurse them out of sight;
Till my two hands, all warm with love,
Fill them with breath, and make them move!

And when Night comes, a grey-haired child
  Shall hobble off to bed;
With rabbits, mice and little birds
  Around his face and head;
Where in your toys his secret lies —
To keep his childhood till he dies.

605.   Broken Hearts

My dog creeps into my shadowed form,
  And takes my foot to rest his head;
It is his love of me, I know,
  That warms his cold, hard bed.
Women have died of broken hearts,
  And men have reached the same disaster;
But the likeliest thing to die is a dog
  That waits for its dead Master.
The King is dead, by millions mourned,
  That bared their heads, or wept, or sighed;
The dog, that waited for him in vain,
  Has broken its heart, and died.
So end two lives, and one so small a thing —
  It never knew its Master was a King.

606. Success

Sharpen your claws, Pussy-cat,
  For a bird newly flown;
While a bird cleans its beak
  For a snail on a stone.
Powder your face, fair Woman,
  Still thinking of Man.
If the cat gets a bird,
  She will purr all she can;
If a bird gets a snail,
  We shall hear a sweet carol.
When a Woman gets Man,
  Tell me — why must she quarrel?

607. Rich Companions

While I have these two rich companions left,
  Wine for my Body, Music for my Mind —
Shall I complain that Life has lost its youth,
  And say that Fate is cruel and unkind?

Come, then, let Wine and Music help each other;
  That when my Wine has closed both eye and ear,
I'll hear in dreams a Music more divine,
  Refined by something more than common air.

Fill up the glass and turn the small round knob —
  Bring in those sweet far-travelled melodies:
Wine for my Body, Music for my Mind —
  Can Age find any richer friends than these?

493

608. The Loneliest Mountain

The loneliest mountain, with no house or tree,
  Still has its little flower so sweet and wild;
While I, a dreamer, strange and but half known,
  Can find no equal till I meet a child.

609. Pride and Humility

He passed me by in April, Lord,
  With what an awful frown!
He held an eyeglass to his eye,
  And looked me up and down.

He passed me by in August, Lord,
  With what a chastened mind!
He held a woman by her arm,
  And walked beside her — blind.

610. The Load of Pearls

Will no one stop that Blackbird now,
  Before he sings himself to death?
Tell him there is no life on earth
  Enjoys an everlasting breath.

He sings because a tree in May
  Is flower all over, low and high:
A cherry tree, whose load of pearls
  Brings diamonds into every eye!

611. Taking Stock

A pipe to smoke, and ale that's mulled,
  With walnuts fresh enough to peel;
The voice of Love, that comes and goes,
  And brings a kiss between each meal;
A day that's hot, for a shady tree,
  A night that's cold, for a cosy bed;
A brain that starved for lovelier dreams,
  A body light, and daintily fed;
A search for keys no man can find,
  To turn the lock of Life and Death:
With these my stock, my song is done—
  And, tell me, do I waste my breath?

612. Worms

Silkworms have dressed the fairest women,
  Glowworms have their own starry climes;
Straight from his breakfast on a worm,
  The bird begins his morning chimes.
    Maggots, so fat and short,
    Tapeworms, so thin and long:
     'All these are able' —
Say Anglers, when they speak the truth —
'To fill a bowl with fish for some man's table.'

613. Silent Eyes

There is a bird that, in her throat,
    Turns half her song to laughter:
She is the woman for my ears —
    But who shall I kiss after?

Find me a woman for my eyes,
    Who'll waste no time in song;
To spend with her a silence that
    Exceeds the sweetest song.

Take her, who loves to hear a voice,
    With notes that fall or rise —
While I enjoy the spawny light
    That spreads in silent eyes.

614. The Deed

When I, made merry with the wine,
    Had left my roystering band,
I saw a cold and bloodless man —
    No poorer in the land;
And, gathering all my money left,
    I filled his trembling hand.

But who looked into his Father's eyes —
    Whose was the voice of pain?
'If he had done this thing,' said Christ,
    'With his clear heart and brain —
Could I not bear a second Cross,
    And die for Man again?'

615. A Cat's Example

For three whole days I and my cat
Have come up here, and patiently sat —
   We sit and wait on silent Time;
He for a mouse that scratched close by,
At a hole where he sets his eye —
   And I for some music and rhyme.

Is this the Poet's secret, that
He waits in patience, like this cat,
   To start a dream from under cover?
A cat's example, too, in love,
With Passion's every trick and move,
   Would burn up any human lover.

616. Trust

Once I was wise when, in my Youth,
   I went my way alone;
Before this world betrayed my trust,
   And turned my heart to stone.

Or is it all in God's good time,
   In keeping with His plan —
That I may put more trust in Him,
   The more I lose in Man?

617. Common Joys

See how those diamonds splutter and choke —
  What greedy things they are for light!
That pearl, whose pulse less wildly beats,
  Is far more restful to my sight.
Soon tired of all these glittering toys,
  With my delight and wonder gone —
I send my thoughts, like butterflies,
  To dream on some old spotted stone.

So, when the Skylark sings no more,
  And I have seen the graceful Swallow;
When I have heard the Blackbird too,
  And many a bird in field or furrow:
Then to my Sparrow I return,
  Who scolds me well for what he misses —
And thinks a common chirp at times
  Pays all his debts, like children's kisses.

618. Speed

Think, Man of Flesh, and be not proud
  That you can fly so fast:
The little Worm can creep, creep, creep,
  And catch you up at last —
Catch up with you at last.

Though you outfly the swiftest bird,
  And laugh as you go past,
Think how the Worm comes, creep, creep, creep,
  To catch you up at last —
Catch up with you at last.

619. Armed for War

Is life on Earth a viler thing
  Than ever was known before?
Who shall we ask — the wise old man
  Whose years have reached five score?

When we have questioned Church and State,
Is there anyone else to ask?
Is it the Baby, three weeks old,
  That wears a gas-proof mask?

Is it the Infant armed to meet
  A poisoned earth and sky —
A thing too weak to lift its hand
  To rub a sleepy eye?

620. The Tugged Hand

I have no ears or eyes
  For either bird or flower;
Music and lovely blooms
  Must bide their lighter hour;
So let them wait awhile —
  For yet another day

Till I at last forget
  The woman lying dead;
And how a lonely child
  Came to his mother's bed
And tugged at her cold hand —
  And could not make it play.

621. Days and Years

How softly now my Days go by —
  How quietly the Moments glide!
Yet, underneath, I feel the rush
  Of a swifter, stronger tide.

And though my Days glide softly by,
  I ache from the throbs and fears
Of a terrible tide that, underneath,
  Is carrying off my *Years*!

622. Following a Bee

Of primrose boys
  April has many;
He seems as fond
  Of them as any;
He shows the world
Those boys in gold.

But violets are
  His girls, whom he
Shuts up in some
  Green nunnery:
So does he prove
His deepest love.

April, a girl
  Of yours is found;
High walls of grass
  Hemmed her around:
April, forgive me —
I followed a bee.

623. Woman

We're but the Shadows of these Women Suns,
  We creep behind, and still they lead the way;
We're but the Tides, and Women are our Moons,
  We come and go, and quietly obey.

We worship them to-day and call them saints,
  We follow them from love, and praise their beauty;
To-morrow comes and, following them from fear,
  We limp behind to do a husband's duty.

They lead the way, and men must follow still,
  We're but their slaves, be it from love or fear;
And when they fail to coax or scold with words,
  We'll find our certain Master in a Tear.

624. The Last Years

A dog, that has ten years of breath,
Can count the number left to me,
  To reach my seventy as a man.
In five years' time a bird is born,
Whose shorter life is then my own,
  Reducing still the human span.

Soon after that, a butterfly,
Who lives for but a year or less,
  Reminds me that the end is near;
And that, when I have lived his life,
A shorter life is still to come —
  Which brings the Summer's insect here.

501

And when at last that insect comes,
That lives for but a single day,
  He makes my life his very own:
Man, dog, and bird and butterfly
And insect yield their separate lives —
  And Death takes all of us as one.

625. All in June

A week ago I had a fire,
  To warm my feet, my hands and face;
Cold winds, that never make a friend,
  Crept in and out of every place.

To-day, the fields are rich in grass,
  And buttercups in thousands grow;
I'll show the World where I have been —
  With gold-dust seen on either shoe.

Till to my garden back I come,
  Where bumble-bees, for hours and hours,
Sit on their soft, fat, velvet bums,
  To wriggle out of hollow flowers.

626. Men that Think

Be damned, you cheeks, be damned and sink;
Body, bend double, sag and shrink;
Go dry, poor Skin, go thin and dry;
Sweet Light, collect in neither eye;
Body, be damned — shall I not find
Your faults redeemed by my unfailing Mind?

A Mind that's strong enough to bear
A Dream-child every day of the year;
A Spirit full of young desire,
With growing pains, to reach up higher —
Is there no joy for men that think?
Body, be damned, bend double, sag and shrink!
Fools have their second childhood, but the Great
Still keep their first, and have no second state.

627. The Dead Tree

I had a cherry tree, one day,
  Against my garden wall;
There came a heavy wind by night,
  And made it crash and fall.
I hired a man, and gave him gold,
  To lift my tree up straight.
He nailed it back, nor missed one twig,
  And knew it was too late.
He knew my tree was old and dead,
  Yet worked with fiendish glee:
How lovely he has nailed his Christ
  On my dead cherry tree!

628. Music's Tragedy

Had birds no season for their precious songs,
  What would we call them but a common pest?
Since Music's now a manufactured thing,
  Potted and churned in every house we pass —
Think of the birds, how they more wisely sing.

503

That Paradise we dreamed of years ago,
    When Music, rarely heard, was thought divine,
Is for the 'Damned', and not the 'Happy Blest';
    Since, fed by force, with Music cheapened so —
Is there no quiet place to sleep or rest?

629.   The Worms' Contempt

What do we earn for all our gentle grace?
A body stiff and cold from foot to face.

If you have beauty, what is beauty worth?
A mask to hide it, made of common earth.

What do we get for all our song and prattle?
A gasp for longer breath, and then a rattle.

What do we earn for dreams, and our high teaching?
The worms' contempt, that have no time for preaching.

630.   Life

The quality of life on earth
    Is all that dreams could make it be;
And all I ask for in this world
    Is but increase in quantity.
My corn and wine — how sweet are these!
    How precious is this living breath!
Is it not Man's ingratitude
    That looks for better after death?

631. Nailsworth Hill

The Moon, that peeped as she came up,
    Is clear on top, with all her light;
She rests her chin on Nailsworth Hill,
    And, where she looks, the World is white.

White with her light — or is it Frost,
    Or is it Snow her eyes have seen;
Or is it Cherry blossom there,
    Where no such trees have ever been?

632. A Change of Voice

I heard a Lady near my door
    Talking to one she knew:
Was this the voice I used to hear,
    So tender, soft and true?
Was this the voice that charmed me once,
    Before the Marriage vow?
But why should Man, securely bound,
    Expect that accent now!
Why should she charm him as a wife,
    Knowing she has him chained for life;
And why should she call him her 'Honey' —
    Knowing the wretch has no more money?

633. Slippers

When Youth is gone, and Beauty too,
    And Blood is wild no more —
How can they prove, when old and weak,
    That Love is still in power?
Will, when their Kisses die for warmth,
    And flesh has no desire,
They fetch each other's slippers from
    The cupboard to a fire?
And will they sit together there,
    To sleep or sew, or read;
And if one hears a sigh, or coughs —
    Will not the other heed?

634. Looks

What knowledge do my Ears provide,
    What do I learn from books?
I trust my Eyes for what I think,
    And feed on silent looks.

The things I hear with my two Ears
    Still cry aloud for proof;
But what I see with my two Eyes
    Must be the very truth.

The woman that's behind my back,
    To hide her looks from me —
Knows not the face of him I watch
    Stirs to her treachery.

635. The Mind Speaks

Poor Body, sitting there so calm,
  With scarcely any breath —
Are we rehearsing that last act,
  When we shall meet with Death?
Our fire of life is burning low,
  And we can feel the cold —
Yet we have had a glorious time,
  When all our days are told.
Rest, tired Body, rest in peace,
  And trust the Mind, this hour:
With thoughts too kind to tempt the flesh
  To act beyond its power.

636. That Golden Time

When will it come, that golden time,
  When every man is free?
Men who have power to choose their tasks
  Have all their liberty.

They'll sweat and toil who love to feel
  Their muscles swell and move;
While men whose minds are more to them,
  Create the dreams we love.

When will it come, that golden time,
  When every heart must sing?
The power to choose the work we love
  Makes every man a king.

637. The Muse

I have no ale,
   No wine I want;
No ornaments,
   My meat is scant.

No maid is near,
   I have no wife;
But here's my pipe
   And, on my life:

With it to smoke,
   And woo the Muse,
To be a king
   I would not choose.

But I crave all,
   When she does fail —
Wife, ornaments,
   Meat, wine and ale.

638. Tyrants

Peace makes more slaves than savage War,
Since tyrants, backed by their Land's Law —
Needing no deadly armament —
Can force a people to consent
To toil like slaves for little pay,
In shops and factories all day;
Make human moles, that sweat and slave
In dark, cold, cheerless rooms; who have
No blood, to make them well again,
If foul Disease should give them pain.

508

The cold, proud rich they, without cares,
In comfort live; like surly bears
That eat and sleep in caves of ice
The Heavenly Sun has painted nice;
Tyrants that would, to have their rent,
Turn tenants' Christmas into Lent,
For fast instead of feast. What, free!
When masters, who hate Liberty,
Can in their height of power and greed
Force weaker men to serve their need?
Dogs may rear cats, the cat a rat,
And wolves stay hunger, loving what
They could devour — so masters may
Make men their care instead of prey.
The Fly has many eyes: I guess
A Spider can see more with less:
One Tyrant, though not right, is strong
To punish thousands for no wrong.

639. To a Butterfly

We have met,
   You and I;
Loving man,
   Lovely Fly.

If I thought
   You saw me,
And love made
   You so free

To come close —
   I'd not move
Till you tired
   Of my love.

640. The Milkmaid's Call

As I walked down a lane this morn,
  I heard a sweet voice cry, Come, Come!
And then I saw ten dull, fat cows
  Begin to race like horses home;
Like horses in their pace,
Though lacking horses' grace.

That voice, which did uplift those feet
  Of cows, uplifted mine likewise;
For, with a heart so light, I walked
  Until the sweat did blind my eyes;
And all the way back home,
I heard her cry, Come, Come!

641. The Milkmaid's Song

A Milkmaid, on a Summer's day,
Was singing, as she milked away.

The heavy, sullen cows had come
Racing when her voice called them home.

A three-legged stool, a pail that glows,
To sit and sing, and milk her cows.

Her cheeks were red, her eyes were bright,
And, like that milk, her neck was white.

The birds around her tuned their throats —
In vain — to take her perfect notes.

The cow gave up the last milk-drop,
And tarried till her song should stop.

'Wilt marry me, sweet Maid?' I said.
She laughed in scorn, and tossed her head.

And she had milked the crimson flood
E'en to my heart's last drop of blood.

642. Beauty's Danger

How can she safely walk this earth,
And not be robbed of all her worth,
By bulls and bees that may catch sight
Of her lips waving their red light.
Birds could make bedding of her hair,
And her ripe lips could tempt wasps there;
If Summer's moths should see her eyes,
They'd drop on them, and never rise,
But, filled at once with mad desire,
Would soon put out those lamps of fire,
With their lives sacrificed: no gem
Shines on Night's ebon breast like them.
Even the hawk a foe might prove,
To see her bosom in a move;
And thinking there she hid young mice,
Or birds, that would not sleep in peace.
For never doth that bosom rest;
If she doth hold her breath, there must
Follow a storm; the only boat
That ever on that sea did float
Is this blessed hand of mine: when I
As helpless as a boat must lie —
When seamaids' music makes the Breeze
Drop on the sails and sleep. O she's
An everlasting spring, that flows
When all my other springs do close.

643. City and Country

The City has dull eyes,
    The City's cheeks are pale;
The City has black spit,
    The City's breath is stale.

The Country has red cheeks,
    The Country's eyes are bright;
The Country has sweet breath,
    The Country's spit is white.

Dull eyes, breath stale; ink spit
    And cheeks like chalk — for thee;
Eyes bright, red cheeks; sweet breath
    And spit like milk — for me.

644. A Summer's Noon

White lily clouds
    In violet skies;
The Sun is at
    His highest rise.

The Bee doth hum,
    Every bird sings;
The Butterflies
    Full stretch their wings.

The Brook doth dance
    To his own song;
The Hawthorn now
    Smells sweet and strong.

The green Leaves clap
　　Their wings to fly;
Like Birds whose feet
　　Bird lime doth tie.

Sing all you Birds,
　　Hum all you Bees;
Clap you green wings,
　　Leaves on the trees —

I'm one with all,
　　This present hour:
Things-far-away
　　Have lost their power.

645.　A Swallow that Flew into the Room

I give thee back thy freedom, bird,
　　But know, I am amazed to see
These lovely feathers, which thou hast
　　Concealed so many years from me.

Oft have I watched thee cut the name
　　Of Summer in the clear, blue air,
And praised thy skilful lettering —
　　But never guessed thou wert so fair.

It is, maybe, thou hast no wish
　　For praise save for thy works of grace:
Thou scornest beauty, like the best
　　And wisest of our human race.

513

646. Now

When I was in yon town, and had
   Stones all round me, hard and cold,
My flesh was firm, my sight was keen,
   And still I felt my heart grow old.

But now, with this green world around,
   By my great love for it! I swear,
Though my flesh shrink, and my sight fail,
   My heart will not grow old with care.

When I do hear these joyful birds,
   I cannot sit with my heart dumb;
I cannot walk among these flowers,
   But I must help the bees to hum.

My heart has echoes for all things,
   The wind, the rain, the bird and bee;
'Tis I that — now — can carry Time,
   Who in that town must carry me.

I see not now the great coke fire
   With ten men seated there, or more,
Like frogs on logs; and one man fall
   Dying across the boarded floor.

I see instead the flowers and clouds,
   I hear the rills, the birds and bees:
The Squirrel flies before the storm
   He makes himself in leafy trees.

647. The Poppy

Sweet Poppy, when thy beauty's gone,
Thy leaves will fall, thy life be done.

No sooner do thy leaves decay.
Than thou dost throw thy life away.

Thou dost not keep them like the Rose,
When she her crimson charms doth lose.

Whose smudgèd face for days is seen,
Which neither dew nor rain can clean.

Thou dost not shrink and dry at last,
To mock that beauty of thy past.

The first soft breeze that comes along
Shall strip thee — when thy leaves go wrong.

And when to-morrow we look there,
The place is clean where thy leaves were.

Thou dost not linger on, like man,
Till thou art bent, and dry, and wan.

'So let me die when my charms fade,
Like that sweet flower' — said Beauty's maid.

'So, like that Poppy, let me die,'
Said Genius — 'when my springs go dry.'

515

648. March

There's not one leaf can say to me
It shines with this year's greenery.
A stoat-like Wind, without a sound,
Doth creep and startle from the ground
The brown leaves, and they fly about,
And settle, till again found out.
But Spring, for very sure, is born:
E'en though I see, this misty morn,
The face of Phœbus cold and white,
As hers who sits his throne at night;
For I can hear how birds — not bold
Enough to sing full songs — do scold
Their timid hearts to make a try.
The unseen hand of Spring doth lie
Warm on my face; the air is sweet
And calm; it has a pleasant heat
That makes my two hands swell, as though
They had gloves on. Spring makes no show
Of leaves and blossoms yet, but she
Has worked upon this blood in me;
And everything of flesh I meet
Can feel, it seems, her presence sweet.

649. The House Builder

The Rain has lost more music keys,
One harp the less for Summer's Breeze;
The Sheep have lost one of their shades,
The Cows one place to rub their sides;
The crash has come, the Oak lies now,
With all its ruined branches, low.

And I am filled with angry pain;
But if I speak, it were as vain
As though a butterfly, poor fool,
Should try to move a stuggy bull!
Where this Oak stood a house must be,
Not half so fair as a green tree;
The crash that made my last hope fall,
Was music to that builder's soul.
No beauty in the bark he sees,
Nor leaves; the boughs and trunks of trees
Shape into planks before his eyes,
To build a house that he will prize.
He'd rather sit inside walls four,
With plaster roof and wooden floor,
Than under a green tree and hear,
As I have done, the birds' notes clear
Among the leaves in Summer. Yet,
What is this life, if we forget
To fill our ears when Nature sings,
Our eyes search for her lovely things?
Of which she keeps a wondrous store,
And charges us our love, no more.

650. A Luckless Pair

Poor, luckless Bee, this sunny morn;
   That in the night a Wind and Rain
Should strip this Apple-tree of bloom,
   And make it green again.

You, luckless Bee, must now seek far
   For honey on the windy leas;
No sheltered garden, near your hive,
   To fill a bag with ease.

My Love was like this Apple-tree,
   In one sweet bloom, all yesterday;
But something changed her too, Alas!
   And I am turned away.

651. The Change

Now Winter's here; he and his ghostly Winds
That day and night swing on the branches bare.
There's February, with his weak, running eyes,
And dog-like nose, that's always damp and cold.
November, who doth make Heaven like one cloud;
And, if he shines at all, his sunsets are
A ghastly white; no sound of birds — save, now
And then, a pheasant hiccups like a child.
There's cold December too; he takes the Brook,
And lodges him in a strong tomb of ice —
The last sweet voice that Nature charms us with.
I cannot help but think of Autumn now,
Ere any leaves begin to fall, and when
He made the dark and sullen forest smile,
And gave the trees gold tresses for their dark;
And was, as I have heard, so generous
That men could feed their pigs on his rich fruit.
And I go farther back: how Spring did clothe
The aged Oak — whose four tremendous arms
Might well be bodies of still noble trees.
And how Spring's sparkling meadows stormed the
   Clouds
With little black balls that went singing up;
And how rain-arrows struck the earth so hard,
Giving no wound to little Leaves and Buds,
But only tickling them to laugh and dance.

And I think too of Summer in her prime —
The tidal wave of Summer's yellow fields;
And her gold tresses, cut and loose on earth,
With merry men and women there all day
Laughing and combing them; when Swallows made
Bewildering dives of forty feet and more;
And Winds sang only loud enough in trees
To give Love confidence for whispering.
And now the world's so bare and cold by day:
It seems but yesterday I welcomed Night
That she hung out her silver orb so cool,
In place of Day's red danger-lamp, which forced
Me into shade all day.

652.   Selfish Hearts

Without a thought
    If death brings in
Joy for our virtue,
    Pain for our sin —

Know this hard truth:
    They live on earth
The sweetest life,
    Who, rich from birth,

Do then maintain
    A selfish mind;
To moans are deaf,
    To tears are blind.

Weep for the poor
    You find in books:
From living poor
    Avert your looks.

Then dance and sing,
  Dress, sail or ride;
Go in your coach
  To halls of Pride.

A selfish heart,
  And rich from birth,
No sweeter life
  Can be on earth.

To match the joy,
  There lives but one:
The beggar who
  Lives all alone.

With selfish heart,
  And shameless, he
Begs bread at huts,
  And almshouse tea.

O selfish pair!
  I know not which
Is happiest —
  So poor, or rich.

The decent poor,
  The working mass,
In misery
  Their lives must pass.

653. Old Ragan

Who lives in this black wooden hut?
  Old Ragan lives there, all alone;
He cursed a lovely lady once,
  Who let her shadow cross his own.

His tongue is a perpetual spring
  Of oaths that never cease to drop;
Wouldst hear him swear? Speak kindly thus,
  'Good morning, Ragan' — and then stop.

Sometimes a woman thoughtlessly
  Has greeted Ragan in this way;
And she will not forget his look
  And language till her dying day.

He throws his fowls their own eggshells,
  Feeds them on thrice-boiled leaves of tea;
And dead flies on his window-sill,
  He killed when they danced merrily.

A wicked, mean, suspicious man,
  He growls to hear an infant's noise;
He hides behind the walls and trees,
  To frighten little girls and boys.

What made old Ragan come to this?
  Young men did jeer at him and shout;
So women, children and houseflies
  Must bear the old man's vengeance out.

654. A Beggar's Life

When farmers sweat and toil at ploughs,
   Their wives give me cool milk and sweet;
When merchants in their office brood,
   Their ladies give me cakes to eat,
And hot tea for my happy blood;
   This is a jolly life indeed,
   To do no work and get my need.

I have no child for future thought,
   I feed no belly but my own,
And I can sleep when toilers fail;
   Content, though sober, sleeps on stone,
But Care can't sleep with down and ale;
   This is a happy life indeed,
   To do no work and get my need.

I trouble not for pauper's grave,
   There is no feeling after death;
The king will be as deaf to praise
   As I to blame — when this world saith
A word of us in after days;
   It is a jolly life indeed,
   To do no work and get my need.

655. A Vagrant's Life

What art thou, Life, and what am I?
Here, every day that passes by
Doth prove an idle, empty cheat;
And hint at some false scheme to meet
The coming day and get more mirth —
Which will pass by with no more worth.

I fear to give one thing my heart,
That Death or Absence may us part;
And 'tis a misery to live
Alone, and have much love to give.
I envy oft that vagrant poor:
He has no landlady next door;
For beauty he has ne'er a care —
More happy bald than with much hair;
He has no child to save gold for,
No patriot's love calls him to war;
No house to burn, no ship to sink,
No wish for fame; no cause to think
Of landlord, rent, or decent cloth;
No wish for Pleasure's hall: in sooth,
With a plain crust, the Sun o'erhead,
Some straw at night to make his bed,
And drinking water, on his knee,
That is the life for him — and me.

656. Death's Game

Death can but play one game with me —
    If I do live alone;
He cannot strike me a foul blow
    Through a belovèd one.

To-day he takes my neighbour's wife,
    And leaves a little child
To lie upon his breast and cry
    Like the Night-wind, so wild.

And every hour its voice is heard —
    Tell me where is she gone!
Death cannot play that game with me —
    If I do live alone.

657. The One Real Gem

Wealth, Power, and Fame — aye, even Love,
  Are but an hour's delight, and go;
But Sleep's a blessing to hold fast
  Till her warm dew becomes Death's snow;
All men that scorned Sleep in the past,
  For any thing beneath the Sun,
  Will rue it ere their life be done.

Much it perplexed of late to know
  What made my heart with joy so light;
Until I thought of how sweet Sleep
  Did, for so many hours each night,
Keep me in her delicious deep:
  Charmed me each night with her sweet powers,
  In one unbroken stretch of hours.

All-powerful Sleep, thou canst give slaves
  Kings for attendants; and their straw
Becomes in thy soft hands like down;
  Thou one real gem, without a flaw,
That purely shineth in Life's crown;
  For Wealth, and Power, and Fame are paste,
  That into common ashes waste.

658. A Merry Hour

As long as I see Nature near,
I will, when old, cling to life dear:
E'en as the old dog holds so fast
With his three teeth, which are his last.
For Lord, how merry now am I!

Tickling with straw the Butterfly,
Where she doth in her clean, white dress,
Sit on a green leaf, motionless,
To hear Bees hum away the hours.
I shake those Bees too off the Flowers,
So that I may laugh soft to hear
Their hoarse resent and angry stir.
I hear the sentry Chanticleer
Challenge each other far and near,
From farm to farm, and it rejoices
Me this hour to mock their voices;
There's one red Sultan near me now,
Not all his wives make half his row.
Cuckoo! Cuckoo! was that a bird,
Or but a mocking boy you heard?
You heard the Cuckoo first, 'twas he;
The second time — Ha, ha! 'twas Me.

659. Love's Birth

I heard a voice methought was sweet;
   Skylark, I mused, thy praise is done;
That voice I'd rather hear than thine
   With twenty songs in one.

And she, in sooth, is fair, thought I,
   Looking at her with cold, calm eyes —
As the Lily at May's feet, or Rose
   That on June's bosom lies.

I heard one day a step; a voice,
   Heard in a room next door to mine;
And then, I heard long, laughing peals,
   For *him!* from Rosaline.

Again she laughs; what, mocking me?
　　I shook like coward in the night —
Who fears to either lie in dark
　　Or rise to make a light.

For weeks I cursed the day I met
　　That fair sleep-robber, Rosaline;
Till Love came pure from smoke and flame —
　　I swore she should be mine.

And in her house I held her firm,
　　She closed her eyes and lay at rest;
But still she laughed, as if a bird
　　Should sing in its warm nest.

660.　To a Flirt

You'll get no help from me;
　　Make me no pool
To train thy looks to take
　　Some other fool.

No effigy of straw
　　To set in flame;
That gives another joy
　　And me the shame.

No tree on which to cut
　　His name and yours;
To be passed laughing by
　　In future hours.

I'll not prepare your nest —
    You sly house-sparrow;
Prepare your heart for him —
    Like a poor Swallow

Driven away, when I
    Have helped his passion;
Condemned and banished at
    Love's quarter session.

You'll get no help from me,
    To make him prove,
With jealous looks and words,
    His backward love.

661. Nature's Moods

I like the showers that make the grass so fresh,
And birds' notes fresher too; and like the Mist,
Who makes thin shadows of those heavy hills,
That carried in the light a hundred fields,
A score of woods, and many a house of stone.
Or see the jealous Sun appear, and make
That Mist, Morn's phantom lover, go;
And drive him to the farthest hill in sight,
On which he'll make his last and dying stand;
A lover, he? Ah, no; a vampire, who
Comes out of Night's black grave to suck Morn's
    blood.
I like to see the Sun appear at last,
To meet the Clouds, Clouds armed with arrow-
    rain;
And see him lift his rainbow banner high.

527

Or see upon a misty night how Stars
Half ope their eyes and close, as if in doubt
To keep awake or not; how sometimes they
Do seem so far and faint, I almost think
My eyes play false, and they are Fancy's stars.
I welcome Nature in her every mood:
To see a hundred crows toss wild about,
Blowing in Heaven's face like balls of soot,
As they make their delirious cries, sure signs
Of coming storm — not half a one, I hope.

662. A Familiar Voice

Ah, what fond memories that voice doth bring!
Even to strangers sweet: no others sing
Their common speech, like men of Cambria's race;
How much more sweet to me then was that voice!
It filled me with sweet memories; as when
I heard one hum the March of Harlech Men,
Dying, five thousand miles from home! Now we
Lived in a city dark, where Poverty,
More hard than rocks, and crueller than foam,
Keeps many a great Ulysses far from home,
With neither kings nor gods to help him forth.
Tell me, sweet voice, what part of that dear earth
Thou callest thine? I asked, to please my whim:
His answer could not cool my pride in him.
For Wales is Wales; one patriotic flame
From North to South, from East to West the same;
There is no difference in our Cymric breed
Of Highlander and Lowlander; no creed
Can enter there to make their hearts divide;
Nay, Wales is Wales throughout, and of one pride.

So, in that city, by stone walls confined,
We of our native land spake with one mind.
We could breathe in vast spaces there: the eye
Could lead proud Fancy in captivity
Mile after mile adown the valleys long,
The kindest hearts in all the world among.
One woman's tears could moisten all the land,
As in that very hour was known: band upon band
Of Cymry swarming from their collieries
To search the hills, in hours of sleep and ease,
For one lost child; a woman's grief could claim
The fiery hearts that tyrants ne'er could tame.
The noblest hearts on earth are in those hills,
For they make national their local ills;
Theirs are the hearts of oak, in truth they are,
So soft in peace, yet knotted hard in war;
Of such an oak as, smoothed down by Pain
Shows flowers of Pity deep in its clear grain.
We did compare this City dame with neat
And simple Jenny Jones, with her charms sweet
As are shy berries under shady leaves,
Hiding from light to sweeten of themselves;
This City dame, with plumes and satin trail —
An empty craft that carries finer sail
Than one whose hull is full of pearls and gold;
For, save in song, our Jenny is not bold.
And so we talked till, with an oath, we swore
We would return and never wander more.

663. The Cheat

Yes, let the truth be heard,
  Bacchus, you rosy cheat:
That you do rob this world
  Of pictures and songs sweet;
You give men dreams, 'tis true,
But take their will to do.

You send them sleep as kings —
  They wake as trembling slaves;
Sent singing to their beds,
  They rise like ghosts from graves;
They drink to get will power —
Then wait a sober hour.

They shake, like leaves with stems
  Part broken on a tree;
As bees from flower to flower,
  Men go from spree to spree;
Until their days are run,
And not one sweet task done.

664. When I Returned

When I returned to that great London Town,
  And saw Old Father Thames, one August night,
Looking at me with half a thousand eyes;
  When I at morn saw how the Heavenly light
Could burnish that dull gold on dome and spire —
I lost all instinct, like a horse near fire.

No thought of ragged youths, and ghastly girls
  Whose metal laughter oft had pained my ear,
For many a pleasant hour; but soon, Alas!
  So shaken was my mind by Traffic's stir,
I felt an impulse mad to shriek out loud,
As if my voice could quiet that vast crowd.

Soon saw how false that empty glitter was,
  For men did drop of hunger there, and die;
There I saw many a homeless man, with death
  The silver lining to his cloud — then I
Saw woolly sheep, fat cows in meadows green,
In place of such men ragged, pale and lean.

665. The Thieves

Thieves, Death and Absence, come
No more to my heart's home:
Behold my chambers bare,
I make no thing my care.

As fast as I aught bring
In place of stolen thing,
One of ye two doth come
Again to my heart's home.

Henceforth I'll leave it bare,
Cold winds shall enter there;
For nothing keep I can —
Of plant, or beast, or man.

666. Sweet Music

Ah, Music, it doth sound more sweet
　　Than rain or crispèd leaves; or when
Beauty doth stroke a kitten rose,
　　And screams, to feel her fingers then
Scratched by its little claws.

Drowned, Music, in thy waves, I saw
　　My whole long Past before me go;
Now, rouse me with a merry shout —
　　Such as charm children, when Winds blow
The light they love clean out.

Laugh thee, sweet Music, like those girls,
　　When each was fit, but none were wed;
As they did banter a shy boy,
　　Who could not raise on high his head
And face their wicked joy.

667. Sweet Youth

And art thou gone, sweet Youth? Say Nay!
　　For dost thou know what power was thine,
That thou couldst give vain shadows flesh,
　　And laughter without any wine,
From the heart fresh?

And art thou gone, sweet Youth? Say Nay!
　　Not left me to Time's cruel spite;
He'll pull my teeth out one by one,
　　He'll paint my hair first grey, then white,
He'll scrape my bone.

And art thou gone, sweet Youth? Alas!
  For ever gone! I know it well;
Earth has no atom, nor the sky,
  That has not thrown the kiss Farewell —
Sweet Youth, Good-Bye!

668. Time's Justice

Alas! we live in days of shame,
That men, inventing some new game
For Pleasure's fools to idle time,
Are welcomed more than men of rhyme,
And men that master sound or paint;
And Genius must be still content
That, though not heeded now at all —
Great men are seen when their stars fall.

What fools we are! Here one man tramps
Collecting fossils, eggs or stamps;
Others in that dull, useless state
Of toads that kernel rocks; men great,
Though efforts they do make untold —
As misers make to reach their gold,
When sick and dying — could not wake
One thought in these for Beauty's sake.

The great man's work, when his life's past,
Will ripen like plucked fruit at last;
So let not Genius fear but what
Time will do justice to his lot,
And give no more or less; in sooth,
The world could not feel half the truth
If Genius had no power to see
One step beyond reality.

Take you no fear but Time is just;
He'll not give Genius to the dust,
With soul and common body joined;
You great man, now deemed mad of mind,
Scorned and abused like some white crow
That comes to make white feathers show
Inside a black crows' rookery —
Courage! Time proves thy sanity.

669.   Solitude

Yes, Solitude indeed: for I can see
Trees all around and, to the west of me —
So near I could almost throw there a stone —
A mountain and a forest stand in one!
I've watched that mountain-top an hour and more,
To see some bird-discoverer sail o'er
That mighty wave of earth and settle here —
For to go back that way he would not dare.
And, did I see that bird, 'twould give such joy
As in days gone, when I, a little boy
Saw lying in a dock the ten-foot boat
That did across the deep Atlantic float;
With one old man, who strapped himself fast down
Three days and nights, knowing that he must drown,
If once a Wind or Wave could lift him free.
Yes, this is Solitude, for I can see
Nothing around but mountains and their trees,
And all the sweet flowers close, and birds, and bees.
The bees, that drink from tankards every size,
Colour and shape, do heave no feeble sighs,
But murmur loud their praise; and every bird
Sang sweet — till but a moment since they heard

534

A Blackbird's startled shriek, when suddenly
He saw me motionless beneath a tree,
And made them dumb in leaves and out; and made
Even tame Robin look around, afraid.
I see a house or two adown the lane,
But no sign there of human life; in vain
The Cuckoo makes his strange but cheerful note,
To get an answer sweet from Childhood's throat.
In this green valley, deep and silent, roam
Cattle that seem to have no other home,
Nor dream of any from their open vale.
And now I see a wall and gate, so stale
And old — black without paint; which seems to me
Could tell some sweet, half dreadful history.
And then I walked and saw a field close by,
And what was seen there opened wide my eye;
A man with a white horse and, this I swear,
Both of them in their sleep were ploughing there.
Then home I went and, till I reached that place,
I never saw another mortal's face.
A week here now; not one hard living tramp,
Of England's many, finds this quiet camp,
To cheat with ready lies and solemn looks
Me, when a dreamer I come straight from books;
And still I would with gladness, now and then,
Be cheated by those happy, wandering men.

670. The Trickster

When first I left a town,
   And lived in Nature's parts,
I heard the march of men,
   And whistles, horses, carts;
And it to me did seem
Nature was but a dream.

I heard blows struck outside,
   And bodies fall all day,
And laughter, shrieks, and groans;
   And who, think you, did play
These mad pranks on my mind?
It was the merry Wind.

He blubbered oft near by,
   Against the corner stone;
Like sulking child, who'll not
   Come in, nor yet be gone —
To whom full well 'tis known
His mother's home alone.

671. Vain Beauty

Ah, what is Beauty but vain show —
   If nothing in the heart is sweet;
As oft the spider finds a moth —
   All wings and little meat.

Thy look as warm as Autumn's is,
   As false — both he and thou art cold;
Then, since thou art unkind and vain,
   Let thy true worth be told.

Worms form thy flesh, and 'tis that flesh
    Makes thee so beautiful to see;
When dying thou refuse them food,
    They'll help themselves to thee.

Thy laugh was falser than men make
    Ere they in dreadful battle fall;
I found thee false, thy looks deceived
    Like short men that sit tall.

Beauty can make thy two lips red —
    But not thy voice sound soft and sweet;
Beauty made thy cheeks smooth, but gave
    Thine eyes no pleasant heat.

I see thee move like a vain horse
    Whose neck is arched to his knee;
His head will soon drop there through age —
    And age will so bend thee.

Age with his frost will warn thee soon,
    And pinch and mark thee here and there;
Will dry thy lip, and dim thine eye,
    And pull out thy long hair.

The flowers that spread their charms too far
    Must soon be served like common weeds;
With my respect love also died —
    No longer my heart bleeds.

672. A Month Ago

A month ago, ah happy me!
  I found a pool with no man by;
Which clouds had made so deep to see,
  As was the height from earth to sky;
It was a lovely day in spring,
And flowers did bloom, and birds did sing.

I hummed with bees, I stared with sheep,
  I whistled with the birds for joy;
I shook the butterflies from sleep,
  Their time the better to employ;
And when night came I laughed with glee,
When I the Moon's sad face did see.

A month ago, ah happy me!
  O woeful, woeful days since then!
For I a banished man must be,
  Out of the land of happy men;
On me a woman trained her charms,
To win another to her arms.

673. The Trusting Young

Ah, little bird, thou art not old;
Thou knowest no danger in this world,
So full of trust, like all young things.
A child knows not the adder stings;
Adders are lovely worms to it;
Tigers would be big cats to pet,
And bears be bigger dogs to love.
But future days too soon will prove
To every child and bird, life's state

Divides itself with love and hate.
So, when I see thee come so near
And, though I threaten, take no fear,
I think of days when thou wilt find
As many cruel things as kind.
All trusting young things come to this;
Look how a loving child would kiss
The civil landlord that did come
To turn it out of house and home;
Nor guessed her mother's look of grief
Was through that law-supported thief.

674. Childhood's Hours

My heart's a coffin cold,
   In which my Childhood lies
Unburied yet; and will —
   Until this body dies.

I think me every hour
   Of those sweet, far-off days
That draw so very close,
   And show their pretty ways.

Where'er I am they come,
   Those ghosts, my Childhood Hours;
They run up to my knees,
   Laughing and waving flowers.

They run up to my knees,
   They shout and cry Cuckoo!
They mock the bleating lambs,
   And like young calves they moo.

Some of their flowers are weeds,
    Are weeds, and nothing more;
But sweeter far they smell
    Than roses at my door.

It is a merry crew,
    And I curse Time that he
Has made me what I am —
    A man and mystery.

675.   In Days Gone

I had a sweet companion once,
    And in the meadows we did roam;
And in the one-star night returned
    Together home.

When Bees did roar like midget bulls,
    Or quietly rob nodding Flowers —
We two did roam the fields so green,
    In Summer hours.

She like the Rill did laugh, when he
    Plays in the quiet woods alone;
She was as red as Summer's rose —
    The first one blown.

Her hair as soft as any moss
    That running water still keeps wet;
And her blue eye — it seemed as if
    A Violet

Had in a Lily's centre grown,
    To see the blue, and white around —
'Twas tender as the Glowworm's light
    On a lost mound.

540

And, like the face of a sweet well
  Buried alive in a stone place —
So calm, so fresh, so soft, so bright
  Was that child's face.

676. Go, Angry One

Go, angry One, and let tears cold
Put out the fires thine eyes now hold;
Let those dark clouds, that make my pain,
Clear themselves pure with thine eyes' rain;
Let Thy cheeks' roses, that once stood
Unblemished by wild Passion's blood,
Be washed by thee in penance dew,
To gain back their first happy hue;
Recover thy voice, sweet and low,
That has such little music now.
But let not anger frost, and kill
The trembling flowers of Love that will
Come pleading unto you for me —
Which would for both great pity be.
Go, angry Beauty, and get calm;
And, when thou art all spent of harm,
Look how I come with greater love;
And anger once again will move
Thee, my wild Pet — but not so strong
That you will think my kisses wrong.

677. Dead Born

A perfect child, with hands and feet,
  With heart and bones;
Which no man's hand could fashion out
  Of clay or stones.

541

Yet this, Alas! is but cold clay;
    The mortal breath
Is lacking, for this perfect child
    Is born in death.

Oft have I seen its mother's joy —
    A new-made wife;
And knew she fed on secret hope
    For her child's life.

And now her heart breaks; she can hear
    No sweet cries wild;
There needs no joyful soothing for
    Her dead-born child.

678. The Sweetest Dream

Nay, no more bitterness from me;
The past is gone, so let it be;
And I will keep smiles softer than
The sad smiles of a dying man
For a child comforter — to give
My sweetest dream, that still must live.
My sweetest dream, that comes more bold;
Of one sweet, simple child of old;
Who, though a queen, and a great one,
Would wear her jewels like a nun;
When miser leaves unlocked his door,
I may forget her — not before.

679. On The Death of a little Child

Her pretty dances were her own,
    Her songs were by no other sung;
And all the laughter in her house
    Was started by her own sweet tongue.

This little dance and song composer,
   This laughter maker, sweet and small,
Will never more be seen or heard —
   For her the Sexton's bell does toll.

The shining eyes are closed for aye,
   And that small, crimson mouth of mirth;
The little feet, the little hands —
   All stiff and cold inside the earth.

680. Love's Power

I ask not of high tide or low,
   That ships may out of port or in;
When thou dost come, and not before,
   Commerce doth on my mind begin.

Until I see thee come like spring,
   My spirits' streams are locked in ice;
But navigation opens, Love,
   As soon as I can hear thy voice.

Thy touch can launch a fleet of boats
   Sunk to their decks with bales of bliss,
To take the tide of my blood-veins
   Straight to my Heart's Metropolis.

681. War

Ye Liberals and Conservatives,
Have pity on our human lives,
   Waste no more blood on human strife;
Until we know some way to use
This human blood we take or lose,
   'Tis sin to sacrifice our life.

543

When pigs are stuck we save their blood
And make black puddings for our food,
   The sweetest and the cheapest meat;
And many a woman, man and boy
Have ate those puddings with great joy,
   And oft-times in the open street.

Let's not have war till we can make,
Of this sweet life we lose or take,
   Some kind of pudding of man's gore,
So that the clergy in each parish,
May save the lives of those that famish
   Because meat's dear and times are poor.

682. Self-Love

She had two eyes as blue as Heaven,
   Ten times as warm they shone;
And yet her heart was hard and cold
   As any shell or stone.

Her mouth was like a soft red rose
   When Phœbus drinks its dew;
But oh, that cruel thorn inside
   Pierced many a fond heart true.

She had a step that walked unheard,
   It made the stones like grass;
Yet that light step has crushed a heart,
   As light as that step was.

Those glowing eyes, those smiling lips,
   I have lived now to prove,
Were not for you, were not for me,
   But came of her self-love.

Yet, like a cow for acorns that
    Have made it suffer pain,
So, though her charms are poisonous,
    I moan for them again.

683. In the Wood

I lie on Joy's enchanted ground:
    No other noise but these green trees
    That sigh and cling to every breeze;
And that deep solemn, hollow sound
    Born of the grave, and made by Bees.

Now do I think of this packed world,
    Where thousands of rich people sweat,
    Like common slaves, in idle fret;
Not knowing how to buy with gold
    This house of Joy, that makes no debt.

What little wealth true Joy doth need!
    I pay for wants that make no show;
    I pay my way and nothing owe;
I drink my ale, I smoke my weed,
    And take my time where'er I go.

684. Love and Immortality

My wonder is the great bright sun,
    Beneath whose looks we live and die
Whose strong bright arm of light can lift
    The water into the Heavens high;
I marvel too at beauty's power
In flesh and rock, in tree and flower.

And yet, in spite of these fine things,
   I have no hope in life to come —
Save that my spirit, like my flesh,
   Will find in common grass a home;
I have no hope of life at last
Outshining this when it is past.

Love, only Love, can change my mind;
   I for that passion great will claim
Immunity from time and space,
   From floods of water and of flame;
A perfect immortality
Must qualify that love in me.

685. To a Working Man

You working man, of what avail
   Are these fine teachings of the great,
   To raise you to a better state;
When you forget in pots of ale
   That slavery's not your common fate.

You victim to all fraud and greed,
   Shun now that mind-destroying state:
   Go, meet your masters in debate:
Go home from work and think and read —
   To make our laws is your true fate.

686. Treasures

He hailed me with a cheerful voice,
   I answered him with ready lips;
As though we sailed the briny seas,
   And hailed from passing ships.

'Come in,' quoth he, 'and I will show
　Thee treasures few men saw before.'
He from his pocket took a key
　And opened wide his door.

He seemed no more than other men,
　His voice was calm, his eyes were cold;
He was not tall, he was not short,
　Nor seemed he young nor old.

I'll see some treasures now, methought —
　Some work in silk and ivory;
Some painted trays and vases quaint,
　Things with a history.

I saw at once some glittering beads
　That seemed like berries fit to eat;
Such as make children leave the woods
　Crying for their home sweet.

'Aye, aye,' quoth he, 'a little maid
　Played with them fifty years ago;
She's perished on the scaffold since —
　That's why I prize them so.

'Pray sit thee down in comfort now,
　For I have treasures rich and rare.'
He went upstairs, I sat me down
　And round the room did stare.

That room looked strange; a little fire,
　The lamp burned low, the hour was late;
A horse outside cropped grass — the sound
　Seemed like the steps of Fate.

The furniture in that man's room
　Seemed part of one large, deadly plant
Which if I touched would hold me fast,
　To perish soon of want.

Aye, I confess, I trembling stayed,
    Thralled by an unexplained desire;
I shook like negro in his hut,
    Sick at a little fire.

I heard him tumbling things about,
    Methought I heard a murder call
And blows; and then the blows did cease —
    I heard a body fall.

Then all was still, how still it was!
    I heard him breathing hard; at last
I heard him with a load caught in
    The narrow stairway fast.

And now he shows his face again;
    I see a bundle on his arm,
A dress, a sheet, a boot — and things
    Too simple to alarm.

'Now list,' quoth he, 'I told thee once
    That I had treasures rich and rare:
This sheet did smother a small babe,
    It was a baron's heir.

'This long, black dress a poisoner wore —
    Her head was chopped off with an axe;
'Tis priceless unto those that made
    Her figure show in wax.

'This is the boot, one of a pair,
    The other matters not' — he said;
' 'Twas with this boot a murderer kicked
    To bits his dead man's head.

548

'These bones were found upon a raft,
    And brought to shore by seamen true:
Bones of a little boy, picked clean
    By a cannibal crew.

'When Bill Black murdered Liza Green,
    As she sat down to pickled pork,
He finished her sweet supper with
    This very knife and fork.

'This scarf, which ties them all in one,
    Was my own father's, he one day
Hanged himself to a beam by it —
    I've other things, so prithee stay.'

He whistling went upstairs again,
    I softly crept towards the door
And vanished in the night, nor saw,
    Nor wished to see him more.

687. Beauty's Revenge

Proud Margery rang her peal of bells;
    'If you despise all womankind,
Take care, young man,' she said, 'take care
    No woman ever plagues your mind' —
The young man smoothed his own soft hair.

And how it came about, who knows,
    It is for womankind to tell;
Before a full-blown rose could fade,
    That man was suffering passion's hell
For Margery, that merry maid.

She brought ripe cherries to his sleep,
 Her teeth and eyes they shone at night;
'I am,' he murmured in his dreams,
 'A poor black ruin blessed with light —
From Margery come those heavenly beams.'

He dreamt he saw her hair at hand;
 'My soul,' he sighed, 'is little worth,
My life till now had little hope,
 But I will find my heaven on earth
By holding to this silken rope.'

He told his love to Margery soon,
 She bird-like cocked her cruel head,
She rang her peal of bells again:
 'Nay, I despise you men,' she said —
'Good-bye, young man, and take no pain.'

688. Dreaming of Death

When I, awake, have thoughts of Death,
 Two friends can ease me of my grief:
First comes Philosophy, who says,
 'Fear brings Death soon, and Life is brief;'
Then comes Old Age with looks so calm,
 In spite of Death, and he so near,
That when I see his happy face,
 It banishes my fear.

But when in sleep I dream of Death,
 Fear cuts me then with a sharp knife:
The Death that comes to me in dreams,
 Is but to feel a stronger life;
For only my poor body dies,
 My mind is still to this life bound;
I hear the merry world go by,
 But cannot make a sound.

689. The Stars at Work

I see the busy stars at work,
　　And question what they do
There comes a voice — 'They knit a shroud,
　　A dead man's shroud for you.'

'No, no,' a second voice doth say,
　　'I'll tell thee what they make:
They knit a veil a lady'll wear
　　Some morning for your sake.'

Yours is the knowledge, lady, speak;
　　The truth is known to thee;
Is it a shroud or bridal veil,
　　Death or sweet life for me?

690. The Temper of a Maid

The Swallow dives in yonder air,
The Robin sings with sweetest ease,
The Apple shines among the leaves,
The Leaf is dancing in the breeze;
The Butterfly's on a warm stone,
The Bee is suckled by a flower;
The Wasp's inside a ripe red plum,
The Ant has found his load this hour;
The Squirrel counts and hides his nuts,
The Stoat is on a scent that burns;
The Mouse is nibbling a young shoot,
The Rabbit sits beside his ferns;
The Snake has found a sunny spot,
The Frog and Snail a slimy shade;
But I can find no joy on earth,
All through the temper of a maid.

691. The Grey-haired Child

Thy father was a drunken man,
   He threatened thee with a sharp knife;
And thou, a child not ten years old,
   Lay trembling for thy life.

Lay trembling in the dark all night,
   Sleep could not seal thine eye or ear;
Thy hair, which was a dark rich brown,
   Is now made grey by fear.

692. The Winged Flower

Bright Butterfly,
Dreaming with thy
Wings spread lengthways;
Full of black eyes,
And black bars rolled
Across red gold,
Straight from thy lips
To wings' white tips:
Wert thou a flower,
Until some power
Made thee to fly —
Then, ere we die,
Oh, let me know
Where such flowers grow.
Lead where they lie,
Now, lovely Fly.
On this leaf wet,
Dreaming worlds yet
Greener than ours —
Show me those flowers
Just when they rise
Live Butterflies.

552

693. The Little Man

Last night I sat in thought,
  When, near my bended head,
I saw a little man,
  And this is what he said:
Of all the eyes and ears
  That in this great world be,
There's not one eye or ear
  Takes any note of thee.'

'Peace, hold thy froward tongue,
  Thou mocking Imp,' said I;
'Joy, that is man's true aim,
  Until the hour we die;
A dream that gives us joy,
  Though vain, is our sweet friend:
Man's *deeds* are but vain dreams
  That soon must have an end.'

694. Sound and Grace

My love laughs sweeter than a brook
  That has been drinking rain all day;
She like a blackbird sings, when he
  Has not one feather dry, in May.

When I can hear her laugh like that,
  My hand starts forth to clutch her gown;
Lord, if she dances while she laughs,
  My mind makes plans to pull her down.

695. A Mother's Science

I heard a man once say this world
  Was but a speck in space;
A leaf upon a shoreless tide,
  That had no resting-place.

I told him then how vast this world
  Was to my own poor mind;
Of all the places seen, and still
  My child I could not find.

I told that man where I had been,
  I mentioned towns around;
And still my boy, in all these years,
  Is never to be found.

696. Man

I saw Time running by —
Stop, Thief! was all the cry.
I heard a voice say, Peace!
Let this vain clamour cease.
Can ye bring lightning back
That leaves upon its track
Men, horses, oak trees dead?
Canst bring back Time? it said.
There's nothing in Man's mind
Can catch Time up behind;
In front of that fast Thief
There's no one — end this grief.
Tut, what is Man? How frail!
A grain, a little nail,
The wind, a change of cloth —
A fly can give him death.

Some fishes in the sea
Are born to outlive thee,
And owls, and toads, and trees —
And is Man more than these?
I see Man's face in all
Things, be they great or small;
I see the face of him
In things that fly or swim;
One fate for all, I see —
Whatever that may be.
Imagination fits
Life to a day; though its
Length were a thousand years,
'Twould not decrease our fears;
What strikes men cold and dumb
Is that Death's time *must* come.

697. Love's Happiness

Blow, blow, thou Eastern wind,
  Since Love can draw thy sting;
The South blows to my mind,
  And does sweet odours bring —
If only Love is kind.

Spout, spout, you frowning cloud,
  Since Love cares not for rain:
With every spout allowed,
  You beat on me in vain —
As though I wore Death's shroud.

Rumble, you thunderstorm,
  Since Love's voice cannot fail
To sing more loud and warm –
  Like a fine nightingale
Paced by your angry storm.

Then thunder, cloud, or wind,
  Come either, stay or go;
If Love to me is kind,
  Rumble, or rain, or blow
Comes easy to my mind.

698.   Circumstance

Down in the deep salt sea
  A mighty fish will make
Its own strong current, which
  The little ones must take;
Which they must follow still,
No matter for their will.

Here, in this human sea,
  Is Circumstance, that takes
Men where they're loth to go;
  It fits them false and makes
Machines of master souls,
And masters of dull fools.

699.   Slum Children

Your songs at night a drunkard sings,
  Stones, sticks and rags your daily flowers;
Like fishes' lips, a bluey white,
  Such lips, poor mites, are yours.

556

Poor little things, so sad and solemn,
    Whose lives are passed in human crowds —
When in the water I can see
    Heaven with a flock of clouds.

Poor little mites that breathe foul air,
    Where garbage chokes the sink and drain —
Now when the hawthorn smells so sweet,
    Wet with the summer rain.

But few of ye will live for long;
    Ye are but small new islands seen,
To disappear before your lives
    Can grow and be made green.

700. To a Rich Lady

Though thou hast silk to wear, and though
Thou'rt clad in it from head to toe —
Still in your hair, that soft warm nest,
My mind would hatch its thoughts and rest.

Though thou hast gems as well, and though
They brighter than the dewdrops glow —
Still would I take my full supplies
Of warmth and light from those two eyes.

Though thou hast cars to drive, and though
Thou'rt driven as the winds that blow —
Still would I find a greater pleasure
To see thee walk an easy measure.

Though thou hast rooms to spare, and though
More than friends need, that come and go —
Still would I ask for no more space
Than where two bodies could embrace.

701. A Woman's Glory

A woman's glory is not hair,
  It is her voice so soft and sweet;
Her hair can be what'er she wills,
  Her voice will stand no counterfeit;
So let her sing, and laugh in tones
Of water caught by rocks and stones.

When woman works from home or drinks,
  And has no time or love to charm
Her young with song between their meals,
  The world and they must suffer harm:
They'll stone dumb creatures, and they'll yell
Around the blind like imps from hell.

702. Beauty's Bait

When Beauty scents with love her bait,
What artful secrets meet their fate;
What things we darkly hide with care,
Leap out before we are aware.

Thinking of girls in flesh and blood,
And not of any shadowy brood —
What poor tame sport will Beauty find
When I confess to her my mind.

When I shall tell of girls whose looks
Came out of painted cloth or books,
Then Beauty, erstwhile full of thought,
Must laugh when such poor things are caught.

703. O Happy Blackbird

O happy Blackbird, happy soul,
  I hear in song's delirium now:
Thou dost forget the days just past,
  Of cold and hunger in the snow.

Would that man's memory were the same;
  For he, alas! must backward cast
His misery-fearing eyes and fill
  The future with his troubles past.

Thou hast no gift of Hope, like man,
  To ease thee of a present pain;
But where's a man, in all this world,
  Who would not sacrifice that gain,
O happy Blackbird: for the power
  To use like thee his present hour.

704. To a Bore

I walk to look,
  To think, and feel
Things that to you
  Make no appeal.

Wert thou the same —
  More joy for thee
To walk without
  My company.

But now — a fool
  Walks out with thee,
As sure as one
  Walks out with me.

559

705. Captives

In this deep hollow, lying down,
   I, looking up at Heaven, can see
You pretty little clouds shut in
   By green hills all around — like me.

And all you simple, little clouds
   Seem glad at my captivity:
Without a thought that I can smile
   As much at you as you at me.

706. The Two Spirits

My friend, mad drunk, struck at his foe,
When I received the cruel blow;
No sooner saw my broken tooth,
He wept, and wiped my bloody mouth.

Then came a message from his wife —
'Come now, and see his last of life.'
But when I reached his room and bed,
The man was lying cold and dead.

Now when I stood beside his bier,
I felt two spirits standing near;
The one said — 'Look: his knuckles show
The toothmark where he struck a blow.'

'Think not of that,' the other said —
'Have pity on him cold and dead.'
'You took no vengeance for that blow,'
The first one said — 'it's too late now!'

Shame on my soul for vengeance nursed,
That, laughing in my heart, I cursed
The hand, now dead, that broke my tooth —
Although it wiped my bloody mouth.

707. The Long Sleep

They press the pillow on their mother's face and head;
They take her by the arm to pull her out of bed —
And still that mother sleeps and will not wake and play.

They laugh and pull, and still their mother will not heed;
The pillow pressed, and yet no breath she seems to
      need —
For still their mother sleeps and will not wake and play.

In pity for those babes a neighbour's head is bowed;
In pity for her grief those children sob aloud —
And more than ever wish their mother'd wake and play.

708. The Child and the Man

Dreaming I was a child,
    And met a man,
My fears of him were wild —
    Away I ran.

The man ran after me:
    'Why run away,
My little boy,' said he —
    'From me this day?'

I looked with my eyes sad,
    When I was caught;
His face seemed not so bad
    As I first thought.

'I am yourself,' said he:
  'It gives me pain
To see you run from me —
  Don't run again.'

'Poor man,' said I, 'what made
  You look so strange?
No wonder I'm afraid,
  At such a change.'

He sobbed too much to speak,
  He could not tell;
And then my heart did break
  With sobs as well.

709. In a Garden

Far from the sound of commerce, where the bees
Make hollow hum that bears it half in mind,
I live; and when those flowers of early spring —
The Daffodils of March, that own unshared
All Nature's world, nor live to see their peers,
Primroses, Violets, and Anemones —
Are overwhelmed in June's green riot, I
Sit more in my small garden, where the flowers
Are large and strong. Blue Irises are there,
Dahlias, and heavy lidded Tulips, too;
Snapdragons, Roses, Stocks, and Marigolds,
Solomon's Seals and Canterbury Bells;
Tall Columbines that never raise their heads,
Sweet Peas and Asters, Mignonette and Pinks,
And cat-eyed Pansies with their velvet skin;
And Poppies, too, that with their richer hues
Make butterflies take wing or lie unseen;

Lilies so fair they challenge all the world,
And hold in silver tumblers their gold dice,
Ready to throw and win; and many a flower
Is there whose large, soft breast is strong enough
To suckle three or four bees at one time.
Those flowers I love, and take more pride in them
Than sailors take in wearing scarves of silk.
I watch with joy the little new-born buds,
How they just peep from half-closed eyes at morn,
And wake to find their dreams of dewdrops true.
There do I sit all through a summer's day —
Days turn without my knowledge into nights.
I sit so motionless at times that birds
Perch on the boughs that almost touch my head,
Before they see I am a thing of flesh.
So, with the poet's double sight and hearing,
I see another face behind the flower's,
I hear another voice inside the wind's —
A face and voice much sweeter than their own.
Helped by Thought's quiet midwife Solitude,
My mind brings forth a family of young dreams.

710. The Child Chatters

Good morning to my dolly first,
  Good morning to my cherry tree;
Good morning to my little chicks,
  For them I love to see.

Good morning to my bow-wow-wow;
  Good morning to my bonnet new;
Good morning to my little self,
  To Dad and Mammie too.

Good morning, God which art in Heaven,
    I hope you slept last night quite well;
And please don't vex your head so much
    About the devil in hell.

And if he bothers you too much,
    And you're afraid, and you sleep bad,
Then, God which art in Heaven, you must
    Have whisky, like my Dad.

711. The Emigrant

Youth has no ties,
    So let him roam;
Where'er he goes,
    Young blood's at home.

But you, with wife
    And children three,
Must leave England,
    And cross the sea.

Leave her to men
    That love her less;
Thy love too great
    For bitterness.

When such fine souls
    I see depart,
A patriot's love
    Must leave my heart.

712. The Collier's Wife

The collier's wife had four tall sons
   Brought from the pit's mouth dead,
   And crushed from foot to head;
When others brought her husband home,
Had five dead bodies in her room.

Had five dead bodies in her house —
   All in a row they lay —
   To bury in one day:
Such sorrow in the valley has
Made kindness grow like grass

Oh, collier, collier, underground,
   In fear of fire and gas,
   What life more danger has?
Who fears more danger in this life?
There is but one — thy wife!

713. Stars

One night I saw ten stars take wing —
   Like flowers to butterflies — and fly;
Then I lay down to sleep, a child,
   Though when I woke a man was I.

But when I saw the stars again,
   So steadfast in their heavenly home;
The same ten thousand years ago,
   The same ten thousand years to come —

Methought, what are they laughing at —
    How close our cradles are to graves?
Do they, in their eternal pride,
    Make merry at our little lives?

And sure, the Moon was laughing too;
    The great, white Moon, that I could see
Shaking her sides, low in the west,
    Like a big rattle in a tree.

714. Come, Let Me Close

Come, let me close thine eyes with kisses —
    And those two lips that day and night
Are opened to a cherry's size,
    And cry for Love to kiss them tight.
Let me enjoy thy bosom now,
    Sweet Lady, let my head rock there;
When it is wedged between thy breasts,
    Throw over it thy silken hair.

Let me lie close before He comes
    To clasp thy bosom like a leech:
I mean that babe, who'll lie between,
    Over whose body I must reach;
That tyrant babe, whom thou wilt love
    Above all earthly things the best:
Though laughing he will trample, kick
    And knuckle into each soft breast.

566

715. In Silent Groves

My walk is now in silent groves,
  With grass and moss beneath my feet;
Which no true poet minds can leave
  Until inspired with fancies sweet.
So quiet there that you can hear
  Grasshoppers in the grass so green;
The insect-cuckoos that will call,
  And still remain unseen.

In silent groves, where lovers go
  To tell those dreams when they confess
That love that's jealous of the air,
  And whispers in a wilderness.
There's no black scandal in these groves —
  The foul disease that still breaks forth
In other parts, as fast as one
  Weak part is healed by Truth.

716. The Rev. Ebenezer Paul

He begs from rich men for the poor,
  And robs the poor of Christmas dinners.
Ah, cruel Time, to keep alive
  For all these years such hoary sinners!
This hard, old man with silvery locks,
  With false, white teeth — see how he fawns!
Feel in that hair, and I'll be damned
  If thou'lt not find the Devil's horns!

This stack of infamy, that keeps
    Dark, greedy thoughts like rats within;
This stack that harbours gentle looks,
    Like snakes with their cold, smiling skin;
This gospel-monger, old and bland,
    Who prays aloud for other sinners —
He begs from rich men for the poor,
    And robs the poor of Christmas dinners.

717. The Shameless One

She comes to see her brother John,
    She's with a man not met before;
To bring her brother's house to shame,
    She comes a hundred miles and more.

And when her brother leaves his home,
    She finds her sisters Maud and May;
She's drunk, and with another man,
    And both her sisters hide away.

She'll follow them from place to place,
    She'll find them yet, be sure of that;
And John will be a shivering dog
    Before the eyes of a black cat.

The beggar-man has not more nits
    Than she has sins, yet she'll not die:
The lightning, that would blind a child
    A second time, has passed her by.

718. We Arm to Fight

We arm to fight the Kaiser's troops,
  And every man will do his part;
One song was mine, a call to arms,
  To cheer my country's heart,
    My love—
  To cheer my country's heart.

Yes, I who have the power of song
  To arm maybe a hundred men,
Have made one call, and only one,
  And armed no more than ten,
    My love—
  And armed no more than ten.

For now we meet, and my one cry
  Is 'Molly, Molly,' night and day;
We fight the foe, and I am dumb:
  Oh, kiss my shame away,
    My love!
  Oh, kiss my shame away!

719. My Lady Comes

Peace, mournful Bee, with that
  Man's deep voice from the grave:
My Lady comes, and Flowers
  Make all their colours wave;
And joyful shivers seize
The hedges, grass and trees.

569

My Lady comes, and leaves
    Above her head clap hands;
The Cow stares o'er the field,
    Up straight the Horse now stands;
Under her loving eyes
Flowers change to butterflies

The grass comes running up
    To kiss her coming feet;
Then cease your grumble, Bee,
    When I my Lady meet;
And Arch, let not your stones
Turn our soft sighs to groans.

720.   To my Thoughts

Stay home and hear the birds and bees,
    And see the blossoms grow;
And mock them both — when Echo mocks
    The bird that cries 'Cuckoo';
For Love, alas! — now understood —
Has many a feather stained with blood.

Though you are my own children born,
    I cannot keep you home;
For though I lock my body up
    Inside an iron room,
You thoughts can still pass through the walls,
To follow her who never calls.

721. How Late

Now thou hast made me blind,
  And I can only see,
In all the world, what comes from thee;

Now thou hast made me deaf,
  And I can only hear
Thy voice, or body's motion near;

Now thou hast made me dumb,
  And my two lips are mute,
Till yours have bid them follow suit;

Now blind and deaf and dumb
  To all the world but thee —
How late thou art forsaking me!

722. Brothers

They lived together day and night,
  Two brothers, all alone:
Six weeks had gone, and neighbours said —
  'We see no more than one.

Where is thy brother Charlie, Tom?
  And is he sick?' they said.
Said Tom, that man so queer and quaint —
  'My brother's still in bed.'

And every night they heard his voice,
  Down on the stairs below:
'And are you still in bed and sick —
  How are you, Charlie, now?'

They forced the doors and entered in,
  Found Charlie on the bed:
'I see a dead man here alive.'
  The old physician said.

'For see the worms! They bubble here
  In pools upon his flesh:
They wag the beard that's on his chin —
  This body is not fresh.'

Then came a voice all sharp and clear,
  Down on the stairs below:
'And are you still in bed and sick —
  How are you, Charlie, now?'

723. The Girl is Mad

She changes oft — she laughs and weeps,
  She smiles, and she can frown;
Should tears of sorrow fill her eyes,
  Then laughter shakes them down:
The girl is mad — and yet I love her.

She smiles, and swears her jealousy
  Would tear out my two eyes,
And make me swallow them by force:
  These words are no strong lies,
For she is mad — and yet I love her.

'Ha, ha!' says she; 'I've killed two men,
  And you're the third I'll kill!'
If I keep time with her fierce love,
  'Tis certain that she will:
The girl is mad — and yet I love her.

724. Passion's Greed

His constant wonder keeps him back
  From flying either far or straight;
Confined by thy great beauty here,
  My life is like that butterfly's,
With every source of wonder near.

Let me go burning to my death:
  Nothing can come between our minds
To ease me of this passion's greed:
  We'll bite each other's neck like dogs,
And ask our fingers if we bleed.

725. A Safe Estate

If I hear Robin sing in mirth,
  I for no company shall pine;
Millions of souls, indeed! on earth —
  I know two only, his and mine.
I like Red Robin, he doth draw
  More close than many of my kin;
The last face yestere'en I saw,
  His first this morn came peeping in;
For him my curtain is half drawn,
To follow on the look of Morn.

He who loves Nature truly, hath
  His wealth in her kind hands; and it
Is in safe trust until his death,
  Increasing as he uses it;

573

'Tis proof 'gainst water, thief, and flame;
  He'll not lay wild hands on his life,
As one who, in his health and prime,
  Lets out his blood with a sharp knife,
When of ten ships but nine returned,
Or out of houses ten one burned.

726. The Distinction

This Talent is a slip, or shoot,
  Cut off the family tree;
To train with care and educate
  Which withers if let be.

But Genius is a seed that comes
  From where no man doth know;
Though left uncared, aye, hindered too,
  It cannot help but grow.

Talent's an outlet of Life's stream
  Whose waters know no change;
But Genius bringeth in from far
  New waters, sweet and strange.

727. The Lament of Age

Why must I dig this old mine still,
  Deep in the dark, the damp, and cold,
  Just for a speck or two outdoled!
It in my youth gave little toil
  To find its top yield nugget gold.

My precious yields they came and went,
  My mine worked out in every run:
  I hear the young ones making fun,
Who must, alas! grow old and spent,
  And lose their gold as I have done.

The top is rich enough for youth,
  Who needs must dig as he grows old —
  Deep in the dark, the damp, and cold;
Until he learns the woful truth —
  The more he digs the less his gold.

O shafts and beams that propped upright
  This mine for eighty years and more —
  For I can count my years four score —
Now that my lamp gives feeble light,
  Fall, that the earth may close me o'er!

728. Heigh Ho, the Rain

The Lark that in heaven dim
  Can match a rainy hour
  With his own music's shower,
Can make me sing like him —
  Heigh ho! The rain!

Sing — when a Nightingale
  Pours forth her own sweet soul
  To hear dread thunder roll
Into a tearful tale —
  Heigh ho! The rain!

575

Sing — when a Sparrow's seen
  Trying to lie at rest
  By pressing his warm breast
To leaves so wet and green —
  Heigh ho! The rain!

729. Love's Inspiration

Give me the chance, and I will make
  Thy thoughts of me, like worms this day,
Take wings and change to butterflies
  That in the golden light shall play;
Thy cold, clear heart — the quiet pool
  That never heard Love's nightingale —
Shall hear his music night and day,
  And in no seasons shall it fail.
I'll make thy happy heart my port,
  Where all my thoughts are anchored fast;
Thy meditations, full of praise,
  The flags of glory on each mast.
I'll make my Soul thy shepherd soon,
  With all thy thoughts my grateful flock;
And thou shalt say, each time I go —
  How long, my Love, ere thou'lt come back?

730. Whom I Know

I do not know his grace the Duke,
  Outside whose gilded gate there died
Of want a feeble, poor old man,
  With but his shadow at his side.

I do not know his Lady fair,
  Who in a bath of milk doth lie;
More milk than could feed fifty babes,
  That for the want of it must die.

But well I know the mother poor,
  Three pounds of flesh wrapped in her shawl:
A puny babe that, stripped at home,
  Looks like a rabbit skinned, so small.

And well I know the homeless waif,
  Fed by the poorest of the poor;
Since I have seen that child alone,
  Crying against a bolted door.

731.   Sweet Birds, I Come

The bird that now
  On bush and tree,
Near leaves so green
  Looks down to see
Flowers looking up —
  He either sings
In ecstasy
  Or claps his wings.

Why should I slave
  For finer dress
Or ornaments;
  Will flowers smile less
For rags than silk?
  Are birds less dumb
For tramp than squire?
  Sweet birds, I come.

732.   The Helpless

Those poor, heartbroken wretches, doomed
    To hear at night the clocks' hard tones;
They have no beds to warm their limbs,
    But with those limbs must warm cold stones;
Those poor weak men, whose coughs and ailings
Force them to tear at iron railings.

Those helpless men that starve, my pity;
    Whose waking day is never done;
Who, save for their own shadows, are
    Doomed night and day to walk alone:
They know no bright face but the sun's,
So cold and dark are human ones.

733.   When the Cuckoo Sings

In summer, when the Cuckoo sings,
    And clouds like greater moons can shine;
When every leafy tree doth hold
    A loving heart that beats with mine:
Now, when the Brook has cresses green,
    As well as stones, to check his pace;
And, if the Owl appears, he's forced
    By small birds to some hiding-place:
Then, like red Robin in the spring,
    I shun those haunts where men are found;
My house holds little joy until
    Leaves fall and birds can make no sound;
Let none invade that wilderness
    Into whose dark green depths I go —
Save some fine lady, all in white,
    Comes like a pillar of pure snow.

734. The City's Ways

Ye say the City stunts the child,
    And robs its bone of half its growth;
And makes less rich the mother's milk,
    Which is her baby's blood, forsooth.

Ye say the City drained its blood —
    But hath it done no more than that?
What made the child to stone the dog?
    What made him pinch and scald the cat?

True, it makes shoulders narrower,
    And maketh men as dwarves to be:
But what hath made them worse than that,
    Demons of hell for cruelty?

Wouldst know the City's cruel ways?
    The homeless dog and cat do know;
And bony nags that cannot last
    For long the pace they're whipt to go.

Or ask the ox, strange from green fields,
    And from the farmer's kindly ken;
Now chased to death with curse and blow,
    By wild things that do seem like men.

I gave no thought how cruel 'twas,
    Until I saw in kindly keep
The grazing ox, the ploughing horse,
    So stout and strong, and fearless sheep.

A good law, for both man and beast:
    Let all flesh food — for a thousand pities —
Enter to us as lifeless meat,
    And goad no live thing through our cities.

Why think of them, though goaded, cursed,
　　Of horses, oxen, sheep, in sooth;
The City's far more hard on men —
　　Some starve, some slave, and some do both.

735. The Dying

He fumbles in the clothes for want of thought,
　　And we, in life, health, fearing death, supply
His dazèd brain the power for clearer work —
　　Imagination to his dying eye.

Locks, bolts, nor bars make coward's heart secure:
　　When I at night see stars shine overhead,
And in the morning dew upon the green,
　　Ah! then I tremble to lie cold and dead —

That I, whom life showed nothing to make laugh,
　　Shall grin at last and know no reason why;
And have no smell when Summer brings her flowers,
　　And have no ear for birds close where I lie.

736. Time's Rule

Time called me out of a dark room
　　In a green place to play;
He gave me flowers, fruits, and sweets,
　　I laughed all day.

I sang all day; I danced; I moved
　　With motion light and free:
Like th' little bird whose weight is scarce
　　More than a bee.

The sunny days made golden years,
   Till Time told his fast rule:
'I send my happy children all
   To a good-school.'

Then to Experience me he took,
   The Master of Life's school;
Who snatched away my flowers and sweets
   And called me fool.

And made me suffer, made me weep,
   In daily teen and pain;
Would I were back, moaned I, in that
   Green place again!

Time heard my plaint; 'that place,' said he,
   'Hath now no fruit or flower.'
'Then take me back to that dark room
   For evermore.'

737. A Familiar Face

O for an old familiar face,
   To see the child outgrow the man!
'Shun him,' they cry, 'that man from jail:
Shun him, that slave to Bacchus ale;
   Shun him, who swears for all he can.'
Nay, what care I for that? I trace
My way through him to scenes of joy;
   I know him not as one who spent
   Part of his life in jail; he went
To the same school with me a boy,
   Which fills my heart with sweet content.

A thousand times I've set my mind
  Sternly 'gainst Bacchus and his race;
I've seen with pity men go mad,
And women going to the bad;
  But Chance hath brought my way a face
Which shows the boy I love behind.
'Say, how is little Jane, who went
  'To school between us two?' 'Oh, she
  Is well; and babies' — 'Babies!' — 'Three'.
And in the name of wonderment,
  Bacchus hath ta'en a hold on me.

738. The Calm

A bird sings on yon apple bough,
And bees are humming near; and now
I think of my tempestuous past,
And wonder if these joys will last.
After a storm of many years,
There comes this calm to lay my fears.
In vain it comes: an anxious eye
Looks for a sign in every sky
For tempest; for it cannot be,
Methinks, that peace will stay with me.
Anon this mind forgets its past.
And then methinks this calm will last.
Then walk I down my lane to see
Sweet Primrose, pale Anemone.
Shy Violet, who hid from sight,
Until I followed a bee right
To her — now while the cries of Spring
Do make things grow, to run and leap.

But are these pleasant days to keep?
Where shall I be when Summer comes?
When with a bee's mouth closed, she hums
Sounds not to wake, but soft and deep,
To make her pretty charges sleep?
As long as Heaven is true to Earth,
Spring will not fail with her green growth,
Nor Autumn with his gold; but when
Troubles beset me, I seek men;
From Nature, with her flowers and songs,
To lose myself in human throngs;
From moonlit glade to limelit scene,
To playhouses from bowers green;
From mossy rock to painted mortar,
To Traffic's wheels from running water;
And from the birds' melodious calls
To lose myself in human brawls.

739.   Strange People

There was a man I knew,
   Cruel to child and wife;
To see a pig despatched,
   And blood upon a knife,
Made him so sick he retched.

There was a man I knew,
   Soft-spoken, he was loved;
He took a club and struck
   A fowl which lived and moved
When he that fowl did pluck.

There was a man I knew,
 Refused no stranger ale;
But Mrs. Jones's head
 Wagged with this woful tale —
'His children moan for bread.

'A farthing's worth of milk
 His little girl gres for,
But quarts of ale drinks he,
 And rum and whiskey raw, —
Said Mrs. Jones to me.

Now these three men I knew,
 Were Tom, and Dick, and Dave;
Dick freely paid for drink,
 Till Mrs. Jones she gave
That hint, which made me think.

740. The Happiest Life

Take from the present hour its sweets,
For, as thou nearest Death's vast sea,
To empty thy Life's river there —
Thou wilt see flowerless banks of sand,
And naked rocks on that drear coast.

We rush through life as though it were
A race to grab new-opened land;
We live as though Life's pleasures were
Piled at its end, and when 'tis reached,
We moan them passed in years long gone.

We either do outrace old Time
Unto an end where no joys are,
Or lie us down in present ease,
In gluttony, or drunken sloth,
And make Time bear us sleeping on.

Man makes his life a burning fret,
Yet beasts do know a shady spot,
And know what herbs are good; proud man
Knows not how much, or what to eat,
And drinks fire-juice in Summer's prime.

We must clear out our vain desires,
Which covet more than gold can buy;
We must live more in Nature's way;
For what we want is th' drunkard's ease
Sans drugs to give us after pain.

We all are one at last; when Death
Hath glazed the eye of cruel Czar,
Which made so many mortals quail —
Bury it soon from flies. Ye gods,
Flies on that eye which cowed down men!

741. The Primrose

No more, from now, called pale and wan,
   As though a pitiful weak thing!
A sickly offspring of weak Sun
   And youngish Spring.

Thy father's golden skin is thine,
   And his eye's gleam; but his bold rays
Are tempered by thy mother's blood
   To softer ways.

For thou hast made the banks ooze gold,
  And make old woods their darkness break;
In them I would not fall at night
  Wert thou awake.

Here is the Primrose family:
  The first born is full blown and tall;
Two in half bloom just reach his chin,
  Three are buds small.

Then, since the first born healthy seems —
  No drooping one I've chanced upon —
It would be speaking false to call
  Them pale and wan.

They mean the Primrose plucked and withered,
  Not growing in his golden shine,
Who'd prove by him how Phyllis looks
  When she doth pine.

Indeed, where find a hardier flower?
  Born when the Spring wind chilly blows,
Still beautiful in Summer's days —
  O rare Primrose!

742. The Homeless Man

Wake up yon wretch in rags,
Remove such filthy bags
From doorsteps clean enough:
Seems like some shaming stuff
That scavengers must take
Early, ere people wake.

The homeless man his mind
Is like old Autumn's wind,
Who here and there in doubt
Doth cast his leaves about,
Against high banks some thrown,
And some in water blown.

So with the homeless one;
The Law must move him on,
For did he sit to sleep
He might fall in Death's deep —
So shocking to the eye
Of decent passers-by.

A tunnel traveller he:
No sight of sunny lea
No bursting to the light;
This traveller of the night,
No glimpse of heaven doth know —
But woe, for ever woe.

A trespasser is he,
Wherever others see:
The child would pelt his bones,
As one — they'd hurl their stones —
With homeless dog or cat,
And only fear stops that.

With prayer-books in their hand,
Where beggar takes his stand,
Church people hurry past;
Perchance one comes at last
With jug to fetch some ale,
He'll hear the beggar's tale.

Six butterflies take hours
To suck such sweets from flowers
As one bee in less time:
Work's want is beggar's crime;
Who'll give employ to one
Worn to a rag and bone?

743. Violet to the Bee

O you false knight in shining mail,
  Who visited my early hours —
My days are numbered by our scorn,
  Since Beauty spurns Love's flowers.

For true my charms are withered much,
  And dry my body is and lax;
My eye like to a burning wick
  That doth outlast its wax;

But for old times' sake look on me,
  On your first love, who ne'er did fail
To give sweet favours when you came
  'Scaped out of Winter's jail.

Only Primrose was here and I
  When April turned to hard hail-stones
The soft rain-drops, and you did make
  In pity such deep groans.

But now the earth is peopled more,
  And you have power to make love's choice;
You are much occupied these days,
  I know it by your voice.

For when you lie on bosoms fair,
    In blissful moments, you are dumb;
Which proves to me your many loves,
    Since you now seldom hum.

You're in your highest heaven just now,
    In apple blossoms overhead;
And your sweet sting it is will make
    Those blossoms' apples red.

Ah! I care not how soon Death comes,
    To bury me on this steep bank;
This flower of Life in other hand
    Than Love's — Oh, it smells rank!

744. In June

I'll enter in June's cool house,
    Where leaves shade over her spring's run;
Sure, but one thing that breathes, the lark,
    Dare now have dealings with the sun;
Embolden'd with such sparkling dews,
He'll do in heaven as he choose.

There is a wood, with leafy boughs,
    Not too far down the hawthorn lane;
When I am in the sun can knock
    Its roof or side, and knock in vain;
Autumn will bring him by-and-by
Some leafless woods wherein to lie.

The little brook beside the road,
  Though running oft from shade to shade,
Is warming still; but if I sleep,
  Perchance, when in that shaded glade,
The faith is mine that June can keep
Out sun or shower, till ends my sleep.

745. The End of Summer

The Dandelion sails away, —
  Some other port for him next spring;
Since they have seen the harvest home,
  Sweet birds have little more to sing.

Since from her side the corn is ta'en,
  The Poppy thought to win some praise;
But birds sang ne'er a welcome note,
  So she blushed scarlet all her days.

The children strip the blackberry bush,
  And search the hedge for bitter sloe;
They bite the sloes, now sweet as plums —
  After Jack Frost had bit them so.

'Twas this Jack Frost, one week ago,
  Made watchdogs whine with fear and cold;
But all he did was make fruits smell,
  And make their coats to shine like gold.

No scattering force is in the wind,
  Though strong to shake the leaf from stem;
The leaves get in the rill's sweet throat,
  His voice is scarcely heard through them.

The darkest woods let in the light,
　　And thin and frail are looking now;
And yet their weight is more than June's,
　　Since nuts bend down each hazel bough.

746.　One we Love

Thou miser, Time, who gave to me
　　Some vigour, grace, and youth more dear —
They were not gifts, but debts and loans,
　　Which I repay thee year by year;
E'en thou, false Time, were not reproved,
Did I grow old with one I loved.
Go, Fame, whose voice is from high hills
　　'Tis death to climb and much heartburn;
Not worldly wealth, nor temporal power,
　　Nor future hopes shall serve my turn —
Not me again shall either move,
So I grow old with one I love.
In ocean's depths, how rude is life,
　　They murder there and make no sound!
Wild beasts are dying off the land,
　　And now 'tis man gives man his wound:
But there's one joy none can disprove —
'Tis to grow old with one we love.

747.　Saturday Night in the Slums

　　Why do I stare at faces, why,
　　　　Nor watch the happy children more?
　　Since Age has now a blackened eye,
　　　　And that grey hair is stained with gore.

For an old woman passed, and she
　　Would hide her face when I did stare,
But when she turns that face from me,
　　There's clotted blood in her grey hair.

Aye, here was hell last night to play,
　　The scream of children, murder cries;
When I came forth at early day,
　　I saw old Age with blackened eyes.

Why do I stare at people so,
　　Nor watch the little children more,
If one such brutal passions show,
　　And joy is all the other's store?

O for the shot in some fierce land,
　　A sword or dagger firmly held:
No brutal kick, no mauling hand,
　　No horrors of the partly killed.

There is the man with brutal brow,
　　The child with hunger's face of care:
The woman — it is something now
　　If she lose pride to dress her hair.

I will give children my best hours,
　　And of their simple ways will sing:
Just as a bird heeds less old flowers
　　And sings his best to buds in spring.

748. April

What happy shouts the children make,
  Since April brought them his warm rains!
When this same April showers his hail
  At their red cheeks behind glass panes,
They know he pelts without avail.

The blossoms drenched, leaves dripping wet,
  'Tis for one moment dark as night;
Then comes a rainbow in the sky,
  And Nature laughs, as children might,
Who had a notion once to cry.

Now, over rocks and down ravines,
  And venturing into mazy nooks,
The Rill doth find his way about;
  And into many a cave he looks,
And laughs — as he knew his way out.

Who can help laugh at April's ways?
  We laugh the more the more he tries
To mimic some old bogey's face
  Under the sunshine of such eyes,
Wherein the thoughts give merry chase.

They would have fields without young lambs,
  Or amber clear of beauty stains;
They would have seas without foam-flowers,
  Who would want April free from rains.
And cloudless his capricious hours.

He shows my lady's shoes in full,
  And makes her form to sway with grace;
Which makes her pout with some annoy,
  But soon come dimples in her face,
And music in her voice of joy.

The laughing girls, half blind and choked,
    Are smothered in their own wild hair;
He took one maiden's yard of it,
    When too close I was passing there,
And whipt my cheeks all red with it.

Now Violet is on the bank,
    And Primrose is not far away;
The Brook doth o'er his margents froth —
    The Wind doth drive him sore this day,
And pucks his face with childish wrath.

We all must sing when April's here,
    Must sing his shine, and sing his shower;
The lark, the throstle, blackbird sing,
    Nor shall their throats improve this hour
In many days of practising.

To smell Primrose's honey-well,
    I would go mad as any bee:
But vain for me come flowers in Spring,
    The Violet, Daffodil to see,
With birds that best in April sing.

749. Whiskey

Whiskey, thou blessèd heaven in the brain,
    O that the belly should revolt,
To make a hell of afterpain,
    And prove thy virtue was a fault!

Did ever poet seek his bed
    With a sweet phrase upon his lips
Smiling — as I laid down my head,
    Pleased after sundry whiskey sips?

I pitied all the world: alas
　That no poor nobodies came near,
To give to them my shirt and shoes,
　And bid them be of goodly cheer.

A blessèd heaven was in the brain;
　But ere came morn the belly turned
And kicked up hell's delight in pain —
　This tongue went dry, this throat it burned.

Oh dear! Oh dear! to think last night
　The merriest man on earth was I,
And that I should awake this morn,
　To cough and groan, to heave and sigh!

Index of First Lines

	PAGE
A Bee goes mumbling homeward pleased,	26
A bird sings on yon apple bough,	582
A cloudless path from East to West,	452
A dear old couple my grandparents were,	161
A dog has bones to spare and hide,	397
A dog, that has ten years of breath,	501
A granted joy can make a careless mind,	428
A jar of cider and my pipe,	110
A little porch with roof and sides	398
A lonely coast, where sea-gulls scream for wrecks	365
A Milkmaid, on a Summer's day,	510
A month ago, ah happy me!	538
A new World calls, in voices loud and strange,	483
A perfect child, with hands and feet,	541
A pipe to smoke, and ale that's mulled,	495
A pretty game, my girl,	283
A silver shilling for his white-haired Granny,	488
A sneeze from Time gives Life its little breath;	292
A summer's morning that has but one voice;	285
A thing that's rich in tears is sweet —	418
A thousand blessings, Puck, on you	156
A Tom Tit clinging upside down,	446
A wealth of stars in Winter time	471
A week ago I had a fire,	502
A woman's glory is not hair,	558
A wondrous city, that had temples there	197
A year's a post, on which	146
Again I sing of thee, sweet youth:	206
Again I wake and cry for light!	416
Ah, Life, we are no sooner dressed	306
Ah, little bird, thou art not old;	538
Ah, little boy! I see	233
Ah, Music! it doth sound more sweet	532
Ah, sweet young blood, that makes the heart	189
Ah, what fond memories that voice doth bring!	528
Ah, what is Beauty but vain show —	536

	PAGE
Alack for life!	64
Alas! we live in days of shame,	533
Ale's no false liar; though his mind	257
All fish and fowl, all fruit, and all you drink,	336
All for the sake of lovely dreams,	490
All from his cradle to his grave,	368
Am I a fool?	145
An hour or more she's gone,	29
And art thou gone, sweet Youth? Say Nay!	532
And now, when merry winds do blow,	98
And will she never hold her tongue,	236
Are those small silver tumps a town,	357
Around that waist, scarce bigger than my neck,	306
As butterflies are but winged flowers,	53
As I go walking down the street	258
As I lay dreaming, open-eyed,	289
As I marched out one day in Spring,	487
As I walked down a lane this morn,	510
As I walked down the waterside	159
As long as I see Nature near,	524
As soon as I began to name a star,	423
Australian Bill is dying fast,	88
Autumn grows old; he, like some simple one,	23
'Away!' I cried, to a spiteful Wasp,	414
Be damned, you cheeks, be damned and sink;	502
Beauty'll be no fairer than	27
Beneath this stone lies one good man; and when	402
Between two rows of trees,	266
Blow, blow, thou Eastern wind,	555
Born to the world with my hands clenched,	224
Bright Butterfly,	552
By my fast horse that knows no rest	404
Can I forget the sweet days that have been,	142
Christmas has come, let's eat and drink —	171
Cold winds can never freeze, nor thunder sour	148
Come away, Death, make no mistake,	367
Come, come, my Love, the morning waits,	362
Come, if thou'rt cold to Summer's charms,	188

	PAGE
Come, let me close thine eyes with kisses —	566
Come, let us find a cottage, love,	259
Come, let us measure	482
Come, lovely morning, rich in frost	421
Come, Melancholy, come, Delight:	433
Come, show the world your mettle now,	328
Come, thou sweet Wonder, by whose power	234
Day after day I find some new delight:	357
Day by day the man in the vale	394
Day has her star, as well as Night,	342
Dead leaves from off the tree	232
Death can but play one game with me —	523
Dinah is young, and I am old;	344
Down in the deep salt sea	556
Down through the trees is my green walk:	348
Dreaming I was a child,	561
E'en though her tongue may by its force	104
Every tick and every tock	284
Far from the sound of commerce, where the bees	562
'Fatty', one day, called 'Red-nosed Scot'	109
Few are my books, but my small few have told	249
Few are my friends,	393
Flowers white and red my garden has;	214
For three whole days I and my cat	497
Forgive me, World, if I outlive my welcome;	425
Four hundred years this little house has stood	408
From my own kind I only learn	288
'Get to thy room,' a voice told me,	30
Girls scream,	84
Give her her ribbon, belt or scarf —	458
Give me a night in June that's clear and quiet,	456
Give me the chance, and I will make	576
Give me the poet's life divine,	220
Give them your silver, let the poor	428
Go, angry One, and let tears cold	541
Go, little boy,	89

U *

599

	PAGE
God's pity on poor kings,	175
Gone are the days of canvas sails!	114
Good morning, Life — and all	167
Good morning to my dolly, first,	563
Good people keep their holy day,	305
Had birds no season for their precious songs,	503
Had I a secret plan by which,	345
Happy the man whose home is still	248
'Have I not bored your teeth,' said Time,	288
Have I now found an angel in Unrest,	275
He begs from rich men for the poor,	567
He comes with a song,	451
He fumbles in the clothes for want of thought,	580
He goes with basket and slow feet,	266
He hailed me with a cheerful voice,	546
He leaves his silver trail behind,	427
He lives his lonely life, and when he dies	171
He passed me by in April, Lord,	494
He takes that woman with his kiss,	429
Hear how my friend the robin sings!	247
Hear me, thou proud, deceitful maid,	155
Her baby brother laughed last night,	59
Her beauty is a wasted thing,	429
Her body's a fine house,	306
Her cheeks were white, her eyes were wild,	93
Her cruel hands go in and out,	80
Her face is full of silent Pain —	466
Her pretty dances were her own,	542
Her sight is short, she comes quite near;	99
Here comes Kate Summers who, for gold,	225
Here in my garden I have lovely stones,	445
Here with my treasured Three I sit,	370
Here you lie, with feathers cold and wet —	443
Here's an example from	138
His car was worth a thousand pounds and more,	445
His chin went up and down, and chewed at nothing,	411
His constant wonder keeps him back	573
How bleak and cold the air is now —	403
How can she safely walk this earth,	511

		PAGE
How I do love to sit and dream		75
How I have watched thy coming, Spring,		279
How kind is sleep, how merciful:		274
How many buds in this warm light		314
How many plates of crumbs, my little friend,		444
How many years since I, a wandering man,		441
How often in my dreams have I beheld		349
How rich hath Time become through her,		216
How sad a face this Knowledge wears!		417
How sad my life had been were't not for her,		125
How slowly moves the snail, that builds		317
How softly now my Days go by —		500
How sordid is this crowded life, its spite		370
How strange that Love should be like this,		460
How sweet is Life, how beautiful,		348
How sweet this morning air in spring,		204
How those wet tombstones in the sun		339
Hunters, hunters,		403
I am a jolly tramp: I whine to you,		65
I am as certain of my song,		481
I am haunted by wonderful places —		425
I am the Poet Davies, William,		268
I ask not of high tide or low,		542
I brought two friends to share my fire,		491
I cannot see the short, white curls		103
I climb a tree to bring them down —		353
I could not love him more —		303
I count my pounds as three times two,		458
I do not know his grace the Duke,		576
I give thee back thy freedom, bird,		513
I had a cherry tree, one day,		503
I had a friend to smoke and drink,		467
I had a sweet companion once,		540
I had Ambition, by which sin		408
I have an orchard near my house,		442
I have no ale,		508
I have no ears or eyes		499
I have no hopes, I have no fears,		274
I have no memory of his face,		359

	PAGE
I have two loves, and one is dark,	366
I hear a merry noise indeed:	191
I hear it said yon land is poor,	250
I hear leaves drinking rain;	75
I heard a Lady near my door	505
I heard a man once say this world	554
I heard a voice methought was sweet;	525
I know a deep and lonely pool — that's where	358
I know my Body well,	426
I know not why I yearn for thee again,	187
I know not why thy beauty should	92
I lie on Joy's enchanted ground:	545
I like the showers that make the grass so fresh,	527
I look on Nature and my thoughts,	271
I love the earth through my two eyes,	335
I loved a ship from early boyhood days;	264
I met her in the leafy woods,	152
I need no glass to help my eyes,	351
I praised the daisies on my lawn,	354
I pray you, Sadness, leave me soon,	149
I questioned Poetry, Say, I said —	402
I saw a black girl once,	176
I saw the fog grow thick,	185
I saw this day sweet flowers grow thick —	151
I saw Time running by —	554
I see at last our great Lamorna Cove,	317
I see the busy stars at work,	551
I see the houses, but I swear	399
I sit beneath your leaves, old oak,	174
I take no pride in body's growth	395
I thought my true love slept;	140
I took my oath I would inquire,	232
I walk to look,	559
I, who had eyes to wander here and there,	346
I who have seen a tiny cloud,	463
If I hear Robin sing in mirth,	573
If I should die, this house is yours,	361
If I were gusty April now,	172
If Life gives friends,	28
If Life is dust, is not dust Life?	347

	PAGE
If my last thoughts contain no wish	475
If nothing takes away our power	407
If these six letters came from birds,	416
If Time and Nature serve us both alike,	360
If, when thy body's end has come,	322
If woman's a delightful creature,	459
I'll enter into June's cool house,	589
I'll have the primrose grow in grass,	352
I'm none of those — Oh Bacchus, blush!	323
In fancy I can see thee stand	107
In summer when the Cuckoo sings,	578
In this deep hollow, lying down,	560
Indeed this is sweet life! my hand	102
Is it for you	102
Is it not fine to walk in spring,	181
Is it that small black star,	82
Is life on Earth a viler thing	499
Is that star dumb, or am I deaf?	361
Is this old Autumn standing here,	426
Is this the Blackbird's richest song —	406
It is a winter's night and cold,	245
It is the bell of death I hear,	251
It may be true the stars are worlds,	418
It was a long, long time ago,	356
It was the night when we expected news from France,	278
It was the Rainbow gave thee birth	107
Jove warns us with his lightning first,	246
Joy, how I sought thee!	173
Kings, who would have good subjects, must	439
Last night I sat in thought,	553
Last night I saw the monster near; the big	238
Last night, though I had fifty souls,	66
Leafy with little clouds, the sky	338
Lend me your precious toys,	492
Let Fortune gift on gift bestow	61
Let me confess, before I die,	289
Let us lie close, as lovers should,	474
Let women long for dainty things,	334

Life's angel half, sweet Sleep, 24
Listen for pity — I impeach 276
Little flocks of peaceful clouds, 218
Little Flower, I hold you here, 449
Lo, I, that once was Fear, that hears 256
London! What utterance the mind finds here! 41
Lord, hear my morning's prayer! 424
Lord, I say nothing; I profess 145
Lord, if that Cloud still grows and swells, 438
Lord, since this world is filled with fire, 431
Love came about the Cuckoo's time, 477
Love is the precious jewel in our Life, 469
Love kissed me in a strange, untruthful hour, 364
Love lights his fire to burn my Past — 463
Love's touch is soft, and Death 355

Man is a bird: 180
Mary and Maud have met at the door, 87
Men that have strength to rule their sex 310
Molly, with hips and ankles plump, 248
Must I live here, with Scripture on my walls, 160
My back is turned on Spring and all her flowers, 175
My birthday — yesterday, 36
My dog creeps into my shadowed form, 492
My dog lies dead and buried here, 442
My dog went mad and bit my hand, 351
My Fancy loves to play with clouds, 105
My friend has a birthday; 409
My friend, mad drunk, struck at his foe, 560
My girl has reached that lovely state 350
My heart's a coffin cold, 539
My little Lamb, what is amiss? 169
My Love could walk in richer hues 243
My love has gone long since, 279
My love laughs sweeter than a brook 553
My Love sits angry: see! 113
My mind has thunderstorms, 166
My purse is yours, Sweet Heart, for I 186
My sacrament of wine and broken bread 450
My silver love is shared by all, 477

		PAGE
My song is of that city which		192
My song, that's bird-like in its kind,		285
My walk is now in silent groves,		567
My walls outside must have some flowers,		86
My wandering days have run their course,		406
My windows now are giant drops of dew,		446
My wonder is the great bright sun,		545
My years to come are numbered on two hands,		455
My youth is gone — my youth that laughed and yawned		320
My youth was my old age,		179
Nature has made my mind a mint,		287
Nay, no more bitterness from me;		542
Night is the only time I live,		311
Night, Lightning, Thunder, Rain.		212
No answer, yet I called her name,		339
No bitter tongue, no grief for what is gone,		432
No house of stone		153
No idle gold — since this fine sun, my friend,		270
No lilies all for milk,		412
No more, from now, called pale and wan,		585
No more of that, you butterfly,		255
No morning breaks but he would pack,		217
No spoilt, no pampered child am I,		485
Not even when the early birds		343
Not only is my love a flower		221
Not till my spirit's naked and ashamed,		450
Not while her charms are still in flower,		486
Now do I hear thee weep and groan,		54
Now how could I, with gold to spare,		183
Now I can see what Helen was:		90
Now I grow old, and flowers are weeds,		77
Now, Joy is born of parents poor,		85
Now shall I walk,		203
Now that she gives my love consent,		291
Now that the tears of love have reached		309
Now thou hast made me blind,		571
Now, when my roses are half buds, half flowers,		400
Now Winter's here; he and his ghostly Winds		518
Now, you two eyes, that have all night been sleeping,		396

	PAGE
O for an old familiar face,	581
O happy Blackbird, happy soul,	559
O those sweet notes, so soft and faint; that seemed	144
O what a life is this I lead,	84
O you false knight in shining mail,	588
Of primrose boys	500
Oft have I thought the Muse was dead,	341
Oh for a glass of wine!	307
Oh, happy wind, how sweet	109
Oh, sweet content, that turns the labourer's sweat	270
On Christmas day I sit and think,	405
On what sweet banks were thy pure fancies fed,	305
Once I was wise when, in my Youth,	497
Once, in that cave, I heard my breath:	340
Once more I see the happy young	318
Once on a time, in Pontypool,	489
One hour in every hundred hours	242
One kiss to open up the day,	470
One morning, when the world was grey and cold,	313
One night I heard a small, weak voice,	332
One night I saw ten stars take wing —	565
One night poor Jim had not a sou,	62
One night, when I was sleeping all alone,	367
One night when I went down	154
Our love this day is ten years old.	464
Peace makes more slaves than savage war,	508
Peace, mournful Bee, with that	569
Peace to these little broken leaves,	332
Play, little children, one and all,	254
Pleasure is not the one I love:	335
Pools but reflect his shape and form,	413
Poor Body, sitting there so calm,	507
Poor, luckless Bee, this sunny morn;	517
Poor souls, who think that joy is bought	316
Proud Margery rang her peal of bells;	549
Rainbows are lovely things:	329
Robin on a leafless bough	76

606

	PAGE
Say, silent Moth,	82
Say that the House that makes our Laws	449
Say what you like	78
See how her arms now rise and fall,	351
See how her body pants and glows,	401
See how the glow-worm's light is found	304
See how those diamonds splutter and choke —	498
See what a light is in those painted clouds!	350
See where he rides, all hot and fast —	429
See where Young Love sits all alone,	333
Seek not to know Love's full extent,	469
Shall I collect for this world's eyes	207
Shall I confess my love?	409
Shall I have jealous thoughts to nurse,	366
Shall I this night, amazed and full of wonder,	412
Sharpen your claws, Pussy-cat,	493
She brings that breath, and music too,	228
She changes oft — she laughs and weeps,	572
She comes to see her brother John,	568
She died when I was wild and young,	434
She fears not me —	397
She flies from my shadow,	465
She had two eyes as blue as Heaven,	544
She pecks the earth for every second,	470
She sends her portrait, as a swallow,	318
She walks as lightly as the fly	234
Should her flirting prove a danger,	478
Silkworms have dressed the fairest women,	495
Since I have seen a bird one day,	277
Since Love cries out for money, still,	479
Since music is Love's milk and keeps him strong,	472
Since you have turned unkind,	343
Sing for the sun your lyric, lark,	241
Sing out, my Soul, thy songs of joy;	137
Six summers old was she, and when she came	239
Sleeping in some green bower, and wrapped	337
So innocent, so quiet — yet	333
So many birds have come along,	63
Some banks cropped close, and lawns smooth mown and green,	34
Some little creatures have so short a life	346

607

Some poets die consumed by love 432
Somehow this world is wonderful at times, 149
Sometimes he roars among the leafy trees 76
Sometimes I blow and praise a bubble, 454
Sometimes I hear fine ladies sing, 166
Sometimes I watch the moon at night, 268
Stand with eyes fixed, the Cuckoo calls — 419
Stay home and hear the birds and bees, 570
Still comes no answer to my greatest question — 434
Stop, feathered bullies! 150
Stung by a spiteful wasp, 250
Summer has spread a cool, green tent 101
Sweet are thy dreams, thou happy, careless boy; 212
Sweet Chance, that led my steps abroad, 215
Sweet child, thou wast my bird by day, 219
Sweet Margaret's laugh can make 100
Sweet Night, that like an angel comes 204
Sweet Poesy, why are thou dumb? 97
Sweet Poppy, when thy beauty's gone, 515
Sweet Stay-at-Home, sweet Well-content, 168

Take from the present hour its sweets; 584
Tell me, Fancy, sweetest child, 141
Tell them, when you are home again, 280
Ten Junes to hear the Nightingale, 473
That day she seized me like a bee, 251
That grass is tender, soft and sweet, 315
That is your little playmate, Jane, 437
That paradise the Arab dreams, 203
That speckled Thrush, that stands so still, 472
That woman there is almost dead, 273
The bird of Fortune sings when free, 183
The bird that fills my ears with song, 480
The bird that now 577
The birds are pirates of her notes, 178
The boding Owl, that in despair 148
The Butterfly loves Mignonette, 52
The cat has her milk, 483
The City has dull eyes, 512
The cold ice-sucking wind has gone, 419

	PAGE
The collier's wife had four tall sons	565
The Dandelion sails away, —	590
The dog was there, outside her door,	272
The drinking man maybe hath gold, and then	66
The gentle wind that waves	229
The great white Moon is not so fair —	261
The hand that rocked his cradle once	415
The Harvest Home's a home indeed;	147
The healthiest place for Love is here,	462
The healthiest trees bear fruits that fail,	467
The homeless man has heard thy voice,	181
The Lark that in heaven dim	575
The laws of Beauty and its patterns	462
The lilac in my garden comes to bloom,	337
The little ones are put in bed,	158
The loneliest mountain, with no house or tree,	494
The man who tells me he has seen a ghost,	358
The midwife nearly drowned my son,	314
The mind, with its own eyes and ears,	205
The Moon his mare, all silver bright,	430
The Moon is beautiful this night	325
The moon is full, and so am I;	252
The Moon, that peeped as she came up,	505
The music's dull — I trust my Ears;	431
The nearer unto Nature's heart I moved,	331
The nightingale I had not heard,	242
The oak bears little acorns, yet	371
The owl has come	449
The Peacock, that fine-feathered bird,	473
The power was given at birth to me	331
The quality of life on earth	504
The Rain has lost more music keys,	516
The seed-time of this lovely life,	456
The shade and colour of her eyes can wait,	340
The sky is clear,	170
The small birds peck at apples ripe,	202
The Spring was late in coming, so,	263
The Sun has his spots, the Moon has her shadows,	457
The Swallow dives in yonder air,	551
The Vision came, all grey and cold,	415

609

	PAGE
The witness to my document	487
The woods and banks of England now,	307
The World dictates my life from day to day,	435
The World has shared my joy and pain,	421
The World is poor, and Love is lonely,	485
The world is sleeping, and the earth is dark,	401
The world may charge a man with sin,	309
The Worlds march on and circle in their place,	452
The years passed by, and my pure love	330
There came a man to sell his shirt,	60
There goes mad Poll, dressed in wild flowers,	177
There is a bird that, in her throat,	496
There, on a branch, he stands alone,	398
There was a battle in her face,	81
There was a house where an old dame	100
There was a man I knew,	583
There was a poet once who died,	440
There's many a pool that holds a cloud	336
There's not one leaf can say to me	516
There's 'Scotty' Bill, four score of years,	55
These butterflies, in twos and threes,	446
These flowers survive their lover bees,	411
They ask me where the Temple stands,	281
They hear the bell of midnight toll,	182
They killed her lamb, and no one wept,	433
They lived apart for three long years,	225
They lived together day and night,	571
They press the pillow their mother's face and **head**;	561
They say wild creatures hide themselves,	441
They sleep together in one den,	209
They're creeping on the stairs outside,	236
Thieves, Death and Absence, come	531
Things that are dear to me at home	410
Think, Man of Flesh, and be not proud	498
Think not her face is patched with pink,	23
Thinking of my caged bird indoors,	227
This apple-tree, that once was green,	260
This bag of cherries for my Love:	480
This curly childhood of the year,	440
'This house is worth a thousand pounds,	468

	PAGE
This is a joy no laughter shakes,	482
This is God's poorest lambing time,	484
This is Love's silent hour, before the tongue	290
This is the hour of magic, when the Moon	313
This is the morning bright and clear,	451
This life in London — what a waste	369
This life is jolly, O!	184
This life is sweetest; in this wood	106
This morning, as I wandered forth,	261
This night, as I sit here alone,	227
This Talent is a slip, or shoot,	574
This, then, is Pleasure's bower,	407
This time of year, when but the Robin sings,	423
Those poor, heartbroken wretches, doomed	578
Thou art now always kind, O sleep:	190
Thou canst not understand my words,	237
Thou comest, May, with leaves and flowers,	230
Thou dost not fly, thou art not perched,	214
Thou foul-mouthed wretch! Why dost thou choose	112
Thou hadst no home, and thou couldst see	179
Thou miser, Time, who gave to me	591
Thou shalt not laugh, thou shalt not romp,	210
Thou that in fury with thy knotted tail	284
Though bees have stings, I doubt if any bee	475
Though floods shall fail, and empty holes	254
Though I am all for warmth and light,	436
Though I must sleep, and give my body rest,	436
Though I sit brooding here, with my eyes closed,	474
Though I was born in April's prime,	278
Though rising early with the Lark —	448
Though thou hast silk to wear, and though	557
Though you are gone and I am left alone,	347
Three things there are more beautiful	313
Thy beauty haunts me heart and soul	215
Thy father was a drunken man,	552
Thy water, Alteryn,	267
Till I went out of doors to prove	253
Time called me out of a dark room	580
To think my thoughts all hers	92
To-day I acted Christ,	481

	PAGE
To-morrow they will come. I know	110
Tormented day and night by fleas,	453
Twice in one hour I've seen this lovely Night,	433
Two spirits in two bodies, Love,	460
Under this tree, where light and shade	413
Wake up yon wretch in rags,	586
We arm to fight the Kaiser's troops,	569
We children every morn would wait	57
We have met,	509
We have no grass locked up in ice so fast	258
We have no mind to reach that Pole	269
We live to read each others' soul —	438
We poets pride ourselves on what	262
We wait our turn, as still as mice,	230
We're but the Shadows of these Women Suns,	501
Wealth, Power and Fame — aye, even Love	524
Welcome, New Year, but be more kind	116
Welcome to you rich Autumn days,	221
What an enchanted world is this,	352
What art thou, Life, and what am I?	522
What can I find in my wild orchard,	461
What can I find in the city shops,	461
What cant, oh, what hypocrisy	338
What county sends me this surprise,	281
What do I stare at — not the colt	394
What do we earn for all our gentle grace?	504
What exultations in my mind	243
What favourite flowers are mine, I cannot say —	422
What glorious sunsets have their birth	466
What happy mortal sees that mountain now,	231
What happy shouts the children make,	593
What is this life if, full of care,	140
What knowledge do my Ears provide,	506
What lies I read, that men of strength	322
What little bird is this that sings?	201
What lovely dark blue flames, O Spade,	354
What lovely meadows have I seen in the Sun,	356
What makes thee weep so, little child,	208

What man was in the Moon last night? 420
What moves that lonely man is not the boom 222
What music, Lord, these birds must feel, 448
What power of will — to follow now, 417
What shall we call thee — mouse o' the air, 33
What, still another woman false, 265
What strange commotion, Love, 447
What sweet, what happy days had I, 391
What swords and spears, what daggers bright, 392
What thoughts are mine when she is gone, 256
What tyrant starved the living out, and kept 58
What work is going on down underground, 341
When all your bitter grief is gone, 439
When April scatters coins of primrose gold 228
When at each door the ruffian winds 182
When Autumn's fruit is packed and stored, 308
When Beauty scents with love her bait, 558
When diamonds, nibbling in my ears, 311
When dogs play in the sun outdoors, 263
When farmers sweat and toil at ploughs, 522
When first I left a town, 536
When from this mighty mountain's top 223
When I am old, and it is spring, 201
When I am sick and dark depression 437
When I, awake, have thoughts of Death, 550
When I came forth this morn I saw 53
When I complained of April's day, 395
When I did wake this morn from sleep 81
When I had crossed the hill at last, 359
When I had met my love the twentieth time, 315
When I had money, money, O! 91
When I had thought my end was near, 444
When I in praise of babies speak, 219
When I look into a glass, 320
When I, made merry with the wine, 496
When I pass down the street and see 329
When I put out my thoughts to grass 396
When I returned to that great London Town, 530
When I sailed out of Baltimore, 282
When I stand here alone at night, 454

	PAGE
When I was in yon town, and had	514
When I was lying sick in bed	342
When I was old, and she was young	476
When I was once a wandering man,	443
When I was once in Baltimore,	142
When I was sitting near a stream,	447
When I went down past Charing Cross,	364
When I went in the woods this morn to sleep,	117
When I went wandering far from home,	369
When leaves begin to show their heads,	275
When Love has lost his bite and sting,	478
When Love is strong in married couples,	461
When Mary Price was five years old,	324
When musing near a quiet stream,	222
When on a summer's morn I wake,	205
When our two souls have left this mortal clay,	245
When Poll stays here, her Jack goes there,	484
When primroses are out in Spring,	143
When she threatened to leave me,	471
When she was but a little child,	392
When starving cattle see	490
When these sweet spirits, my most faithful friends,	455
When this strange world speaks ill of me,	424
When thou hast emptied thy soft purse,	158
When tigers flee from fire, the deer	157
When we are young and wake from sleep,	345
When we forget that Nature gives	457
When we're together, how the moments fly!	465
When will it come, that golden time,	507
When, with my window opened wide at night,	344
When yon full moon's with her white fleet of stars,	253
When young, I kissed a miser man,	435
When Youth is gone, and Beauty too	506
Where are you going to now, white sheep,	152
Where did you sleep in the Country, Lad?	453
Where she is now, I cannot say —	310
Where wert thou, love, when from Twm Barlum turned	28
While I have these two rich companions left,	493
While joy gave clouds the light of stars,	271
'While we enjoy this meat, my Son,	491

Whiskey, thou blessèd heaven in the brain   594
White lily clouds   512
Who are these men with quiet smiles —   486
Who bears in mind misfortunes gone,   312
Who can abide indoors this morn,   94
Who dreams a sweeter life than this,   210
Who is this man that, brain on fire,   479
Who lives in this black wooden hut?   521
Who knows the name and country now,   422
Who knows the perfect life on earth?   365
Who stands before me on the stairs: 240
Who taught fair Cleopatra how to bring   321
Who would not be a poet, when   464
Why did we think no power in Heaven   468
Why did you kill that harmless frog?   247
Why do I stare at faces, why,   591
Why does a woman change her moods?   363
Why must I dig this old mine still,   574
Why should I pause, poor beast, to praise   56
Will no one stop that Blackbird now,   494
With all our mirth, I doubt if we shall be   304
With all thy gold, thou canst not make   223
With mighty leaps and bounds,   276
With this one friend — I ask no more   405
With thy strong tide of beauty I must go,   312
With thy true love I have more wealth   147
Within that porch, across the way,   273
Without a thought   519
Without contentment, what is life?   307
Workhouse and Bedlam, Refuge, Den,   476
Working her toothless gums till her sharp chin   244
Would I had met you in my days of strength,   363
Would that the Powers that made my eyes so keen,   414

Ye Liberals and Conservatives,   543
Ye Saints, that sing in rooms above,   38
Ye say the City stunts the child,   579
Ye who have nothing to conceal,   115
Yes, I will spend the livelong day   139
Yes, let the truth be heard,   530

	PAGE
Yes, Solitude indeed: for I can see	534
You berries once,	211
You false church clock, whose long-drawn chimes	360
You interfering ladies, you	291
You Nightingales, that came so far,	83
You working man, of what avail	546
You'll get no help from me;	526
'You'll have a son,' the old man said —	321
Your Laurel Hedge, with its broad leaves,	488
Your life was hard with mangling clothes,	286
Your songs at night a drunkard sings,	556
Youth has no ties,	564